1 & 2 TIMOTHY
AND
TITUS

BELIEF

A Theological Commentary
on the Bible

GENERAL EDITORS

Amy Plantinga Pauw
William C. Placher[†]

1 & 2 TIMOTHY
AND
TITUS

THOMAS G. LONG

WJK WESTMINSTER
JOHN KNOX PRESS
LOUISVILLE · KENTUCKY

First edition
Published by Westminster John Knox Press
Louisville, Kentucky

16 17 18 19 20 21 22 23 24 25—10 9 8 7 6 5 4 3 2

Book design by Drew Stevens
Cover design by Lisa Buckley
Cover illustration: © David Chapman / Design Pics / Corbis

Library of Congress Cataloging-in-Publication Data
Long, Thomas G., 1946- , author.
 1 & 2 Timothy and Titus : a theological commentary on the Bible / Thomas G. Long.
-- First edition.
  pages cm -- (Belief: a theological commentary on the Bible)
 Includes bibliographical references and index.
 ISBN 978-0-664-23262-7 (hardback) -- ISBN 978-0-664-26205-1 (pbk.) 1. Bible.
Timothy--Commentaries. 2. Bible. Titus--Commentaries. I. Title.
 BS2735.53.L66 2016
 227'.8307--dc23
                                                                    2015031928

*For George Leitz, who was my mentor in
ministry far more than he ever knew.*

Contents

2 TIMOTHY

TITUS

Publisher's Note

William C. Placher worked with Amy Plantinga Pauw as a general editor for this series until his untimely death in November 2008. Bill brought great energy and vision to the series, and was instrumental in defining and articulating its distinctive approach and in securing theologians to write for it. Bill's own commentary for the series was the last thing he wrote, and Westminster John Knox Press dedicates the entire series to his memory with affection and gratitude.

William C. Placher, LaFollette Distinguished Professor in Humanities at Wabash College, spent thirty-four years as one of Wabash College's most popular teachers. A summa cum laude graduate of Wabash in 1970, he earned his master's degree in philosophy in 1974 and his PhD in 1975, both from Yale University. In 2002 the American Academy of Religion honored him with the Excellence in Teaching Award. Placher was also the author of thirteen books, including *A History of Christian Theology, The Triune God, The Domestication of Transcendence, Jesus the Savior, Narratives of a Vulnerable God,* and *Unapologetic Theology.* He also edited the volume *Essentials of Christian Theology,* which was named as one of 2004's most outstanding books by both *The Christian Century* and *Christianity Today* magazines.

Series Introduction

Belief: A Theological Commentary on the Bible is a series from Westminster John Knox Press featuring biblical commentaries written by theologians. The writers of this series share Karl Barth's concern that, insofar as their usefulness to pastors goes, most modern commentaries are "no commentary at all, but merely the first step toward a commentary." Historical-critical approaches to Scripture rule out some readings and commend others, but such methods only begin to help theological reflection and the preaching of the Word. By themselves, they do not convey the powerful sense of God's merciful presence that calls Christians to repentance and praise; they do not bring the church fully forward in the life of discipleship. It is to such tasks that theologians are called.

For several generations, however, professional theologians in North America and Europe have not been writing commentaries on the Christian Scriptures. The specialization of professional disciplines and the expectations of theological academies about the kind of writing that theologians should do, as well as many of the directions in which contemporary theology itself has gone, have contributed to this dearth of theological commentaries. This is a relatively new phenomenon; until the last century or two, the church's great theologians also routinely saw themselves as biblical interpreters. The gap between the fields is a loss for both the church and the discipline of theology itself. By inviting forty contemporary theologians to wrestle deeply with particular texts of Scripture, the editors of this series hope not only to provide new theological resources for the church but also to encourage all theologians to pay more attention to Scripture and the life of the church in their writings.

We are grateful to the Louisville Institute, which provided funding for a consultation in June 2007. We invited theologians, pastors, and biblical scholars to join us in a conversation about what this series could contribute to the life of the church. The time was provocative and the results were rich. Much of the series' shape owes to the insights of these skilled and faithful interpreters, who sought to describe a way to write a commentary that served the theological needs of the church and its pastors with relevance, historical accuracy, and theological depth. The passion of these participants guided us in creating this series and lives on in the volumes.

As theologians, the authors will be interested much less in the matters of form, authorship, historical setting, social context, and philology—the very issues that are often of primary concern to critical biblical scholars. Instead, this series' authors will seek to explain the theological importance of the texts for the church today, using biblical scholarship as needed for such explication but without any attempt to cover all of the topics of the usual modern biblical commentary. This thirty-six-volume series will provide passage-by-passage commentary on all the books of the Protestant biblical canon, with more extensive attention given to passages of particular theological significance.

The authors' chief dialogue will be with the church's creeds, practices, and hymns; with the history of faithful interpretation and use of the Scriptures; with the categories and concepts of theology; and with contemporary culture in both "high" and popular forms. Each volume will begin with a discussion of *why* the church needs this book and why we need it *now*, in order to ground all of the commentary in contemporary relevance. Throughout each volume, text boxes will highlight the voices of ancient and modern interpreters from the global communities of faith, and occasional essays will allow deeper reflection on the key theological concepts of these biblical books.

The authors of this commentary series are theologians of the church who embrace a variety of confessional and theological perspectives. The group of authors assembled for this series represents more diversity of race, ethnicity, and gender than any other commentary series. They approach the larger Christian tradition with a critical respect, seeking to reclaim its riches and at the same time to acknowledge its shortcomings. The authors also aim to make available to readers a wide range of contemporary theological voices from many parts of the world. While it does recover an older genre of writing, this series is not an attempt to retrieve some idealized past. These commentaries have learned from tradition, but they are most importantly commentaries for today. The authors share the conviction that their work will be more contemporary, more faithful, and more radical, to the extent that it is more biblical, honestly wrestling with the texts of the Scriptures.

William C. Placher
Amy Plantinga Pauw

Acknowledgments

Of the many colleagues and friends who gave great help in the writing of this commentary, I want to express particular gratitude to five of them: Kimberly Wagner, my tireless and most capable research assistant; New Testament scholars, friends, and conversation partners, Luke Timothy Johnson and Steven Kraftchick; my dear and patient friend of many decades, Craig Dykstra; and my pastor during my college years, George Leitz, who modeled faithful ministry for me and to whom this volume is dedicated.

Introduction:
Why the Pastoral Epistles?
Why Now?

The "Pastoral Epistles" (which is the name by which the letters 1 Timothy, 2 Timothy, and Titus have collectively been called since the eighteenth century) are among the most neglected books of the New Testament. Most pastors have preached from these letters only rarely, and they are usually explored only lightly, if at all, in Bible studies. Although they present themselves as letters from the apostle Paul to two of his young pastoral protégés, Timothy and Titus (thus the name—the "Pastoral Epistles"), they were almost surely written several decades after Paul's death, and their main focus is on establishing—or reestablishing—order, discipline, and theological soundness in congregations that have gone—or are threatening to go—off the rails.

The fact that congregations sometimes get into trouble, occasionally escalating to nasty church fights, and require remedial intervention is nothing new, of course, but it rarely makes for stirring and inspirational reading. As one accomplished preacher said of the Pastoral Epistles, "Frankly, they're not my go-to books." That's understandable. We would rather read accounts of the church cruising smoothly down the highway of faith, proclaiming the gospel faithfully, compassionately showing the love of Christ, standing tall for social justice. In the Pastoral Epistles, though, we see the church on the mechanic's lift in the garage, and we are given guidance for performing an ecclesial engine overhaul.

Ironically, though, the very traits that have caused the Pastorals to be overlooked by earlier readers may, in fact, make them urgently important for readers today. In a time when churches were full

1

and relatively prosperous, it was easy to imagine that healthy and confident congregations were the norm and troubled churches the exception. But in North America now the picture has drastically changed; it is the whole church that is in trouble. The membership numbers for traditional denominations are in precipitous decline, and most local congregations are becoming grayer, smaller, and sometimes discouraged. The preferred religious choice among many of our youth is "none of the above," and churches with impressive buildings that once housed large and vibrant Sunday congregations now find only a handful gathered for worship. People look around at the vacant pews and wonder, "What happened? Where are the young people? Are we dying?"

Even congregations that have bucked the trend and seem to be growing and strong are often confused about what it means to live as Christians in the fragmented culture in which we find ourselves today. The lines marking off the difference between healthy and unhealthy congregations are often blurred: many worship spaces look and feel more like pop concert arenas and entertainment venues than sanctuaries, some churches operate more like corporate entities than pilgrim communities, people seem to know more about the lives of superficial celebrities than they do of the saints, and North American Christianity sometimes seems more beholden to consumerist values than to the gospel.

One could despair about all this church decline and wonder why God doesn't put a stop to it. Or, more fruitfully, one could take a theological view of this shaking of the foundations. The church as we have known it is under stress, but maybe God doesn't stop the pressure and the upheavals because God started it. As Ecclesiastes says, there is "a time to break down, and a time to build up." We do know, at the very least, that God is in the middle of the church's turmoil, tearing down what we have known in order to build up a church more faithful and full of life.

And that is where the Pastoral Epistles come into play. Some of the issues faced in these letters are our issues once again—the lure and peril of "spirituality" for Christians, the character of authentic worship, the qualities needed for sound leadership, the relationship between family life and the "family" of the church. And even in those matters in these letters that seem remote from our current situation, the author approaches them with the elements we need as we address our own challenges: a love for the church, a firm gospel compass in hand, and a clear and courageous voice. As Christians in North America venture out from the ruins of the churches we once knew seeking new ways of being church, the Pastoral Epistles can refresh our memory about what really counts in Christian community and the profound importance of trustworthy leaders.

Hearing these ancient documents as wisdom for our day will require a generosity of spirit on our part. Taken at face value, the Pastoral Epistles have some jagged edges and tend to divide the house. On the positive side, these three letters, unlike other New Testament epistles, are addressed to individuals rather than churches or groups of people, and they often bear the marks of a tender and loving personal correspondence. Also, there are passages in these letters that soar in beauty and theological power, for example the moving portrait of Paul at the end of his life as one who has "fought the good fight . . . finished the race . . . kept the faith" (2 Tim. 4:7) or the encouragement given to Timothy as a pastor to reclaim the zeal for ministry that was there on the day of his ordination, "to rekindle the gift of God that is within you through the laying on of my hands" (2 Tim. 1:6). Reverberating through these letters is a love for the gospel and for the church, which finds expression in a yearning that all of the faithful would "take hold of the life that really is life" (1 Tim. 6:19).

On the negative side, however, there is a concern for church order and decorum in these letters that many readers find brittle and stern, perhaps even repressive. Beyond this, some of the instruction given in the Pastorals is quite conventional, reflecting typical codes of behavior expected in Greco-Roman households of the era rather than a new gospel-inspired ethic. The writer of these letters seems at times to forget, or perhaps ignore, his own teaching about the transformative power of Christ. Other teaching in these letters is downright shocking, even repugnant, to readers today. For example, the author says, "I permit no woman to teach or to have authority over a man" (1 Tim. 2:12), and he advises, "Tell slaves to be submissive to their masters . . ." (Titus 2:9). Also, the author sometimes does not mind his tongue, speaking of some members of the community as "silly women" (2 Tim. 3:6) and seeming to agree with the slur that all people from the island of Crete are "liars, vicious brutes, lazy gluttons" (Titus 1:12).

How do we approach these letters, then, which both attract and repel at the same time? Some of the reading strategies that I have chosen to employ in this commentary are as follows:

1. To read the Pastoral Epistles in their own context, that is, in light of the circumstances, issues, and possibilities inherent in the situation being faced by the author.

In Sierra Leone in the 1950s, the noted church historian Andrew Walls began his long teaching career. Being at that time a young and aspiring professor with an Oxford and Cambridge pedigree, Walls delivered learned lectures to his African students on the documents and history of the early church. They dutifully took notes, but, as Walls says, "You could see from their faces that it didn't penetrate."[1]

But then Walls made a startling discovery. He began to worship in local African Christian congregations, went to meetings with the Sierra Leonean pastors, and immersed himself in the life of the indigenous churches. One day in the classroom, when he was lecturing to his students about the second-century church, it suddenly struck him that he "was actually living in a second-century church."[2]

After that moment of insight, Walls read the documents of the early second-century church with new eyes, aware now that he was looking at living examples of that literature all around him. He read, for example, the long sermon-like document known as 1 Clement and would recognize that he had heard similar sermons in the African context. "Yes," he said, "I'd hear sermons like that, and just as long." He read Ignatius on martyrdom, "and though I had not actually seen anybody going to martyrdom, you saw the same sort of

---

1. Tim Stafford, "Historian Ahead of His Time," *Christianity Today,* 51/2 (February 2007): 88.
2. Ibid.

intensity."[3] He said to himself, "Why did I not stop pontificating and observe what was going on?"[4]

Reading the Pastoral Epistles with insight and understanding requires, I think, a similar shift in perspective. As readers, we have to imagine our way into a late first-century Christian community in Asia Minor. Reading these letters in context does not mean forgoing our own judgments about what these texts finally say to us, to our faith, and to the church in a quite different world today, but it does mean suspending that judgment long enough to try to make an empathetic connection to the author in his own time and place. We read these letters keeping in mind novelist L. P. Hartley's famous dictum, "The past is a foreign country: they do things differently there."[5]

I have written this commentary while serving on the faculty of a university divinity school in the United States, a school in which men and women in roughly equal numbers are preparing for positions of responsibility and religious leadership. Our faculty and students come from all over the world, represent many theological traditions, and are of many ethnicities, backgrounds, and theological worldviews. We are located in the American South, and some of our students are the descendants of nineteenth-century African slaves, while others are the great-great-grandchildren of slave owners. Some of our students are heterosexual and others are homosexual, all preparing for ministry in a time when church attitudes and rules are changing rapidly and dramatically.

In other words, I live in an environment where the church seems global, multicultural, and complex, and major change seems not only possible but inevitable and desirable. Not only that, the community in which I work is filled with people who see themselves as empowered to create that change and as called to help transform the world toward ever more just societies. We are aware of our past— its rich traditions and its shameful times and historical burdens— but we are also aware that the future can and must be different. In short, when some social structure is out of alignment with the values

3. Ibid.
4. Ibid.
5. L. P. Hartley, *The Go-Between* (New York: New York Review of Books, 2002), 17.

of the gospel, whether it be the government, the economic system, the church, or even the theological school itself, we see ourselves as having the responsibility to do all we can to change the world and make it right.

It would be easy to think that the author of the Pastoral Epistles operated in such a world as ours, but he did not. In his world, to be sure, some things could be changed, but the basic structures of society were seen as much more fixed and permanent than we view them. In our world, young people can flash messages over social media, gather a crowd in a public square, and eventually accomplish the almost unthinkable: topple a government. The author of the Pastorals, however, could not envision such a possibility, There would, for example, always be an emperor. One could imagine many ways of relating to the emperor—pray for the emperor, not pray for the emperor, pray *to* the emperor, refuse to pray to the emperor, obey the emperor, resist the emperor, die for the emperor, die at the hands of the emperor—but a world without an emperor? Unimaginable. Therefore, the author of the Pastorals, given his context, will consistently offer advice about how to move the pieces on the chessboard. We sometimes lose patience with him because we expect him to throw out the chessboard and to change the game itself.

Two experiences in particular have given additional shape to my understanding of the context of these letters. First, before I became a seminary teacher, I briefly served as the pastor of a small congregation, long enough to discover the difference between the gospel expressed in pure terms and the gospel as actually lived out in the messy lives of people and congregations. In times of calm and when I was at my pastoral best, I could speak to my congregation as a caring shepherd, with grace, patience, and compassion. But there were other times when some brush fire had broken out in the church, and, desperate to keep the fire from spreading, I could hear myself barking shrill orders like a desperate fire chief. Just so, the author of these letters is not writing as a systematic theologian. He is writing as a pastor to real congregations, congregations in trouble, and the brush fires are starting to spread. As New Testament scholar John P. Meier said, "The Pastorals are often accused of being pedestrian and bourgeois. As every bishop knows, they are simply realistic."[6] Therefore, when the mood suddenly darkens in these letters and the author's voice becomes bossy or even caustic, I don't always respond with joy or appreciation, but as a former pastor myself, I do think I understand.

I remember some years ago seeing, on one of the network television morning news shows, an interview with a learned psychiatrist. He had just written a wise and compassionate book about his years working in a psychiatric hospital and treating patients with severe mental illness. At one point in the interview he recalled having seen, in his days as a young medical student, the movie *One Flew over the Cuckoo's Nest*. In the film, Jack Nicholson plays the part of R. P. McMurphy, a small-time criminal who fakes insanity to get out of prison work duty. He is transferred to a psychiatric hospital, which is ruled over by the formidable, stern, and inflexible Nurse Ratched. To the delight of the movie audience, McMurphy ends up leading a spirited rebellion among the patients against her and her rigid rules. Because of the movie (and the Ken Kesey book on which it was based), the name "Nurse Ratched" is now cultural shorthand for oppressive authoritarianism.

The psychiatrist being interviewed said that when he first saw the movie that he, like almost everyone else, "hated Nurse Ratched." She came across as mean, obstinate, and hidebound. But then the psychiatrist, somewhat tongue in cheek, quipped, "Now that I am older, however, and have spent my whole medical career dealing with severe psychiatric cases, I have a deep appreciation for her and her work!" Just so, experience in trying to lead real and challenging congregations can soften how we understand the seemingly stern author of these letters.

Second, while I have not had the extensive experience outside of North America that others, such as Andrew Walls, have had, occasional opportunities to teach and do church-related work in what are sometimes called "less-developed" parts of the globe have tuned my ear somewhat to the problems and issues in these letters. There are many churches in the world today that in important

---

6. John P. Meier, "The Inspiration of Scripture: But What Counts as Scripture? (2 Tim 1:1–14; 3:14–17; cf 1 Tim 5:18)," *Midstream* 38/1–2 (January–April, 1999): 76.

ways are more like the late first-century congregations of the
Pastorals in form and outlook than they are like their contemporary
counterparts in Chicago, Dallas, Minneapolis, or San Francisco.
In these congregations, gender roles are complex but have firmer
boundaries and definition than they do generally in North America,
the lines between Christian and non-Christian belief and practice
are more sharply drawn than many North American Christians
are accustomed to drawing, and communication is carried more
informally—by word-of-mouth as people travel from one small
church gathering to another. When I see the author of the Pastorals
getting in a knot over whispers and rumors being spread by some of
the women as they move about in the community, I realize I have
seen similar communication patterns—and problems—among
churches today set in village societies. Gossip can be a problem
in any congregation no matter where it is located. But in these
congregations, gossip—regardless of the gender of its source—is
not simply a nuisance; it can become the primary means of forming
attitudes. Left unchecked, it can bring the church to its knees, and
not in prayer. These congregations breathe much of the same air
as the churches of the Pastorals, and awareness of them has helped
tune me to the context of these letters.

2. To read the Pastoral Epistles as Scripture.

Reading these letters as Scripture does not mean suspending
one's critical faculties. In fact, it could be argued that reading these
texts as holy Scripture requires the sharpening of critical faculties.
But to read these documents as Scripture does mean recognizing
that the church has included them in the canon of Scripture because,
through the centuries, it has heard gospel in them and found its life
formed by them more fully into the pattern of Jesus Christ.

What this kind of reading involves—and this is an often difficult
assignment for a person of my temperament—is openness,
generosity, and humility. As biblical scholar Ellen Davis has
commented about the task of reading difficult biblical texts,

> The difficult text is worthy of charity from its interpreters.
> Interpretive charity does not mean pity but rather something
> more like generosity and patience toward the text. . . .

> Charitable reading requires considerable effort; it is easier
> to dispense with the difficult text. Those who regard a text
> as religiously authoritative are willing to sustain that effort,
> because they perceive it in some sense as a gift from God.[7]

If we understand these letters, then, to be more than artifacts of
second-generation Pauline ecclesiology, but to be in some sense
gifts from God, then at the end of the day we may throw up our
hands in despair about this or that passage, unable to see how such
a word has any divine gift in it. But we will do so only at the end
of the day, not at the beginning. We will sit for a long day, dwelling
humbly with these texts, listening for the gift that God wishes to
give through them. More practically, we will consider each passage
in these letters to consist of the intersection of the gospel and some
concrete circumstance in a late first-century Christian community.
Sometimes we will be able to hear the gospel word clearly. Other
times, though, the circumstance will shout more loudly than the
gospel; so, denied a clear word, we will look instead for the trajectory
of the gospel, the difference it made in the situation.

I say this because the Pastoral Epistles have more than their share
of unsympathetic readers. To be sure, if one wishes to see these
epistles as unfortunate examples of the ossification of the once-
vibrant early church, or as documentary evidence of the resurgence
of a powerful and rigid patriarchy, or as a heavy-handed imposition
of conventional Greco-Roman domestic ethics on the Christian
community, there is plenty of material in these letters to make a
damning case. But to read the Pastoral Epistles as Scripture is to take
on two roles. We do serve, temporarily, as the prosecuting attorney,
putting these texts to the test. But finally we stand as the defense
attorney. We expose these documents to the critical gaze. They
can take it. But in the end, we come around to do what we can to
advocate for them. The good interpreter of Scripture does not make
a false case for the text but does work hard to make the best case for
the text. As Jewish philosopher Moshe Halbertal has argued,

7. Ellen F. Davis, "Critical Traditioning: Seeking an Inner Biblical Hermeneutic," in Ellen F.
Davis and Richard B. Hays, eds., *The Art of Reading Scripture* (Grand Rapids: Eerdmans,
2003), 178. Italics in original removed.

> In the case of the scriptures, there is an *a priori* interpretive commitment to show the text in the best possible light. Conversely, the loss of this sense of obligation to the text is an undeniable sign that it is no longer perceived as holy. Making use of the principle of charity, the following principle can be stipulated: the degree of canonicity of a text corresponds to the amount of charity it receives in interpretation. The more canonical a text, the more generous its treatment.[8]

Some commentators have studied the Pastoral Epistles, compared them to the more daring documents elsewhere in the New Testament, and come to the understandable conclusion that the author has an unfortunately "conservative and conventional social ethics."[9] Perhaps this is correct. When we read him from this distance, the author can indeed sound at times like the repressive Dean Wormer in the movie *Animal House*, especially when he is contrasted to the more radical-sounding Paul of Galatians: "There is no longer Jew or Greek, there is no longer slave or free, there is no longer male and female; for all of you are one in Christ Jesus" (Gal. 3:28) and "For freedom Christ has set us free" (Gal. 5:1).

But generosity demands that the author of the Pastorals receive a closer and better look, that he not be dismissed as merely a stiffer, more buttoned-up version of the "real Paul." Maybe he is, as his critics claim, rigid—temperamentally, theologically, and socially—frightened that he is losing control. On the other hand, though, maybe we get a different picture of him once we consult the weather radar. Maybe, just maybe, he is working like mad to nail a blue tarp on the roof of the church in the middle of a thunderstorm. When the howling winds and pounding rains are threatening to destroy the house, it may not be fair to criticize him for not installing a screen porch and skylights. Perhaps he's just a tightly wound conservative. Or maybe it's that he believes, as the windows rattle in the gale and the shingles fly off the roof, that the church and the gospel are worth conserving.

---

8. Moshe Halbertal, *People of the Book: Canon, Meaning, and Authority* (Cambridge, MA: Harvard University Press, 1997), 29.

9. Jouette M. Bassler, *1 Timothy, 2 Timothy, Titus* (Nashville: Abingdon, 1996), 105.

3. To read these letters not as coming from Paul the apostle but from someone writing in his name, probably near the end of the first century.

The question of who wrote the Pastoral Epistles, once fairly settled, has opened up again in New Testament scholarship. A number of scholars have gone back to the classical view that these epistles were precisely what they present themselves to be, authentic letters from the apostle Paul to two of his protégés in ministry, Timothy and Titus (although "Titus" may be simply a nickname for Timothy).[10] Most New Testament scholars, however, continue to subscribe to the dominant view, which has more or less held sway for two centuries, that these letters come from a later period, probably sometime around 90–100 CE, and that they were composed by an unknown author writing in the name of Paul.

The reasons for this prevailing view are complex, but essentially they rest on three factors: the style of the letters, the situations addressed, and what we know otherwise about the career of Paul the apostle. In short, these letters, while reminiscent of Paul, don't ring quite true to being in his voice, the churches addressed in these letters seem more developed in governance and doctrine than early Pauline churches, and the places and occasions mentioned in these letters don't square up neatly with what we know of Paul's missionary itinerary. Advocates of Pauline authorship have responses to all of these factors (e.g., Paul didn't always sound the same in his authentic letters; why should we expect consistency here?), but the weight of the evidence for these as later epistles seems overwhelming and, thus, persuasive to me.

On the other hand, I don't see these letters as forgeries, someone's attempt to mislead readers into thinking he's Paul. I say more about this in the commentary on 1 Timothy 1:1–2, but I argue that these letters were written late enough that Paul is almost certainly dead (he probably died in the mid-sixties; there is an allusion to his impending death in 2 Timothy 4:6) and that Paul's death would surely have been well known in the circle of Pauline churches. So, none of the original readers or hearers of these letters would have

---

10. For a fine statement of the view that these letters are from the hand of Paul the apostle, see Luke Timothy Johnson, *The First and Second Letters to Timothy* (New York: Doubleday, 2001), esp. 55–99.

been fooled into thinking these were letters from the actual Paul. What they received, instead, was a message from the iconic Paul, the Paul of blessed memory, the Paul who would have said this to us were he here to say it.

Also, if these letters were composed in the late first century, this would be about forty years after the Pauline missionary tours, and so Timothy and Titus are also probably dead, or certainly quite elderly and not the young pastors implied in these letters. I take the view that Timothy and Titus are symbols for pastoral leaders in the churches addressed by these letters. When "Paul" speaks to "Timothy" or to "Titus," he is actually speaking to the leaders in those communities who have remained loyal, or wish to remain loyal, to the Pauline trajectory of early Christianity.

Poet Marianne Moore delightfully described the task of a true poet as creating "imaginary gardens with real toads in them."[11] In other words, a good poem is like an imaginary garden, but the poem should connect with actual life so firmly and palpably that the garden is filled with "real toads." There is a sense in which the Pastoral Epistles are imaginary gardens with real toads. The act of the imagination was the creation of three Pauline-like letters; the real toads are the actual problems and circumstances of the churches that received them.

First and Second Timothy are presented as letters from Paul to Timothy in Ephesus. I take the view that the Christian house churches in Ephesus probably constitute the real destination of these two letters. The tangible problems presented so clearly and forcefully are likely the actual issues in this community. In a way, though, it matters not very much if Ephesus is a symbolic destination rather than an actual one. Maybe the crisis described in these letters was widespread enough that this letter could have been read profitably in a number of settings, but one thing is sure: the problems being addressed—the toads in the garden—are real.

Titus presents itself as a letter from Paul to Titus, whom he has left to organize the church in Crete. This letter has a somewhat less specific feel than do the first two. Some of the same issues are raised,

11. Marianne Moore, "Poetry," in *Complete Poems* (New York: Penguin, 1994), 36.

but they are presented more generally and sometimes as potential rather than actual problems. It may be that the newly forming Christian community in Crete is the actual destination for this letter, or it may be that "Crete" is a symbol for any new church development in the post-Pauline world of the late first century. Again, the precise destination of these letters is an interesting question but not critical to interpretation.

One additional note about a stylistic strategy in this commentary. When I use the names Paul, Timothy, and Titus, I mean to refer to the actual Paul, Timothy, and Titus mentioned in Acts, Galatians, and elsewhere in the New Testament. When I put these names in quotation marks—e.g., "Paul"—I mean to refer to them as symbolic figures. Sometimes it is difficult to know which typography to employ, but I hope it is clear enough to help the reader know which is which.

1 TIMOTHY

1 Timothy 1:1–20

1:1–2

Signing On

1 Timothy is an epistle—a letter—and the author, following the letter-writing rules in play in his own day, signs the letter in the very first line: "Paul, an apostle of Christ Jesus by the command of God our savior and of Christ Jesus our hope" (1:1). In most ages and cultures, letters are patterned according to certain conventions—the address goes here, the signature goes there—and writers of letters typically follow the characteristic literary pattern in vogue. Even if they are surging with urgent emotion or simply eager to get down to the practical business at hand, they do not start writing abruptly and just let the words flow. They follow the accepted style for letters and shape what they write according to the conventional genre—first this element, then that, then the other.

These rules change from culture to culture, of course, but in the Greco-Roman world, the environment out of which 1 Timothy came, the accepted form called for a letter to *begin* with the signature, with the name and identity of the sender. Today, of course, we typically place the signature at the end of a letter: "Sincerely, Elizabeth;" "As always, Bill;" "With gratitude for your loyalty, Superior Car Rental." But in the Greco-Roman world, letters opened more like our office memos[1]—From: Margaret Hogue, To: Jonathan Darnell—and the recipient knew up front who was sending the missive. First Timothy is no exception.

Two aspects of this opening signature are important. First, a signature at the beginning of a letter has a slightly different function

---

1. Katherine Grieb, *The Story of Romans: A Narrative Defense of God's Righteousness* (Louisville, KY: Westminster John Knox Press, 2002), 8.

than a signature at the end. When someone today signs a letter at the end, "Cordially, Steve," this closing signature serves as a kind of summary, drawing the strands of the letter together with a final cinch. It is Steve's way of saying, "Whatever I wrote above, I hope to leave you here at the end on an amiable note. Regardless of how you may have received the words of this letter, whether gentle or harsh, confrontational or comforting, I want you to know that the last word is one of cordiality." But when the signature comes at the beginning of the letter, it does not sum things up; it gets things going. It *aims* the letter by giving the reader a hint of what is coming, a clue to the letter's agenda.

If a friend were to write a letter that began, unconventionally, "This is from Eleanor, your grief-stricken, heartbroken friend," this opening identification would shape our expectation that every word to follow would be coming from Eleanor's friendship and from the deep sorrows of her heart. Just so, when 1 Timothy begins, "Paul, an apostle of Christ Jesus by the command of God our savior and of Christ Jesus our hope," the writer is not just signing his name but setting the compass heading for how we should read what follows.

We find the same aiming feature in the signatures at the beginning of the other Pauline letters in the New Testament. For example, the Letter to the Philippians has a major accent on humility, so it begins with a suitably humble signature, "Paul and Timothy, servants (slaves) of Jesus Christ" (Phil. 1:1). By contrast, the more feisty Letter to the Galatians, written on the defensive because Paul's authority and message have been challenged by adversaries, opens with a plucky signature that already has its fists up, "Paul an apostle—sent neither by human commission nor from human authorities, but from Jesus Christ and God the Father. . . ." (Gal. 1:1). In Romans, a letter consumed with the question of the nature of the gospel, Paul opens by signing his name. Then, instead of saying something simple like "an apostle" or "a slave of Jesus Christ," Paul identifies himself by means of a long and complex series of clauses that, in English translation, ramble for over a hundred words:

> . . . a servant of Jesus Christ, called to be an apostle, set apart for the gospel of God, which he promised beforehand through his prophets in the holy scriptures, the gospel concerning his Son,

who was descended from David according to the flesh and was declared to be Son of God with power according to the spirit of holiness by resurrection from the dead, Jesus Christ our Lord, through whom we have received grace and apostleship to bring about the obedience of faith among all the Gentiles for the sake of his name, including yourselves who are called to belong to Jesus Christ, ... (Rom. 1:1–6)

In other words, here in the Letter to the Romans, Paul identifies himself as connected to almost the whole sweep of biblical history, from the legacy of David to the incarnation of Christ to the resurrection to the mission to the Gentiles.[2] Taken as a whole, it signals to the readers of Romans that this is not just plain old Paul writing, but the Paul who has his whole identity bound up in the full arc of God's salvation story and that everything in the letter should be read in this light. In sum, then, New Testament letter writers do not simply sign their letters with their names but with clues to the readers—aiming, anticipating, and framing what follows.

Second, the signature of a letter not only aims at what follows, it also puts the identity of the writer on the line. Letter writers have always known that signing their letters is an act of commitment and sometimes an act of courage. It constitutes at least a mild statement, "This is who I am, and this is where I stand." Indeed, not to sign a letter, to send it anonymously, is more often than not an act of hiding, deception, and cowardice.

The awareness that one's identity is at stake in a letter often prompts the writers of letters to sign their letters with more than just their bare names. Sometimes we add titles—"John Wilcox, President of the Elmwood PTA," which indicates that Wilcox is not writing generically but out of his role as a PTA officer. Often we add indicators of relationship, such as "Gratefully, Patricia," which signals to the reader that, of all the possible Patricias—the sad Patricia, the angry one, the affectionate Patricia, the shy Patricia, the forgetful Patricia who cannot remember where she left her glasses—this letter is coming from the Patricia filled with gratitude. The same person may sign some letters, "Barbara J. Kensington, Distinguished Professor of Philosophy, Oxbridge College," and other letters, "Love, Barb,"

2. See ibid., 2–4.

depending on which facets of one's identity are being put forward. We even have subtle relational codes built into the signature: "Sincerely, Mark" is somewhat reserved and formal; "Cordially, Mark" conveys a shade more warmth; "Fondly, Mark" a touch of intimacy; and "Love, Mark" a full embrace.

So, given the fact that signatures on letters both aim the letter and reveal the identity of the writer, what does it signal when the author of 1 Timothy begins his letter, "Paul, an apostle of Christ Jesus by the command of God our savior and of Christ Jesus our hope"? We can get at these questions by parsing the various components of this signature:

Paul—As we noted in the introduction, although some New Testament scholars think that 1 Timothy was written by the actual apostle Paul, and probably near the end of his life, most scholars take a different position. They see this letter as written by an unknown author and as coming from late in the first century, probably after Paul was dead (which is the position taken in this commentary). So this is the signature not of the historical Paul the apostle but a literary "Paul."

If someone other than the apostle wrote this letter, what, then, can it mean that it is boldly signed "Paul"? One possibility, of course, is that it is a kind of forgery, a form of identity theft, that someone eager to advance his own views in the church simply wrapped himself in Paul's name and reputation to make his opinions more authoritative. But such an outright deception seems highly unlikely. Private letters in the ancient world did not arrive unannounced in the mailbox, delivered by an anonymous postal worker. They were usually carried personally by travelers, couriers, and trusted companions of the writers. They were written, delivered, and read amid a web of relationships. Moreover, if Paul was dead when this letter was written, surely the recipients (Timothy or whoever else was to read this letter) would almost certainly have known this and hardly been fooled by a letter signed "Paul."

Some have suggested that 1 Timothy was written by a close disciple of Paul, a student of Paul's ideas, and to sign the letter with Paul's name was a way of saying, "This is written in the spirit of Paul." This would place 1 Timothy in the category of the "pseudonymous letter," a common form of letter writing in the ancient world in which a writer would assume the mantle of a respected figure, and it certainly seems closer to the truth than the idea of forgery. But if the first readers knew that this was a pseudonymous letter, one that came from a disciple of Paul and not Paul, the inclusion of biographical material and personal detail applicable only to the "real" Paul seems curious. Ideas can be "in the spirit of," but to describe details about his call to preach and his call to be an apostle (2:7) and to announce the fact that he is about to arrive for a visit (4:13) has a more embodied and personal character than might be expected in a strictly pseudonymous letter.

Still others have proposed that 1 Timothy was written as a forgery and passed off to its first recipients as an old letter from Paul that was lost and only recently discovered. But this smacks more of contemporary sensibilities—we historically aware moderns are the ones who excavate "lost" texts—than of a likely first-century scenario.

The most likely possibility about authorship of 1 Timothy is that the writer of this letter was, as we have assumed, not the historical apostle Paul and also that the original readers of this letter almost surely knew that, but that the letter was to be received as if it were from Paul himself—the full, embodied Paul, present and speaking its words. In the Greco-Roman world, it was not uncommon for someone to write a letter in the voice of a past "hero" and to include in the letter specific personal details and even mundane references, in order to give the letter the feel of an actual letter from the hero.[3] A strong possibility, then, is that the community that received 1 Timothy (and 2 Timothy as well) revered the memory of the apostle Paul and wondered, now that they were facing new challenges and problems, "What would Paul have said about these things?" Seen this way, 1 Timothy was a letter written in Paul's voice to answer this question.

It is well-known that letters convey the quality of presence. As is not the case with other forms of literature—declarations, novels, proverbs, essays, or even e-mails—a letter makes the writer almost

---

3. Patricia A. Rosenmeyer, "Pseudonymous Letter Collections," chap. 8 in *Ancient Epistolary Fictions: The Letter in Greek Literature* (Cambridge: Cambridge University Press, 2001), 197 et passim.

palpable to the reader. To open the envelope, to physically unfold the pages once folded by the writer, to run a finger across the signature in the writer's very hand, to be greeted by name, and to find oneself personally addressed by the letter's conversational language, is to be gathered up into a rare combination of presence and absence unique to the letter form.

The 2012 academy-award-winning film *Lincoln* centered on a critical moment in the presidency of Abraham Lincoln: the negotiations and political maneuverings around the passage of the thirteenth amendment to the Constitution, which abolished slavery. Viewers of the movie watched as Lincoln, portrayed in the winter of 1865, discussed, argued, cajoled, and joked with his cabinet and members of Congress about such matters as "bipartisanship" in Congress, "racial equality," and "peace talks" with the Confederate rebels. Not lost on the audience was the fact that "bipartisanship," "racial equality," and "peace talks" were issues very much in the news in 2012. (In fact, those phrases are anachronisms in the movie: no one spoke exactly that way in 1865. The movie had its eye as much on the present as on the past.[4]) The result was that the film was not merely a historical narrative but was also a vehicle that allowed the most revered American president of the past to speak wisdom to the most vexing political problems of the present. The "Lincoln" of the movie was the real Lincoln, the one who sported a beard, practiced law in Springfield, married Mary Todd, spoke homespun truths, and was assassinated at Ford's Theatre, but he was also the iconic Lincoln, the Lincoln of legend, Lincoln the hero, the Lincoln who transcends time and place to speak to us now.

Just so the "Paul" of 1 Timothy. He is portrayed as the real Paul, the Paul who is "an apostle of Christ Jesus," the Paul who was knocked to the ground on the Damascus Road and summoned to be a teacher to the Gentiles, the Paul who served as a mentor to young pastors like Timothy, the Paul who just might stride through the door in Ephesus at any minute. But he is also the iconic Paul, the ideal Paul, the Paul of legend who transcends time and place to speak wisdom

4. Benjamin Schmidt, "Did Anyone Say 'Racial Equality' in 1865? The Language of *Lincoln*," *The Atlantic*, Jan. 10, 2013, http://www.theatlantic.com/entertainment/archive/2013/01/did-anyone-say-racial-equality-in-1865-the-language-of-i-lincoln-i/266990/.

and encouragement always to the struggling Christian community. In most references in this commentary, we will call him the "Pastor."

An apostle of Jesus Christ by the command of God . . . and of Christ. . . . —Sometimes in his more personal letters, as we have noted, Paul introduces himself with humility—as a "slave" of Jesus Christ (Rom. 1:1, Phil. 1:1) or even as Christ's "prisoner" (Phlm. 1:1). But despite the fact that 1 Timothy presents itself as a quite personal letter written to a beloved colleague, here Paul announces himself not with humility but authority. We do not encounter "Paul the servant" but instead "Paul an apostle of Christ Jesus." In fact, some commentators think the signature should be translated even more boldly as "Paul *the* apostle of Christ Jesus."[5] In other words, the Pastor who wrote this letter reaches into the lengthy and rich curriculum vitae of Paul and draws out an ace to place on the table: This is Paul writing to you, Jesus Christ's very own apostle.

Why the display of credentials? First, as we shall see in more detail later, even though this letter seems to be a piece of personal correspondence—from Paul to my child Timothy—the real audience of this epistle is the church, the whole community of faith. Much of the letter is addressed directly to the church, and even those parts seemingly addressed to Timothy are actually meant to be overheard by the church as words for them (the final words of the letter, "Grace be with you" [6:21b], are in the plural, a clear sign that the true audience is a group and not just an individual). So, while it seems that the letter is written colleague to colleague, pastoral mentor to student, it actually comes from the apostle to the church. Also, in speaking to the church, the Pastor wants to do more than comfort them. He wants to exhort them to a new, or perhaps renewed, way of believing and living. In short, he wants change, and so, as he does in other letters where change is high on the agenda (e.g., Galatians and Corinthians), he appeals at the outset to his authority as an apostle.

But this authority does not reside in Paul *as* Paul, as a human being. Paul's authority does not come because he is the smartest person in the room, or the most eloquent speaker, the most

5. The underlying Greek lacks the article and can be translated literally, "Paul, apostle of Christ Jesus."

charismatic leader, or the savviest strategist. It is, rather, an *apostolic* authority, a derivative authority than comes from the command of God and of Jesus Christ. This is, of course, the fragility and embarrassment of Christian ministry. Right at the point that it wishes to exercise authority, it immediately confesses that is has no authority other than an authority borrowed from God, given by grace, and bestowed in the moment. Ministry comes boldly announcing that it speaks and acts with authority, but truthfully it does not have what it comes to give. Ministers do not own authority, and they can dispense only the authority and wisdom first given to them by the Spirit.

All Christian leadership, in fact, stands on this volatile ground. The president of a global corporation may have authority by dint of a quicksilver intellect, a ruthless personality, a tough skin, and a genius for reading charts, crunching data, and making the tough decisions. Christian leaders, to the contrary, may have charts, data, and native gifts, but finally their authority rests on a call and a prayer, the call from God that sends them to the always perilous places where ministry is done and a desperate prayer that a wisdom beyond their own will be given to them.

In one of his provocative essays, novelist Walker Percy imagines a convention of cutting-edge thinkers—scientists, philosophers, and artists—gathered in a great auditorium in Aspen, Colorado. The purpose of the gathering is to hear speeches about the latest theories, discoveries, and advances in their various fields of knowledge, but in the middle of the proceedings, the building catches fire. A man suddenly rushes to the podium and announces into the microphone, "Come, I know the way out."

Percy observes, "The conferees will be able to distinguish at once the difference between this sentence and all the other sentences which have been uttered from the podium." All the other speakers may be the top authorities in the land. They may have the finest educations, the latest statistics, the most complex theories, but in their speech-making they can provide only information. The man who knows the way out may be none of these things. He may or may not have education, social standing, or scientific expertise, but what he says is more than information, more even than knowledge: it is a combination of wisdom and personal authority—it is, says Percy, *news.*[6] "There is a way out, trust me," he says, "and I know the way."

Because the Pastor, writing as Paul, begins this letter by claiming his identity as an "apostle of Christ Jesus"—and this is the second reason for his use his apostolic credentials—he invites the reader to receive what follows not as information but as news, good news, as a word that does not so much come from him as *through* him from Christ. He is an apostle of Christ, and he is to be trusted as one who knows the way to life.

But there is at least one more reason why the Pastor leads off this letter with Paul's identity as an apostle. He is, he says, an apostle "by the command of God . . . and of Christ Jesus," and by this "Paul" is stating that he is a man who is "under orders." At first this may seem as if "Paul" is pulling rank and committing an act of hubris ("I am God's Master Sergeant with orders from headquarters, so listen up!"), but actually, to the contrary, this is an expression of the writer's humility. "Paul" is saying, "I am not my own here, and I am not acting out of my own desire or agenda. What follows in this letter is not the stroke of my own genius or a personal desire to exert authority but is instead the result of obedience to the God who lies above and beyond my own wisdom."

At one level, "Paul's" testament that he belongs not to himself alone but to God is true of all Christians, indeed of all human beings. As the striking opening entry of the Heidelberg Catechism affirms,

> Q. What is your only comfort in life and in death?
>
> A. That I am not my own, but belong—body and soul, in life and in death— to my faithful Savior, Jesus Christ. He has fully paid for all my sins with his precious blood, and has set me free from the tyranny of the devil. He also watches over me in such a way that not a hair can fall from my head without the will of my Father in heaven; in fact, all things must work together for my salvation. Because I belong to him, Christ, by his Holy Spirit, assures me of eternal life and makes me wholeheartedly willing and ready from now on to live for him.[7]

6. Walker Percy, *The Message in the Bottle: How Queer Man Is, How Queer Language Is, and What One Has to Do with the Other* (New York: Picador, 2000), 138–39.
7. Question 1, The Heidelberg Catechism in Part I, *Book of Confessions* (Louisville, KY: Office of the General Assembly, Presbyterian Church (U.S.A.), 1999), 29.

At another level, by pointing out that he is under the command of God, Paul is naming, and modeling, one of the primary themes of the letter, namely, that being a Christian and living in Christian community are often counter-intuitive activities, and, as such, they require a Gethsemane-like relinquishing of one's own will to the will of God. The writer of this letter will, in the sections of the letter that follow, counter certain teachers who proclaim other paths to spiritual fullness. He will have to take into account the simple truth that sometimes those other paths seem to make more sense and have more appeal than the way of Christ. So experiencing the fullness of Christian life comes through walking obediently where God calls us to go rather than through following one's own crafty religious instincts. As commentator Luke Timothy Johnson says, "Paul works to show that it is not human knowledge or asceticism that saves, but God, just as it is not human effort or riches that form the basis for authentic hope, but only the living God."[8] Here at the outset of the letter, Paul introduces himself as an apostle who has walked just such a path in obedience and faithfulness to this living God.

The command of God our Savior and Christ Jesus our hope. Some readers of this phrase find it to be theologically odd. Why is God called "savior" and Jesus Christ called "our hope"? Isn't God equally the source of hope, and isn't Jesus Christ usually described as the savior? Actually, the writer of the letter would agree. Later in the letter, he emphasizes the salvific role of Christ by saying, "Christ Jesus came into the world to save sinners" (1:15), and still later he affirms that God is the ground of hope when he claims that "we have our hope set on the living God" (4:10). So the point here is not a division of labor—God taking the role of savior and Jesus as the hope-giver—but instead to picture the Christian life as a process, a movement from salvation toward hope: it begins in the saving act of God and comes to its culmination in the hope embodied in Jesus Christ.

For the writer of 1 Timothy, God has called the Christian community to a different way of life, a life characterized by grace, mercy,

8. Luke Timothy Johnson, *The First and Second Letters to Timothy,* The Anchor Bible, vol. 35a (New York: Doubleday, 2001), 160.

and peace. This way of life is comprehensive; it touches on every reality, from how we worship, to how we speak to each other, to what we eat and drink, to the way we raise our children. This way of life is rooted in the saving power of God. Indeed, God is saving the world through grace, mercy, and peace, and when the church embodies these qualities, it is truly the body of Christ, an instrument and an embodiment of God's saving work in the world.

But this way of life is also a wager, a gamble that, despite what reality may seem to be, grace, mercy, and peace will, in the final analysis, be vindicated. Why live with grace in a society where people grab what they can, turn their backs on people in need, resort to violence to get their way, and mock as naive any who try to live with mercy and peace? As a way of life, grace, mercy, and peace can seem hopelessly foolish and naive. The Christian life, then, is a wager that such "foolishness" will, in the end, be shown to be the path of life and the wisdom of God. Jesus himself made that wager, and the resurrection of Jesus Christ is the "down payment" on that wager. Easter is God's validation of the life of Jesus, a life of radical obedience to the ways of God despite the worst that the world could muster, and a promise that those who live this way after him will be validated as well. So the Christian life is lived from salvation, by grace and mercy, and toward *shalom* and hope. To be a Christian is to set out on a journey, from Egypt to the Promised Land, from Exodus to the messianic banquet, from God the savior toward Jesus the hope.

After the signature, the next element that appeared in an ancient Greek letters was the naming of the addressee and the giving of a greeting. And so in 1 Timothy we find, "To Timothy, my loyal child in the faith: Grace, mercy, and peace from God the Father and Christ Jesus our Lord" (1:2).

Timothy was the well-known missionary colleague of Paul. The son of a Jewish mother and a Greek father, Timothy was already a well-regarded member of the Christian community when Paul first met him in the area of Lystra and Derbe, on Paul's second missionary journey (see Acts 16:1–5). In his letter to the Philippians, Paul describes his trust in and affection for Timothy, saying, "I have no one like him who will be genuinely concerned for your welfare. . . .

In October 2006, Charles Roberts, a milk truck driver in rural Pennsylvania, walked into a one-room Amish schoolhouse and shot ten little girls, killing five of them. The distraught, emotionally ill killer then turned his gun on himself and committed suicide. The parents of the children, and the other members of the Amish community, responded in bewilderment and grief, of course, at such an unfathomable tragedy occurring in their midst. But they also responded, to the astonishment of the outside world, with forgiveness toward the killer and his family. They visited his widow, took food to her, spoke words of comfort and reconciliation, and raised money for her and her children. When asked how such deeds of mercy could be possible in the face of such cruel and tragic circumstances, one Amish woman said, "This is possible if you have Christ in your heart."[*]

Some criticized the Amish outpouring of forgiveness as misguided. One commentator suggested that such acts were "uncalled for," "disrespectful of the dead," and run "the risk of denying the very existence of evil."[†] But the Amish were not pretending that evil is not evil, that tragedy is not tragedy, and that the loss of life does not provoke grief. They had mountains of grief and tears over the loss of their children. Yet, at the same time, they were wagering that the hope of the world lies in God's forgiveness and that the Christian community is to do all it can to live and embody that truth now.

[*]"Amish Community Forgives Killer and Raises Money for His Family," *WND Weekly*, October 4, 2006, http://www.wnd.com/2006/10/38231/.

[†]David Gottleib, "Not Always Divine," *Cross Currents*, Oct. 17, 2006, http://www.cross-currents.com/archives/2006/10/17/not-always-divine/.

How like a son with a father he has served with me in the work of the gospel" (Phil. 2:20–22).

On the surface, then, 1 Timothy is a letter from the apostle Paul to a younger man, Timothy, Paul's protégé in ministry. But, as we have seen above, there is textual evidence that the letter is actually addressed not to a single individual but to the larger community. Also, if we are correct about the date of 1 Timothy, Timothy would be at least an aged man, quite possibly deceased, at the time the letter was composed. In congruence with the treatment of "Paul" above, it seems likely that 1 Timothy is a letter from an iconic "Paul" to an iconic "Timothy," having the effect of allowing the community that received this letter to overhear what the revered Paul would have said to the revered missionary worker Timothy about the problems the present community was currently facing. The effect is to allow a community that was in danger of losing its bearings regarding the gospel to recalibrate by reflecting on their current situation in light of their mission church roots.

Those problems, as we shall soon discover, have to do with false teaching rampant in the community, myths and speculations, which the writer is convinced are undermining the truth of the gospel and prompting scorn from those outside the church. So, when Paul greets Timothy with "grace, mercy, and peace" from God and Christ, it is both a standard epistolary greeting and also an implicit critique of the false teaching, which, as we will find out in due course, is marked by a lack of grace, a deficit of mercy, and a disruption of the peace.

On the standard side of the equation, "grace, mercy, and peace" is close to the customary formula for the greeting section of a New Testament letter. The usual Greek letter includes the word *chairein* (greetings), which Paul typically changes to the more theological *charis* (grace) and to which he characteristically appends the Jewish greeting *shalom*, rendered by the Greek word *eirēnē* (peace)—thus the classic Pauline formula "grace and peace" (Rom. 1:7, 1 Cor. 1:3; 2 Cor. 1:2; Gal. 1:3; Eph. 1:2; Phil. 1:2; Col 1:2; Phlm. 1:3; 1 Thess. 1:1; 2 Thess. 1:2). Here, however, the word "mercy" is unexpectedly inserted in the middle, which both reinforces the journey motif started in 1:1 and provides a subtle critique of the false teaching in the community. The Christian life is a journey from salvation to hope, started by the grace of God (and not by some human quest for spiritual knowledge), sustained by mercy (and not by fables, myths, and speculation), which has as its ultimate end the *shalom* of God (and not some abstract spiritual ecstasy).

1:3–11

Trouble in the Church

So far, the writer of 1 Timothy has followed exactly the template of the ancient Greek letter: signature, addressee, greeting. What should follow next is a section called *philophronesis*, which can be roughly translated as "warm and friendly words." Many contemporary letters still include such an element, allowing the writer to make a positive connection with the reader before getting on to the main purpose of the letter—such as, "It was wonderful to see you again at the conference last month" or "I hope you and your family are well and that the weather is cooperating." Paul's letters almost always have such a section, usually theologically nuanced, such as the one in Romans: "I thank my God through Jesus Christ for all of you . . ." (Rom. 1:8).

The Letter to the Galatians is an exception to this rule. In that letter, Paul is so impassioned, so zealous to get on to the crisis in that community, that he skips over the *philophronesis* and gets on immediately to the business at hand. The same is true of 1 Timothy. This epistle presents itself as a mentoring letter sent to a beloved protégé in ministry, "Timothy, my loyal child in the faith." One would expect here a few words of affection, something like, "I give thanks to God always for your loyalty in the faith." But no; there is serious trouble in the community, and "Paul" doesn't waste any time before going right to the heart of the matter.

But what is the crisis that commands such urgency? Here we face a problem of interpretation. Nowhere in the letter, and certainly nowhere outside the letter, are we given a clear and full description of what has gone wrong in this church. The writer of 1 Timothy and its first readers already knew the shape of the distress, so there was no need to spell it out in detail. For the contemporary reader, though, figuring out the central issue of this epistle involves some sleuthing, piecing together hints and clues, combining a phrase here with a fragment there, and sometimes trying to read between the lines. We have some solid pieces of evidence, but we also have to do plenty of educated guessing.

We do know that the problem has to do with what the letter writer considers to be false teaching (the teaching of "different doctrine," 1:3), and it seems to have found its main—though not exclusive—audience among "younger widows" in the congregation (5:11–15). So, to go deeper in understanding this crisis, and in order to gain some perspective on it, we need to pull back and explore these two aspects of the problem: (1) the issue of widowhood in the early church and (2) the character of this false teaching.

1. *The Church and Widows*—No one can say for sure exactly what the social situation was in the church at Ephesus (the likely

destination of 1 Timothy). What was the case in one community of New Testament believers was not necessarily the case in another community. Broadly speaking, though, the church in Ephesus, like most of the early Christian communities, was constituted by a cluster of house-based groups. In contrast to most congregations today, the earliest churches did not routinely gather as single congregations in one building for Sunday worship. They met mainly in homes in small groups, where worship, teaching, and training in discipleship took place. The leaders and teachers of these smaller groups were called "elders" (the Greek term is *presbuteroi*, which technically means "older men" but here means something closer to "experienced leaders"), and these elders were paid a stipend for their leadership (5:17–18). Eventually in the early church, a new office, that of "supervisor" or "overseer" (the Greek term is *episcopos,* which is usually translated "bishop") was established, and these supervisors managed the world of the local elders, but that appears to be a later development in the structure of governance. The author of the Pastoral Epistles seems, at this point, to use the terms "elder" and "bishop" to refer to the same office. He may say "elder" when he wishes to accentuate the teaching function of these leaders and "bishop" when the guiding or ruling function is in view.

One of the key ministries of the early church, and, thus, one of the critical responsibilities of the elders, was the care of widows. In the ancient world, widowhood often meant poverty, and the church saw it as a responsibility to care for the needs of these women in their midst. It is a beautiful idea, of course—caring for the needs of widows—but, as anyone who has been charged with the administration of a charitable program can testify, there are constantly issues and problems.

To begin with, not all widows were impoverished. So a roll was kept of the widows who were actually in need of food and money (5:9), and maintaining that roll fairly was forever a challenge. For example, in the book of Acts there is already a complaint on the part of Gentile believers that Jewish believers, who were apparently in control of the widows list, were neglecting Gentile widows (Acts 6:1).

Second, there was an expectation that widows who received the church's care would reciprocate by using their spiritual gifts to strengthen the life of the faith community. Biblical scholar Jens-Uwe Krause describes what early Christian communities expected of widows:

> The tasks and functions of Christian widows can be described in a few words: prayer for the congregation, fasting, moral instruction of the younger women (but only in private), in some cases assistance at baptism, and supervision of other women during worship.[9]

But not every widow possessed spiritual maturity, of course, so guiding and watching over the work of the widows was yet another job entrusted to the leadership.

Third, there was the question, what exactly is a widow? In contemporary usage, of course, the answer is easy: a widow is a woman whose husband has died. But there is some evidence that, for the early church, the definition of "widow" was more flexible, perhaps hinging less on the loss of a husband and more on singleness and financial need. The term widow may have been applied not only to women with deceased husbands but to any "woman who lives without a man."[10] This could include not only widows in the usual sense but also women who had simply never married, divorced women, and women who had taken vows of chastity. In fact, Tertullian, an early third-century church leader, expresses shock and disapproval over the news that a certain supervisor (bishop) has allowed a teenaged virgin to be placed on the widows roll:

> I know plainly, that in a certain place a virgin of less than twenty years of age has been placed in the order of widows! Whereas if the bishop had been bound to accord her any relief, he might, of course, have done it in some other way without detriment to the respect due to discipline; that such a miracle,

9. Jens-Uwe Krause, *Witwen und Waisen im romischen Reich,* vol. 4: *Witwen und Waisen im frühen Christentum* (Heidelberger althistorische Beitrage und epigraphische Studien 19; Stuttgart: Steiner, 1995) 65. Translation by Charlotte Methuen in "The 'Virgin Widow': A Problematic Social Role for the Early Church," *Harvard Theological Review,* 90/3 (1997): 294.
10. Gustav Stahlin, "χήρα," Theological Dictionary of the New Testament 9 (1974), 440-65, esp. 442.

not to say monster, should not be pointed at in the church, a virgin-widow![11]

Obviously, what happened here was that a young, unmarried woman needed, for whatever reason, financial support, and the local bishop seized on a logical solution: put her on the widows roll. What seems to make this "virgin-widow" idea monstrous to Tertullian was not so much that a young, unmarried woman could be called a "widow" but that she was too young and immature to fill Tertullian's idea of the role of a "church widow," that her youth and inexperience prevented her from setting the wise example expected of widows in the church. Most widows were at least in their sixties and had plenty of life experience, and Tertullian was concerned that this young women would not be "capable of readily aiding all others with counsel and comfort."[12] As Charlotte Metheun notes, "Tertullian's arguments point to a widely-held view that a woman should 'earn' her status as a widow. . . ."[13]

So the role and place of "widows" was already a vexed matter in the early church, and now, at Ephesus, there is a new problem that seems to have its epicenter among the congregation's widows. There were older widows on the roll at Ephesus, but there were also some younger, inexperienced, spiritually immature widows as well, who were, according to the writer, easy prey for bad theology and destructive teaching.

Apparently, a few of the elders at Ephesus had become attracted to some new and questionable ideas about spirituality and the Christian life that were in the air in the late first century, and they found that the younger widows especially were an eager audience for these ideas. The elders no doubt found this attention from the younger widows flattering, but they also discovered it was lucrative. This new teaching received such an enthusiastic reception, some widows, particularly those of independent financial means, were willing to pay

11. Tertullian, *On the Veiling of Virgins*, 9, trans. S. Thelwall, from *Ante-Nicene Fathers*, vol. 4, ed. Alexander Roberts, James Donaldson, and A. Cleveland Coxe (Buffalo, NY: Christian Literature Publishing Co., 1885), 33.
12. Ibid.
13. Methuen, "The 'Virgin Widow,'" 296–97.

dearly to hear it, and these elders found their stipends fattened as a result. There are also hints here and there in the letter that the relationships between the elders and the younger widows were charged sexually, but the language is vague and whether there was sexual misconduct can only be a matter of speculation.

These new theological ideas were spreading rapidly through the community, not only via the teaching of the elders, but also through conversations among the women themselves. The writer is concerned that some of the younger widows were going "from house to house" (probably meaning from house-church to house-church, but perhaps also simply from household to household as these younger women went about their daily activities) spreading the contagion. The effect was not only trouble inside the church but damage to the church's good reputation outside the community (5:14). So the problem was two-dimensional: some of the men were teaching the false doctrine and some of the women were spreading the virus. 1 Timothy is essentially an effort to bring the legendary authority of Paul to bear on this spread of "false doctrine" in the community. In the course of the letter, the whole community will be called to a reformation of Christian practice, the younger widows will be instructed and encouraged to piety, and the offending elders will be disciplined (two of them, Hymenaeus and Alexander, appear to have already been excommunicated [1:18-20]).

2. The False Teaching. What were these new ideas that were catching fire at Ephesus? Again, we have to do the best we can to patch an answer together from bits and pieces in the letter. Here are some themes that seem to have characterized the false teaching:[14]

> (1) *It was concerned with "myths and endless genealogies that promote speculations" (1:4).*

> The term "myths and genealogies" was not invented by the author of 1 Timothy but goes back at least to Plato. Like the phrase "high crimes and misdemeanors," it was already a set literary and philosophical expression that had a variety of

14. Martin Dibelius and Hans Conzelmann, *The Pastoral Epistles,* Hermeneia (Philadelphia: Fortress Press, 1972), 65–67.

meanings, depending on the context. Here the phrase probably indicates that the suspect teachers were tellers of false spiritual stories ("myths") and spent a wearying amount of time and energy (thus the "endless") fishing around in the biblical genealogies looking for secret spiritual truths—perhaps through a certain form of spiritualized exegesis of the Scriptures, developed in some Jewish circles, that involved cracking imagined numerical codes and making bizarre name associations.

(2) *It emphasized other-worldliness and ascetic values (Titus 1:15).*

The false teachers thought that bodily functions, such as sexuality and even eating ordinary food, were unspiritual, so they discouraged marriage as an inferior state, and, for the sake of spiritual purity, called for abstaining from certain food and drink.

(3) *It enthusiastically emphasized the present tense as the time of complete religious fulfillment and deemphasized the claim of the resurrection (2 Tim 2:18).*

The false teachers promised spiritual ecstasy in the present moment and proclaimed that the resurrection of believers was something that had already occurred in a spiritual sense and not a matter of a hope for the resurrection of the body in the future.

(4) *It had a disputational and divisive pedagogy (6:4).*

The false teachers loved argument, wrangling, and disputes. Their method was probably to challenge accepted views of Christian truth with contentious counterviews and opinions, presented as superior to conventional ways of understanding the gospel.

(5) *It implied elitism*, claiming that its core message was a special form of knowledge (6:20—Greek *gnosis*) that transcended the spiritual awareness of "ordinary Christians."

When we survey the whole canvas of this teaching, it looks very much like a quite early form of Gnosticism, which eventually became a complex and highly developed ideology that would bedevil the church a century later.[15] Indeed, Irenaeus and Tertullian, who would battle full blown Gnosticism in later generations, both read the Pastoral Epistles as evidence that Paul had anticipated the very heresy they now encountered. But in reading the pastorals this way, they mistook the bulb for the flower.[16] In the context of the Pastoral Epistles, Gnosticism should really be understood as "gnosticism," lowercase, a set of spiritual impulses rather than a system of thought. Some have argued that the reference in Titus 1:14 to the false teaching as "Jewish myths" means that the heresy was not a form of gnosticism at all but instead a version of Judaism taking root in the church and competing with Christianity. It is far more likely, though, that the false teachers of the Pastoral Epistles were spiritualizers with gnostic tendencies who worked their exegetical alchemy on Old Testament texts, particularly the genealogies and certain sections of the law. Thus, the phrase "Jewish myths," that is, gnostic readings of what were at that time the basic Christian Scriptures.

In sum, then, this "false teaching" conveyed the message that "real spirituality" was to be found somewhere else than in ordinary, everyday living. Commonplace folk might be tied down to mundane realities, like figuring out how to manage a household, raising children, going to work, putting food on the table, and participating in the community's life of worship, but the truly spiritual person, the person who genuinely desires a purer union with God, transcends all of these fleshly constraints and worldly activities in favor of a free-floating, exhilarating, and ecstatic encounter with the divine. Even the Bible is a secret document, open only to the cognoscenti. Humdrum Christians who are spiritually numb might think they are gleaning scriptural truth, but they are foolishly grazing on the surface. Only those with the discernment to crack the Bible's hidden codes can ferret out the real wisdom to be found there.

15. Dibelius and Conzelmann write, "The little that can be known definitely about the opponents points not to the great Gnostic systems, but rather to a Judaizing Gnosticism (with speculation and observances of the Law). . . ." (Ibid., 3).
16. Ibid., 17.

FURTHER REFLECTIONS
1 Timothy and Patriarchy: The Empire Strikes Back?

Biblical texts are inherently ambiguous, and there is always more than one convincing way to read them. The approach of this commentary is to receive 1 Timothy and the other Pastoral Epistles mostly at face value, that is, as letters written to provide gospel responses to practical problems in particular church contexts. We take both sides of that equation—the gospel and the context—seriously and critically.

In recent decades, however, a number of excellent biblical scholars, feminist scholars in particular, have developed an alternative way to read both the message and the context of 1 Timothy (and the other Pastorals). In this view (developed differently by different scholars, of course), the real issue underlying 1 Timothy is not false doctrine taking root among some women in the church but instead the very fact that women were stepping out of traditional gender roles and exercising power and authority. Certain women in the community, the argument goes, were seizing on the freedom offered by the gospel and asserting themselves in leadership roles, and the male authorities were responding unfavorably. Since marriage in the first century by definition curtailed this freedom and placed a woman under the jurisdiction of her husband, these women were employing the category of "widow" as a political protection against male domination and putting themselves forward as teachers with the same authority as male teachers in the church, moving at their own discretion from house church to house church (as did male teachers) and thereby proclaiming a gospel of equality.

According to this view, then, the true purpose of 1 Timothy is not to knock down the heresy afflicting women in the church but to put down the women themselves, namely these strong women who were stepping over the defined boundaries of a patriarchal society. No wonder, then, that 1 Timothy encourages these women to get married, to have children, and to cease and desist from teaching men. As a man whose power is threatened, the author himself wants these women put back in their place. And as for his criticism of the young widows' clothing and sexual behavior (such as in 2:9–10), this is, as one scholar notes, "seen as a disingenuous attempt to discredit an otherwise worthy effort by women to serve within the community."[17] In short, I Timothy can persuasively be seen as a classic case of a threatened patriarchy striking back. The Jesus movement may have encouraged women to exercise their gifts, but now, some decades later, it has gotten out of hand and the men are attempting to suppress it by putting women back into the traditional roles of wife and child bearer.

Unless one retreats to some moist-eyed view of biblical inspiration that would protect every line of this letter as the eternally valid wisdom and will of God, applicable in all times and all places, then this analysis of the patriarchal impulses of 1 Timothy needs to be taken quite seriously, no matter how unsettling it may be. It makes perfectly good sense of many of the details of the letter, and it fits nicely within what we know of the sociological shifts and anxieties over gender taking place in ancient Greco-Roman society more generally. It may well be that 1 Timothy and the other Pastorals are the stubborn stand of an outdated patriarchy attempting to reassert its dominion. As such, we would do well to preach and teach against these letters rather than from them.

More should be said, then, about why this commentary takes a different position, one that lies somewhere between an uncritically positive view of these biblical texts on the one hand and a reading of 1 Timothy (and the other Pastorals) that springs from a hermeneutics of deep suspicion on the other.

I assume, to begin with, that the central problem facing 1 Timothy is exactly what it presents itself to be: false teaching in the Christian community. I further assume that this false teaching was initiated, and for the most part was carried out, by elders, who presumably were all male. Two of these men, Hymenaeus and Alexander, are portrayed as particularly egregious perpetrators of the heresy ("shipwrecks in the faith") and have already been cut off from the community. Before this was a problem involving women, it was a problem about men: men started it.

17. Johnson, *The First and Second Letters to Timothy*, 271.

I also assume that 1 Timothy is about practical solutions for a specific problem. It is not a general treatise on widowhood (or womanhood) and Christianity. In fact, 1 Timothy is not primarily a general treatise on anything, not the structure of leadership in the church, not the nature of Christian marriage, not the formula for faithful parent-child relationships, not the value of wine as a medical remedy for stomach distress—although it speaks about all of these matters and others. 1 Timothy is, rather, a pastoral intervention in a very particular moment in a very particular crisis in a very particular community of faith. All of the concerns of the letter are not abstract speculations but tangible responses to the crisis at hand.

The "young widows" of 1 Timothy are not the source of the mischief. They are, in the view of the writer, the target of it. As a vulnerable population, the widows have become a petri dish in which the virus of false teaching is rapidly multiplying. The writer of 1 Timothy, in an attempt to thwart the infection, takes a technically conservative approach in that he calls for the church to return to the way it was as a social institution before the trouble began, to return to the days when the gospel was first received in power and purity, reminiscent of the time when Paul and Timothy were out there doing mission work among the churches.

The problem is—and here's the rub—that earlier form of the church was not only the place where the newfound gospel found expression, it was also an embodiment of many of the typical structures of the patriarchal society around it. We may well wish that the author of 1 Timothy had challenged the patriarchy inherent in the very solutions he offers. We may grieve over his missed opportunity to take Paul's own words more seriously that "there is no longer male or female; for all of you are one in Christ Jesus" (Gal. 3:28) and to call for a more radical gender equality in leadership. But for the most part, the writer of 1 Timothy does not. He simply assumes the conventional structures. For him, there is only one problem: the house of God is on fire with bad theology, and in the middle of a five-alarm blaze he does not pause to criticize the architecture of the house or the living arrangements inside. He simply turns on the fire hose and tries to douse the flames and to restore things to the way they were before.

Many years ago, I served on a task force that crafted a new marriage service for my denomination. We were particularly concerned at the time to do the right thing regarding the equality of men and women in the rite, and we carefully struck any language in the service that would have implied a different gender status. No father "gave away" the bride in our service, and no woman promised to "serve and obey" her husband. Bride and groom spoke exactly the same vows, made precisely the same promises, stood on equal footing. We were pleased with ourselves for the progress we had made.

Reading our service today, though, one is immediately struck by an unexamined assumption: it is clear we thought the marriage partners would always be a man and a woman. Today, of course, same-sex marriage, while still debated, has attained widespread cultural, legal, and religious acceptance. To read what we wrote in the marriage service several decades ago would give the impression that we were taking a side in the debate, positioning ourselves against same-sex marriage, when actually we weren't. The possibility of same-sex marriage simply wasn't on our radar screen; indeed, most of us on the task force had probably never even imagined it as a social or ecclesial option. But to read now what we wrote then, in the context of today's social debate about marriage, it appears as though we were staking out and defending a certain theological position on same-sex marriage. We were trying to be inclusive in our own time, and we ended up sounding partisan and rigid on an issue we never anticipated.

I take something of the same dynamic to be at work in the Pastoral Epistles. If the author knew that these letters would float above the specific crisis of the day and be put into the Bible to be read as Scripture in later generations; and if he knew how the Spirit would lead the church in future generations to celebrate the gifts and strengths of both women and men; if he knew that one day the very texts he wrote would serve as teaching and preaching resources for strong, faithful, and articulate women pastors; then he might well propose the same solutions for the problems he and his readers were facing, but he would probably ask for the chance to revise and clarify the language he employed to express them. He might want to send phrases like "silly women" and "gossips and busybodies"

(5:13) to rewrite. In his own day, the Pauline community already knew well of strong women leaders and preachers, and, given the way the Holy Spirit has continued to raise up women of power and charisma as leaders in the church, this author might choose to put his advice about the silence and submission of women into a more nuanced context. But the record is the record, and history rarely provides opportunities for such do-overs.

So what we must do as interpreters is to walk the narrow path between reading the Pastorals uncritically and dismissing them as mere patriarchal bluster. They are the attempt by a time-and-culture-bound pastor to speak a word of gospel in the midst of a concrete time-and-culture-bound crisis. Reading the Pastoral Epistles is, in some ways, like opening the door of a family home just as exasperated parents have sent their fighting children to their rooms with the command, "We don't want to hear another word out of either of you!" Such a scene might well be an example of good parenting in the moment of uproar, but we would not want to weave a theology of the Christian family out of this one thread! A wise observer, though, would recognize that such times are not exceptions to parental love but deep expressions of it. We are not called to imitate or adopt the social solutions the Pastor commends but instead to trace our finger along the trajectory of his thought, looking for the impulse of the gospel and following it forward into our own time and place. Doing so will allow us to receive these letters not as restrictive but as instructive, yes, even as inspired by the Spirit—holy wisdom, holy word.

So now at the outset of the letter, the Pastor, author of 1 Timothy, turns to face the main problem at hand in the church: the teaching of false doctrine. He tells Timothy that he has been left at Ephesus exactly for the purpose of stemming the tide of such instruction (1:3). If the problem is wrong teaching, then it might seem as if the Pastor would engage in a point-by-point refutation of the heresy. Significantly, however, he does not, focusing rather on the effects of the teaching, not the content. What are the effects? Bad theology leads to spiritual anxiety—troubled mind games, "speculations" about the nature of life (1:4), and to a loss of meaning (1:6). Good theology and sound teaching, on the other hand, lead to the kind of "love that comes from a pure heart, a good conscience, and sincere faith" (1:5).

At first, this seems to confound common sense. Good theology leads to love? There are plenty of counterexamples, people who can recite the Apostles' Creed flawlessly, list the kings of Israel, and parse the distinction between sanctification and justification who are nevertheless spiteful, selfish, mean-spirited, and destructive. How can the Pastor claim that good theology leads to love? The key is the Pastor's concept of a "good conscience." In popular usage, a person's conscience is an inner voice that negotiates between a person's deeply held view of right and wrong and that person's actual behavior. In times of temptation, one's conscience whispers, "Remember, you know what is right and what is wrong."

But these inner voices, these deep views of morality are actually quite personal and culturally bound. We acquire them from many sources—parents, social norms, tradition, experiences—and thus they differ from person to person and society to society. For some people, taking a sip of wine or viewing a Hollywood movie would trouble their consciences, whereas for others, a fine Chardonnay with dinner or taking in the latest film is the essence of the good life.

So the conscience, popularly defined, is a useful guide, but it is morally ambiguous. It constantly whispers "yes" and "no" as a person navigates the day, making ethical choices; but it is utterly dependent on the inner moral code for which it speaks. Bernie Madoff, who swindled investors out of billions of dollars in history's largest Ponzi scheme, was apparently a devoted husband and father. But his ethical code was governed by a combination of family affection and his own greed, ego, and ambition. With self-indulgence in his soul, his conscience kept whispering "yes" as Madoff selfishly seized whatever he could for himself and his family and slid down the slippery slope of avarice and deceit. Journalists who have visited Madoff, now serving a life sentence in prison, are surprised by what one reporter calls "his lack of conscience." "I could care less about my victims," Madoff tells his fellow inmates, who admire him as the supreme con artist. "I carried them for twenty years, and now I'm doing 150 years."[18] But Madoff does not actually lack a conscience. His conscience was simply what the writer of 1 Timothy would call a "bad conscience," one channeling a corrupt moral core. In sum, one's conscience is only as good as one's heart.

In Saul Bellow's *Mr. Sammler's Planet*, Sammler gazes at the face of his dead friend Elya Gruner as he prays,

> Remember, God, the soul of Elya Gruner, who as willingly as possible and as well as he was able, and even to an intolerable point, and even in suffocation and even as death was coming was eager . . . to do what was required of him. . . . He was aware that he must meet, and he did meet— through all the confusion and degraded clowning of this life . . . the terms of his contract. The terms which, in his inmost heart, each man knows. . . . For that is the truth of it—that we all know, God. . . .

Saul Bellow, *Mr. Sammler's Planet* (New York: Penguin, 2004), 230.

A "good conscience," however, differs from a "bad conscience" in the sense that it brokers not merely one's personal (and thus self-oriented) sense of right and wrong or even society's standards of conventional morality but the way of life given by the grace of God. Living the Christian life is not a matter of formulating some abstract ethical rules and then internalizing them and obeying them. Rather it is experiencing the transforming grace and mercy of God in Christ and then allowing one's life to be shaped by this overwhelming experience. This is what the Pastor calls having a "pure heart," which is not an achievement; it is a gift. A follower of Jesus Christ, he says, is one whose heart has become captive to God, one whose inner being has been transformed by the grace of Christ (he will later say that this is exactly what happened to him [1:12–17]). A disciple is one who has, in the most profound way possible, been "converted," that is changed from the value systems of the world (even good conventional morality) to a radical new understanding of what counts in life. To those whose lives have been transformed by Christ, love is now stronger than hate, even stronger than death. Peace is more to

18. Steve Fishman, "Bernie Madoff: Free at Last," *New York*, June 6, 2010, http://nymag.com/news/crimelaw/66468/.

be treasured than strife. To heal the wounds of life, mercy is the most precious ointment of all. Sins may weigh heavily, but forgiveness outweighs them all. To the prevailing culture, love, mercy, peace, and forgiveness look like chump virtues, like the values of suckers in a world jaundiced by Bernie Madoffs, but believers are persuaded— in fact are wagering their lives—that when history has run its course and the last word is spoken, the love of Christ will be on the throne.

The claim of the gospel is that human beings come fully alive when they embody in their everyday life the love, mercy, and forgiveness experienced in Jesus Christ. This is not an idea that one can come up with on one's one. It is not obvious from experience, cultivated in traditional codes of morality, or available to philosophical inquiry. Indeed, it is quite counter-intuitive and can only be learned through the Holy Spirit. The way the Spirit instructs, however, is not by beaming information magically from heaven but through the faithful preaching and teaching of wise believers, and this is why the Pastor is so zealous about sound teaching in the church. Only when the gospel is faithfully taught can purity of heart be preserved. And only when there is purity of heart can the voice of conscience speak wisely so that people can live out a sincere faith, with mercy, grace, and love.

The aim, then, of sound teaching is not enabling people to get the right answers to theological questions or to preserve some intellectual concept of orthodoxy. The issue, rather, is how do the faithful see the world, how do they discern the difference between what truly gives life and what only appears to be life-giving? The goal of doctrinal instruction in the church is not correct content but renewed, liberated, joyful, faithful, and loving people. "Liberation," as the educator Paulo Freire says, "is thus a childbirth, and a painful one. The man or woman who emerges is a new person. . . ."[19] The truth taught by the church, which is of course the gospel, may be hidden but it is not secret. It is accessible not through ordinary perception or the manipulations of human reason but only through an encounter with the loving God. Just such a free and open encounter is the goal of Christian teaching and preaching. Everything depends on faithful

---

19. Paulo Freire, *Pedagogy of the Oppressed: 30th Anniversary Edition,* (New York: Bloomsbury Academic, 2000), 49.

communication of the truth that the cross-shaped life of love and mercy that Jesus lived, contrary to all appearances and counter to worldly wisdom, is the way of God in the world and the way to fullness of life. As theologian John Howard Yoder put it,

> The point . . . is not only that people who wear crowns and who claim to foster justice by the sword are not as strong as they think—true as that is: we still sing, 'O where are Kings and Empires now of old that went and came?' It is that people who bear crosses are working with the grain of the universe. One does not come to that belief by reducing social process to mechanical and statistical models, nor by winning some of one's battles for the control of one's own corner of the fallen world. One comes to it by sharing the life of those who sing about the Resurrection of the slain Lamb.[20]

In 1:8–11, the Pastor makes what seems to be an unexpected turn by bringing up the proper role of the Old Testament law. We can only assume that, in context, this turn is not as abrupt as it seems because the false teaching at issue in the letter evidently involves some inappropriate use of the law. He begins his discussion of the law with a pun: "the law is good, if one uses it *lawfully*" (1:8)[21] This is somewhat like saying, "Poetry is true, if one reads it poetically." In other words, to read the law as something other than law, to stretch it beyond what it is meant to be, results in mangling its meaning. So how do we read the law lawfully? By recognizing, says the Pastor, that it is "not for the innocent but for the lawless and disobedient" (1:9). In other words, the Pastor sees the basic function of the law as identifying human sin and convicting human sinfulness. To illustrate this, the Pastor provides a catalog of types of sins and sinners. Such lists appear often in Greco-Roman literature, and the Pastors' inventory is basically a collection of what the Pastor considers to be his time's most shocking examples of violations of the Ten Commandments (e.g., not just people who kill but people who murder their mothers and fathers). The Pastor names fornicators, slave traders, and perjurers. Every generation would make a somewhat

20. John Howard Yoder, "Armaments and Eschatology," *Studies in Christian Ethics*, 1/1 (January 1988): 43.
21. Johnson, *The First and Second Letters to Timothy*, 167. Johnson's translation of 1:8.

different list, and today the Pastor might name child pornographers, terrorist bombers, and Wall Street embezzlers.

The false teachers, however, were teaching the law in a different way, somehow pressing it beyond its proper limits, using it not as instruction for sinners but as a guide for "the innocent," that is, as a positive model for spiritual living. It is not entirely clear how they were doing this, but if we connect the dots to the "myths . . . endless genealogies . . . and speculations" mentioned earlier (1:4), we can make an educated guess. It is likely that these false teachers were performing a form of esoteric exegesis of the law, perhaps similar to Kabbalah, in which they sought to find hidden under the actual texts a secret code to the eternal wisdom of the universe. This is like people in the 1970s who listened to Beatles' albums backwards, listening for secret messages smuggled into the recordings. Such approaches to Scripture can be found in every generation, one of the latest being Michael Drosnin's best-selling and misguided *The Bible Code,* in which the author interprets the Torah not by reading the plain sense of the words but by calculating the mathematical relationships among the Hebrew letters on the page. By doing so, he claims that the Torah, for those who have eyes to see, contains secret foreknowledge of such events as the assassinations of President John F. Kennedy and Israeli Prime Minister Yitzhak Rabin.[22]

Apparently, the false teachers in 1 Timothy's community were saying things like, "Now, one of the commandments says, 'You shall not steal,' and some ignorant people might try to tell you that this commandment means only what it says on the surface, namely 'don't steal.' But that's a spiritually immature way to read it. If you have spiritual eyes, you can see hidden truths in this commandment and in all of the commandments. When you read them spiritually you can gain a special knowledge and a righteousness not available to ordinary people." In other words, the false teachers taught that the Bible was a way to the wisdom of God and life, but not the Bible that everybody can read and hear, only the "real" Bible, the "secret" Bible, the Bible hidden beneath the surface, accessible only to the spiritually elite. This was part and parcel of their larger claim that "real spirituality"

---

22. Michael Drosnin, *The Bible Code* (New York: Touchstone, 1998), 13.

takes a person out of this world of ordinary care and into some realm of rarefied wisdom. To this, the Pastor says, "We know better than that. These people are trying to read the law illegally, to read poetry unpoetically. Read the law for yourself. It is exactly what it seems to be, a word addressed to sinners designed to name the shape of their sinfulness, not some secret code for the super spiritual."

While he has the readers' attention regarding the law, the Pastor makes another point by contrasting the external role of the law with the internal role of the "glorious gospel of the blessed God" (1:11). The law merely lists sins from the outside; the gospel shapes lives from within. It is important to note that, in all these discussions, the Pastor is thinking of the law in its most restricted sense, as a list of commandments. Sometimes Christians make the mistake of thinking of Judaism generally as a law-bound, rule-oriented, legalistic religion in contrast to the freedom and grace of the Christian faith. To do so, however, is to misunderstand the Torah in its original context. Recently scholars have given more emphasis to the narrative aspects of the Torah and to its theological relationship to the covenant between God and Israel.[23] Seen this way, the Torah is not simply a collection of laws but is a divine gift that shows the paths of life and defines a total way of being before God. The Torah, then, actually functions in a way analogous to how the Pastor sees the gospel.

In her book on the Torah, Johanna W. H. Van Wijk-Bos makes a helpful distinction between "Torah" (with a capital T), which names the first five books of the Bible and includes the more comprehensive view of the Torah as an encompassing way of life, and "*torah*" (italicized and with a lower case *t*), meaning the specific regulations and instructions of the law code. "You might say," she states, "that the Torah contains *torah*."[24] When the Pastor talks about the law in this letter, though, he means mainly *torah*, specific texts in the Torah that provide lists of "thou shalt nots." Such lists can point out lawlessness, but they cannot do what the gospel does, transform the heart. If a law states, "Thou shalt not drive over twenty-five miles per hour on local streets," this law can certainly reveal speeding and speeders, but it

23. See, for example, Johanna W. H. Van Wijk-Bos, *Making Wise the Simple: The Torah in Christian Faith and Practice* (Grand Rapids: Eerdmans, 2005).
24. Ibid., 4.

cannot inculcate thoughtful, civil, and responsible driving generally. That is a matter of character. Just so, the law can highlight perjurers and liars and convict them of their sin, but only the gospel can shape human beings toward a life of "love that comes from a pure heart, a clean conscience, and sincere faith" (1:5).

1:12–20
The Gospel at Work in Human Life

1:12–14 "Paul's" Experience

This next section of the letter begins, "I am grateful to Christ Jesus our Lord. . . ." This sounds a lot like the usual *philophronesis* or thanksgiving section of a typical Pauline Epistle (see the comments on 1:3–11; also compare Romans, "First, I thank my God through Jesus Christ for all of you . . ."; 1 Corinthians, "I give thanks to my God always for you . . ."; or 1 Thessalonians, "We always give thanks to God for all of you"). Normally, as we noted, this section would come immediately after the greeting (1:2), as a way of establishing a mood of thankfulness and warm relationship before getting down to the business of the letter. But in 1 Timothy the business on the table, false teaching in the community, was too urgent to wait, so only now does the Pastor get around to the thanksgiving.

Normally Paul gives thanks for the *recipients* of his letters (e.g., "We must always give thanks to God for you . . . ," 2 Thess. 1:3), but here the Pastor, writing as Paul, gives thanks for *himself* and his own experience. The reason is that the Pastor wants the readers to think of Paul as a model for what the Christian life is truly about, a strong counterexample to the message of the false teachers. He is saying, in effect, "These so-called teachers claim to show you spiritual ecstasy and wisdom, but remember what happened to me. Genuine religious power and meaning can be seen in my own experience of the mercy of Jesus Christ."

The experience he tells is a well-known one—a story no doubt often-told and treasured in this community—of Paul's own encounter with Christ. It is not a story about illumination, secret whispers, and the cracking of codes about myths and genealogies. It is rather a story of transformation, the grace of Jesus Christ making a new person altogether. It is a story of how Paul, a religious terrorist, a blasphemer, persecutor, and man of violence encountered the surprise of Christ's mercy and forgiveness, a gracious and loving power and presence that overwhelmed him and overflowed into his life, turning a seething enemy of the gospel into a strong and faithful servant of Jesus Christ.

There is some debate among scholars about whether the historical Paul actually told his story, or would have told his story, in such stark before-and-after terms. For example, in their commentary on the Pastorals, Martin Dibelius and Hans Conzelmann doubt that Paul would have used "blasphemer" and "evil doer" to describe his former life, and they assert that "1 Tim presents a portrayal of Paul from post-apostolic times, stylized for use as a missionary paradigm."[25] Luke Johnson, on the other hand, finds a place for the language of this passage in the linguistic repertoire of the authentic Paul.[26] Regardless, 1 Timothy does seem intent on telling Paul's experience in a way that forms a clear contrast to the false teachers. Through grace, Paul moved from being a sinner of the worst sort to an apostle in service of the gospel. He was ignorant (1:13) and unbelieving, a blasphemer and a persecutor of the faithful, and Christ's mercy transformed him into an example of faith worthy of being imitated by others. The false teachers, however, have moved in the opposite direction. Once servants of the gospel, they have now become sinners. Once faithful leaders, they have now become ignorant, unbelieving, blasphemers—blind guides who are leading the people of God astray.

1:15–17 Clues from Worship

In the middle of the autobiographical section, the Pastor inserts two set pieces, two sayings probably drawn from the liturgy of the community:

---

25. Dibelius and Conzelmann, *The Pastoral Epistles,* 28.
26. Johnson, *The First and Second Letters to Timothy,* 178.

1. "The saying is sure and worthy of full acceptance, that Christ Jesus came into the world to save sinners . . . ." (1:15) and

2. "To the King of the ages, immortal, invisible, the only God, be honor and glory forever and ever. Amen" (1:17).

The first saying is probably a creedal-like recitation, and to insert it here allows the Pastor to say, "The very thing you speak so often when you are at prayer is absolutely true and should be deeply affirmed: Christ Jesus came into the world to save sinners." But saying something repeatedly in worship and really taking it to heart are often two different things, and the Pastor wants to give this old saying some new bite. The phrase "save sinners" is here fastened to the recital of Paul's story, which conveys the idea that what is chanted in the creed is precisely what happened to Paul. The saving power of Christ is not an abstract concept, but something that actually occurs in the midst of people's messy lives. As we see in Paul's life, Jesus Christ is a living presence at work in human life, lovingly and mercifully overcoming destruction and dysfunction and enabling human beings to flourish and to arrive at their true fulfillment.

The statement "Christ Jesus came into the world to save sinners" contains an implied contrast with other possible understandings of Jesus' mission (such as those taught by the false teachers). In our own time, the Pastor's emphasis continues to underscore the primary mission of Jesus Christ to save sinners, not merely to serve as a good example of a nice person, to model self-care, to wander around Palestine as a tart-tongued sage, to stimulate peasant insurrection toward Galilean land reform, or to whisper secret gnosis into the ears of spiritual virtuosi. He had bigger fish to fry; he came into the world to rescue a lost and perishing humanity.

This affirmation of Jesus' saving role carries with it an understanding of the plight of humanity. Any concept of salvation always contains an implied question: saved from what? For the Pastor, human beings are not primarily unenlightened, needing to be taught deeper spiritual truths, or incomplete, needing to mature in mystical wisdom, or hungry for the heavenly secrets, needing to be initiated into the esoteric mysteries. Human beings are, rather, sinners, people who have turned away from God and away from the selves God created them to be, joining up with the forces of death and making a "shipwreck" (1:19) of life.

Perhaps no one wrote more powerfully of human captivity to sin and death than did the lawyer and lay theologian William String-fellow. For Stringfellow, death was not just a biological event but "a moral power claiming sovereignty over all people and all things in history."[27] Human beings, he thought, are constantly torn between life and death, and death is powerfully seductive, working its malice through the enticements of what the Scripture calls the "powers and principalities."

> People are veritably besieged, on all sides, at every moment simultaneously by these claims and strivings of the various powers each seeking to dominate, usurp, or take a person's time, attention, abilities, effort; each grasping at life itself; each demanding idolatrous service and loyalty. In such a tumult it becomes very difficult for a human being even to identify the idols that would possess him or her. . . .[28]

Lest this sound too apocalyptically strange, too remote from common experience, Stringfellow reminds us that the powers and principalities are embedded in the everyday realities of life, in everything that is not God but that still presses in on human beings, demanding loyalty and obedience. The power and principalities are at work in

> . . . all institutions, all ideologies, all images, all movements, all causes, all corporations, all bureaucracies, all traditions, all methods and routines, all conglomerates, all races, all nations, all idols. Thus, the Pentagon or the Ford Motor Company or Harvard University or the Hudson Institute or Consolidated Edison or the Diners Club or the Olympics or the Methodist Church or the Teamsters Union are principalities. So are capitalism, Maoism, humanism, Mormonism, astrology, the Puritan work ethic, science and scientism, white supremacy, patriotism, plus many, many more—sports, sex, any profession or discipline, technology, money, the family—beyond

---

27. William Stringfellow, *A Keeper of the Word: Selected Writings of William Stringfellow* (Grand Rapids: Eerdmans, 1996), 66.
28. Ibid., 211.

any prospect of full enumeration. The principalities and powers are legion.[29]

The grip of death on us is a power too strong for us to break
on our own. We cannot think ourselves free, educate ourselves to
genuine humanity, or behave our way to fullness of life. Jesus Christ
comes, then, to do what we cannot do on our own power, to save us
from death—death at the end of life and also death in the middle of
life—and to restore our humanity. I believe, said Stringfellow, "that I
am called in the Word of God—as is *everyone* else—to the vocation
of being human, nothing more, nothing less."[30] This saving power,
this call of the Word, is not, Stringfellow insists, a call to be con-
ventionally religious. "Indeed, all religious versions of the gospel are
profanities."[31] It is a call to be what we were created to be, human
beings who express our deepest humanity by living toward ourselves
and others with the same love and mercy that have been our gifts in
Christ Jesus.

As a young lawyer, Stringfellow experienced the powers and principalities as a temptation to succumb to the trappings of a successful
legal career. He was ultimately set free from this careerist temptation, not because he saw through it, but because, like the Paul of 1
Timothy, he was converted by the gospel to a new way of seeing and
being:

> I . . . elected then to pursue *no* career. To put it theologically,
> I died to the idea of career and to the whole typical array
> of mundane calculations, grandiose goals and appropriate
> schemes to reach them. I renounced, simultaneously, the
> embellishments—like money, power, success—associated
> with careers in American culture, along with the ethics requi-
> site to obtaining such condiments. I do not say this haughtily;
> this was an aspect of my conversion to the gospel, so, in fact, I
> say it humbly.[32]

The salvation of Christ Jesus happens, then, in the present tense,
in the midst of life's pressures and failings, but it also points forward

29. Ibid., 205.
30. Ibid., 31.
31. Ibid.
32. Ibid., 30.

toward eternity. Paul says that he is "an example" (present) for others "who would come to believe in him for eternal life" (future). To be among those who have participated in Christ's salvation is, then, an eschatological reality. In God's eternal life, we already have the identity as children of God and full human beings that, in historical time, we must live for and grow toward. An old spiritual sings, "Oh, nobody knows who I am, till the judgment morning," which means that the true identity of those who belong to God is not fully recognizable in the midst of history but can be known only in the light of God's ultimate victory.

In April 1975, a twenty-one-year-old woman named Karen Ann Quinlan was at a birthday celebration with some friends at a local tavern near her home in New Jersey. Tragically, the alcohol she consumed reacted with sedatives she had already taken. She went into cardiac arrest and was rushed to a hospital, where she quickly slipped into a coma, from which she would never awaken. Her condition steadily deteriorated, and within days she was diagnosed as being in a "persistent vegetative state." Some months later, her body had wasted away to seventy pounds, she was still on a respirator, and except for a few minimal functions, her brain was effectively dead.

Karen Ann's parents, Joseph and Julia Quinlan, were deeply devout Catholics. Unable at that point to have children of their own, they had adopted Karen Ann from a Catholic charity service when she was a few weeks old. When the nun at the charity handed Karen Ann to Julia, she said, "Although this baby comes to you through us, she is a gift from God." But now, they watched in pain and horror as their daughter was kept barely alive on a ventilator. Finally, they made a moral decision: they would remove life support from their beloved daughter. They saw this as the right thing to do, the faithful thing to do, but they quickly ran into legal difficulties, including a threat by the county prosecutor to file homicide charges against them if they acted to remove the ventilator. The Quinlans eventually took their case all the way to the New Jersey Supreme Court, which ruled unanimously that Joseph Quinlan had the right to determine Karen Ann's medical treatment, including the right to discontinue all extraordinary means of life support.

At the trial, Joseph Quinlan took the stand, speaking out of deep sadness, his voice hardly above a whisper. He described his Christian faith and how he had struggled for six months to come to his decision. Her physical condition was irreversible, he said, but his decision was a religious one, not just a medical choice. Having talked many hours with their priest, Joseph and Julia were convinced that their daughter belonged steadfastly to God, that nothing could separate Karen Ann from the love of Christ, and that to allow her body to be kept alive by machines when she could not recover was a sign of a lack of faith. Joseph told the judge that he wanted "to place her completely in the hands of the Lord."[33]

Joseph Quinlan's testimony came out of the Christian faith, with its eschatological vision of life and death. This vision did not spare the Quinlans heartache and grief over the illness and death of their daughter, but it did allow them to see that what had happened to their daughter was not the final word about her and her relationship to God. The court, of course, could not receive Joseph Quinlan's testimony at face value because its origin was not in the legal system or even in ordinary morality but in the hope of Jesus Christ and the eternal promises of God. The court was able to hear what he said as "bearing upon his moral character."[34] In other words, what Joseph Quinlan said about his faith was, to the court, evidence only that he was a good person.

To put this in terms of 1 Timothy, Joseph Quinlan had a view of his daughter and of life that was the gift of the gospel. It could not be derived merely from medical information or from rational ethical thinking. It was not the product of speculation or mystical exegesis. It was taught by his church, but its source was the life and mercy of Jesus Christ. It prompted Joseph and Julia Quinlan to act out of a "good conscience" and to take ethical action in the present, but whether their choices were wise and true could only be seen in an eschatological light, could only be measured by "those who would come to believe in [Christ] for eternal life" (1:16).

---

33. Michael S. Lief and H. Mitchell Caldwell, *And the Walls Came Tumbling Down: Greatest Closing Arguments Protecting Civil Liberties* (New York: Scribner, 2006), 18.
34. The Supreme Court of New Jersey, In The Matter of Karen Quinlan, An Alleged Incompetent, 70 N.J. 10 (1976), 355 A.2d 647.

The key to the obedience of God's people is not their effectiveness but their patience. The triumph of the right is assured not by the might that comes to the aid of the right, which is of course the justification of the use of violence and the other kinds of power in every human conflict; the triumph of the right, although it is assured, is sure because of the power of the resurrection and not because of any calculation of causes and effects, nor because of the inherently greater strength of the good guys. The relationship between the obedience of God's people and the triumph of God's cause is not a relationship of cause and effect but one of cross and resurrection.

John Howard Yoder, *The Politics of Jesus* (Grand Rapids: Eerdmans, 1994), 232.

The second of these liturgical sayings, "To the King of the ages," which is a blessing or benediction, probably functions here in two ways. First it serves as an ascription of praise, an expression of Paul's gratitude for the transforming mercy of Christ. Paul tells his story and then sings the doxology. Second, since the phrase almost surely comes from the community's own liturgy, it would evoke the memory of their worship. As is the case with all of the New Testament letters, 1 Timothy was probably read aloud to the community, and its reading and hearing would have had acoustical impact. In the middle of the retelling of Paul's story and a discussion of false teaching, then, the recipients would have heard the familiar words of the blessing, reminding them that here and now, as the community gathers for worship, is a place of encounter with God. Where is God to be found? In myths and genealogies? No, God is more likely to be found on some dusty Damascus road in the middle of life's crises. Where is the "immortal, invisible" divine to be encountered? In "speculations"? No, right here in this place of worship as the sisters and brothers in faith gather in prayer around the Lord's Table. Indeed, it is to this very experience of worship that the Pastor turns in chapter 2.

1:18–20 Timothy's Character

The Pastor, having already lifted up "Paul" as an example of what the mercy of Christ can do to renew a life, now lifts up Timothy as an example of the ideal local leader. Three traits make him a model.

First, his leadership is an expression of divine charisma, a spiritual gift for leadership and teaching given by God. This is the meaning of the phrase about "prophecies" (1:18), which most likely refers not to predictions about Timothy but to the church's practice of discerning through prayer (and then declaring in a prophetic utterance) who among the community has the gift of leadership. In the background may even be the memory of the commissioning and ordination of the historical Timothy (the reference to "laying on of hands" in 2 Timothy 1:6 may also allude to such an event).

Second, Timothy has faith, presumably of the type named in 1:4, the sort of faith that is rooted not in speculation but in the will and plan of God. And third, he has a "good conscience," which allows him to make everyday ethical decisions on the basis of his faith (see the discussion on 1:5).

In vivid contrast to Timothy, who has both faith and a good conscience, the Pastor in 1:19–20 names two men who have neither, Hymenaeus and Alexander. As for conscience, these men rejected it, and as for faith, they "suffered shipwreck. . . ." Thus "Paul" says that he excommunicated them ("turned over to Satan," 1:20), evidently a temporary disciplinary measure designed to teach them "not to blaspheme." It is hard to know if these are actual people in the community that received the letter, spotlighted because they were egregious examples of the false teachers, or if they, like the historical Paul and Timothy, are figures from a previous generation who are inserted here because the community would remember what happened to them and take warning. Either way, their names are more evidence of the character of the false teaching. Hymenaeus is mentioned again in 2 Timothy 2:17–18 as one who "swerved from the truth by claiming that the resurrection has already taken place," and Alexander is probably the troublemaker "Alexander the coppersmith," named in 2 Timothy 4:14 who did Paul "great harm."

1 Timothy 2:1–3:1a

As we have seen, the church community addressed by this letter was badly broken. False teaching, faulty testimony, a damaged mission, troubled relationships, a tarnished public reputation—these were the marks of a Christian community in disarray. Beginning with chapter 2, the Pastor opens up his physician's bag and begins to apply remedies, both practical and theological, to these wounds.

As we have also seen, the Pastor writes in the voice of the apostle Paul to Timothy, a symbolic trusted leader who is imagined to have been left at Ephesus to "fight the good fight" (1:18) of community repair and restoration. The recipients of the letter get to overhear "Paul" giving advice to "Timothy" in a very direct and personal voice: "I urge . . ." (2:1), "I desire . . ." (2:8), "I permit . . ." (2:12). The goal of this firm advice and instruction is that the church will regain its bearings, get a grip on its theological heritage, and recover an understanding of "how one ought to behave in the household of God" (3:15).

2:1–7
Getting the House in Order: Prayer

The very first item on the list, the first wound to be treated, is worship, specifically the prayer life of the community. This section of the letter forms the longest sustained discussion of prayer in the New Testament.[1] The Pastor is concerned that a healthy life of

---

1. Robert W. Wall (with Richard B. Steele), *1 & 2 Timothy and Titus* (Grand Rapids: Eerdmans, 2012), 79.

prayer and worship be recovered, and as such, he addresses three aspects of prayer, all of which were contested by the false teachers: the scope of prayer, the purpose of prayer, and the proper attitude of prayer (which he will address in 2:8–15). Since these aspects of prayer were matters of dispute, the Pastor works to allow them once again to rotate like planets around the burning sun of good theology, receiving illumination specifically from an understanding of what the God of salvation has done in and through Jesus Christ (2:3–6).

As for the scope of prayer, the Pastor commands that prayer in all its forms ("supplications, prayers, intercessions, and thanksgivings") should be made "for everyone" (2:1). The strong imperative ("I urge . . .") implies that there is a counter practice in play, namely, that at least some people in the community had a more exclusive prayer list and were not, in fact, praying "for everyone." Why was their prayer list narrowed? First, it is difficult to pray for everybody in the community in the middle of a church fight. There were divisions in this church, gossip and acrimony were on the menu every day, so some of these Christians in Ephesus were probably praying for "us" but not "them," for the folks who believed as they did but not for those who didn't. Prayer had become a form of cheerleading for our team against the others. There is also a strong possibility that the false teachers were playing into this discord by suggesting that there were levels of Christians—ordinary Christians and the "truly spiritual" Christians, the ones who had mastered the mystical secrets of divine knowledge. Genuine prayers, then, could be offered only by and for those in the know, those at the highest level.

No, warns the Pastor, this restricted prayer life is both destructive to the community and out of accord with sound teaching. Prayers should be made not just for some but for all. The Pastor then extends this notion of universal prayer with a somewhat surprising twist, namely that prayers for all should also include "kings and all who are in high places" (2:2). The surprise here is that these early Christians lived under the power of Rome, not always a safe or friendly force. However, praying for the worldly authorities is imbedded in the Old Testament ("Pray for the life of the king and his children," Ezra 6:10) and the book of Baruch suggests that even exiles in Babylon were encouraged to pray for King Nebuchadnezzar and his son

Belshazzar, for "we shall live under [their] protection" (Bar. 1:11–12). Praying for the secular rulers was carried forward into Christian practice. The letter of 1 Clement, written probably just slightly later than 1 Timothy, uses prayerlike language to express a similar view:

> You, O Lord, have given the authority of the kingdom to the rulers of this earth through your almighty and unspeakable power, so that we, knowing how you esteem and honor them, might submit ourselves to them, in no way opposing your will. Give them, O Lord, health, peace, concord, and steadfastness, so that they may discharge without transgression the authority You gave them.[2]

The prayers of the church, then, cast the widest possible net. They are for friends and enemies, for those inside the community of faith and those outside, for those of little power and influence and for those in high positions of power and authority. In short, the church prays "for everyone." But why? What is the reason for these all-embracing prayers? The first purpose the Pastor names is "that we might lead a quiet and peaceable life in all godliness and dignity" (2:2). This reason applies to the whole spectrum of Christian prayer,

---

A beautiful prayer, which is included in the service books of several denominations, gathers up the theological connection between prayer and peace expressed by the Pastor:

Holy God, giver of peace, author of truth,
we confess that we are divided and at odds with one another,
that a bad spirit has risen among us
and set us against your Holy Spirit of peace and love.
Take from us the mistrust, party spirit, contention,
and all evil that now divides us.
Work in us a desire for reconciliation,
so that, putting aside personal grievances,
we may go about your business with a single mind,
devoted to our Lord and Savior, Jesus Christ.   **Amen.**

The Book of Common Worship (Louisville, KY: Westminster John Knox Press, 1993), 812.

---

2. A paraphrase of 1 Clement 61:1, based on the 1885 translation by Charles H. Hoole.

but it has particular pertinence in the prayers "for kings and all who are in high places."

Many commentators have complained that this desire for "peace and quiet" sounds pretty bourgeois.[3] This letter is addressed to a church probably in the late first century, and the suspicion is that, by then, the fire had gone out of the belly of the Christian movement. In the early days, Christians lived in the gale force wind of the Spirit, were constantly on the *qui vive*, expected the present age to come to a dramatic end at any minute, were willing to let land and possessions go, and were fearless before the wrath of authorities, the fires of tyrants, and the lions of Caesar. But now, goes this line of reasoning, the years have dragged by, and it is clear that Christ's return is delayed and that Christians will have to learn how to go along and get along for a while in this present age, maybe a long while. Jesus was crucified by the Roman authorities, Paul was dragged before angry mobs and tried by a governor of the empire, but now Christians felt they needed to lay low, to become inconspicuous, and to be known not for their proclamation of a new sovereignty but instead for the fact that they posed no threat to the present one.

But to view this passage in this way, as merely a timid word to "pray for the emperor so he'll leave you alone," misses a good many theological cues in the text. While it is true that the eschatological outlook of the church changed as the decades passed, one could say that in many ways the church's eschatology seasoned over the years rather than slackened. It gained the wisdom of knowing that Christian hope does more than paint a picture of eternity; it also summons a way of living in the here and now. The Pastor who wrote this letter still believed that Christ would appear as victorious Lord "at the right time" (6:14–16), but he was now aware that this expectation and hope must be lived out in an extended historical present. The Pastor knew well that being Easter people did not mean renouncing the world, donning white robes, going to the mountaintop, and singing "I'll Fly Away." Rather it meant the harder task of living the gospel every day in the rough and tumble world of pagan neighbors and worldly powers. Christians are called, the Pastor knew, to serve

---

3. See, for example, the discussion of the "bourgeois" view in Philip H. Towner, *The Letters to Timothy and Titus* (Grand Rapids: Eerdmans, 2006), 171–75.

Christ as Lord in a world of kings and Caesars, presidents and potentates, and to live the life of the citizen of heaven amid the constraints and complexities of this present age.

One way to serve Christ this way was to pray "for kings and all who are in high places," which shows its countercultural implications when we recognize that this command is to pray *for* the emperor and not *to* the emperor. In the ancient world, earthly rulers were commonly viewed as divinized persons worthy of exaltation, worship, and prayers, and the Roman imperial cult demanded prayers and sacrifices. Offering prayers *for* the emperor, as Jouette Bassler has noted, was an "important substitute" for the unthinkable act of praying to Caesar and a signal from the church that it posed no insurrectionist threat.[4] But for the Pastor, the primary motivation for these prayers was theological. Prayers are to be made to the "one God" (2:5) on behalf of the worldly rulers, which makes it clear that the God of Jesus Christ is the one true God, without rival in heaven or on earth, and that even the exalted and powerful Roman emperor is subject to this God. Not only that, the church is to pray not for royal favors or special treatment but for the earthly rulers to do their God-given job, to bring shalom to human society. In other words, God's will for the rulers of this earth is that they will exercise power in such ways that they bring not the clamor of war but the quiet calm of peace, not the suffering of tyranny and oppression but the protection for people to live "in godliness and dignity" as creatures of the living God.

The second reason for praying for everyone, even the earthly rulers, is also theological and christological, and it brings this discussion about prayer to a white hot intensity. The Pastor claims that Christians in Ephesus should be praying for everyone—high and low, near and far, friend and foe—not out of some sentimental cultural ethic of "inclusivity," but rather because of the universal saving intentionality of God. God "desires everyone to be saved" (2:4)—not a few, but *everyone*—and Christ Jesus "gave himself as a ransom for all" (2:6)—not just for some, but for *all*.

When the Pastor's claims that the faithful ought to pray for

4. Jouette M. Bassler, *1 Timothy, 2 Timothy, Titus* (Nashville: Abingdon Press, 1996), 50–51.

Too often we think of hope in too individualistic a manner as merely our personal salvation. But hope essentially bears on the great actions of God concerning the whole of creation. It bears on the destiny of all humanity. It is the salvation of the world that we await. In reality hope bears on the salvation of all men— and it is only in the measure that I am immersed in them that it bears on me.

Jean Cardinal Daniélou, SJ, *Essai sur le mystère de l'histoire* (Paris: Seuil, 1953), 340.

everyone, he says in effect, "Because, *as we all know*, God desires everyone to be saved and to come to a knowledge of the truth." The issue at hand is the proper scope of prayer, not the breadth of salvation, but what the Pastor assumes his readers will take for granted has taken on a theological life of its own. Does the claim that God desires everyone to be saved imply universal salvation? The text simply says that God *desires* the salvation of all, not that all are saved, but as many theologians have observed, if God desires it but doesn't achieve it, this has implications about the power of God. The New Testament as a whole is somewhat ambiguous about whether every human being will be redeemed, and we should be cautious about going beyond what we are given. The main thrust, however, of this and other texts, is toward a God whose mercy is wide and whose saving love embraces the whole of creation. As William Willimon has said,

> You know how, through the ark of Noah, God rescued a righteous remnant, allowing the many to perish. But do you know the full implications of the story told by 1 Timothy, suggesting that God's plan is now more bold than to rescue a religious elite (that is, everyone in this room) from an otherwise botched creation? No one is more convincing than Paul in proclaiming that God's present desire is restoration of all things in Christ:
>
>> In him we have redemption through his blood, the forgiveness of our trespasses, according to the riches of his grace that he lavished on us . . . he has made known to us . . . to gather up all things in him, things in heaven and things on earth. (Eph. 1:7–10)
>
> You can't miss that *to gather up all things in him*. Paul has

poetically sailed beyond the merely personal, "Jesus died for
my sins," or "I know that I will be in heaven." God's desire, in
Jesus Christ, is akin to God's cosmic desire in Genesis 1 and
2. God is still busy bringing worlds into being that were not.
The restless Creator became the relentless Redeemer. The
Redeemer is the same fabricator of the chaos whom we met
as Creator. The work of the cosmic Christ is cosmic salvation.[5]

Through Christ, God has bound Godself to us, and us to God, in the most
radical way imaginable. And this binding is not occasional or temporary. It
cuts to the heart of who we are, while speaking volumes about the person that
God is and the actions that God undertakes. Precisely because the scope of
the Son's intercession is as broad as the humanity that he assumes, precisely
because Jesus is "exalted at the right hand of the Father" (Acts 2:33, cf. Acts
7:55–6 and Mark 16:19), there is good reason to suppose that God's saving
work has no limits. It's not theological overreach to hope that salvation will
come to all. Such hope follows directly from an awareness of God's love and
power, articulated by Christ and distributed, mysteriously, by Christ's Spirit.

Paul Dafydd Jones, "A Hopeful Universalism," *The Christian Century,* 129/13 (June 27, 2012): 27.

God is at work in the world doing saving work—calling all human
beings to their full humanity, summoning worldly rulers to their
proper labor for justice, healing the estrangement between humanity and God—and prayer is one of the powerful ways that Christians
actively participate in this divine saving action. We pray for everyone, including ourselves, not so people won't have their feelings hurt
if they are left out, but so that they, and we, will be reconciled to God
and restored to fullness of life as creatures of God. We pray for the
emperor, claims the Pastor, not so he will be appeased but for a more
dramatic purpose—so he will be *saved.* The prayer is a plea for the
redeeming power of God to capture the emperor's will and to guide
his scepter so that he rules justly and is restored to his proper role as
an ambassador of God's peace.

---

5. William H. Willimon, *Who Will Be Saved?* (Nashville: Abingdon Press, 2008), 46.

"The Lord's Prayer itself, as William Stringfellow has pointed out, is an act of exorcism: 'Whether many who redundantly and ceremoniously recite the Lord's Prayer are cognizant of it or not, the fact remains that the invocation of the name of God, followed at the end of the prayer by the plea "deliver us from evil" . . . constitutes an act of exorcism.' The church understood itself as an alternative community living in resistance to the principalities and powers of the world; it thus had to struggle constantly to live free from captivity to the 'collective possession' of the society around it."

Charles L. Campbell, *The Word before the Powers: An Ethic of Preaching* (Louisville, KY: Westminster John Knox Press, 2002), 56.

FURTHER REFLECTIONS
The First Letter to Timothy and the Letter from the Birmingham Jail

This approach to prayer for "all who are in high places" walks a narrow line in Christian ethics. It can easily slip into an assumption that Christians are called always to be decent, quiet, law-abiding citizens, content for the sake of social peace to let the politically powerful have their way. But the Pastor here is not urging the Christian community to become obedient to Caesar for the sake of peace, but, to the contrary, to pray that Caesar will become obedient to the will of God, to rule with justice, and to provide the conditions for peace to prevail in society.

In 1963, eight white clergy in Alabama, no doubt believing that they were in the irenic spirit described in 1 Timothy, wrote an open letter urging Martin Luther King to cease demonstrations and civil disobedience on behalf of civil rights. "We further strongly urge," they wrote,

> . . . our own Negro community to withdraw support from these demonstrations, and to unite locally in working peacefully for a better Birmingham. When rights are consistently denied, a cause should be pressed in the courts and in negotiations among local leaders, and not in the streets. We appeal to both our white and Negro citizenry to observe the principles of law and order and common sense.[6]

6. "Public Statement by Eight Alabama Clergymen," Mass Resistance, April 12, 1963, http://www.massresistance.org/docs/gen/09a/mlk_day/statement.html.

In his "Letter from Birmingham Jail," King responded:

> One may want to ask: "How can you advocate breaking some laws and obeying others?" The answer lies in the fact that there are two types of laws: just and unjust. I would be the first to advocate obeying just laws. One has not only a legal but a moral responsibility to obey just laws. Conversely, one has a moral responsibility to disobey unjust laws. I would agree with St. Augustine that "an unjust law is no law at all"
>
> Now, what is the difference between the two? How does one determine whether a law is just or unjust? A just law is a man-made code that squares with the moral law or the law of God. An unjust law is a code that is out of harmony with the moral law. To put it in the terms of St. Thomas Aquinas: An unjust law is a human law that is not rooted in eternal law and natural law. Any law that uplifts human personality is just. Any law that degrades human personality is unjust. All segregation statutes are unjust because segregation distorts the soul and damages the personality.[7]

In important ways, King's reply is actually more in accord with the theology of 1 Timothy than the "working peacefully" petition of the Alabama clergy. King, citing Aquinas, recognized that the true role of human law, and thus of the worldly authorities, is to serve God's law, and only those laws that uphold human dignity serve God's law. When the Pastor urged prayers for the emperor so that they could lead a "peaceable life," his passion is not for the *Pax Romana* but for the peace of God.

In 2:5–6, the Pastor moves into a rhythmic, hymn-like description of the saving act of God in Jesus Christ. Some translations, such as the NRSV, set this as poetry to support the idea that the Pastor is here likely quoting a hymn or a creed, but this is not necessarily the case. In fact, as the clauses unfold, they constitute a cumulative theological argument pointedly pertinent to the issues being addressed in the letter. Each phrase of the statement works as a double-edged

7. Martin Luther King Jr., "Letter from Birmingham Jail," April 16, 1963, Bates College, http://abacus.bates.edu/admin/offices/dos/mlk/letter.html.

sword, cutting away false doctrine first in the culture and then inside the church:

"For there is one God."—In a polytheistic culture, this is a bold monotheistic claim. There is only one God, and this God's name is not Augustus or Nero or Zeus or Diana, but the God of Israel, the God of Jesus Christ. To the Christians at Ephesus, this claim serves as a reminder of the continuity of the gospel with the traditional Jewish understandings of creation, providence, and redemption, and it possibly also serves as a corrective to the "myths" (1:4) about cosmic powers being promulgated by the false teachers.

"there is also one mediator between God and humankind, Christ Jesus"—Again the sword cuts in two directions. No divine emperor stands between God and humanity, so this statement about Jesus Christ is again a countercultural claim. But it is also true that this statement works inside the community as a claim against the false teachers. As Robert W. Wall has noted, "God's offer of universal salvation is tendered by a single ambassador; any other source is bogus."[8] Therefore, there are no legitimate teachers of secret spiritual knowledge, no speculative wisdom available only to the spiritual elite. The bridge to God is Christ and Christ alone.

"himself human"—This emphasis on the humanity of Jesus is not a reflection of a low Christology but instead a trumpeting of the incarnation. The hope of humanity does not rest on some quasi-divine earthly king. "The mediator is not a divinized emperor; the mediator is a human being."[9] And Jesus was no spiritual gas, no mystical presence floating above time and circumstance; he was flesh and blood. Much as is the case with the Gospel of John ("the Word became flesh and lived among us" 1:14), there is the shock of human corporeality here, the weight of embodiment. The false teachers were frothing up proto-gnostic whipped cream. Real spirituality, they intoned, is to transcend bodily constraints and to ascend into the heights of secret and pure godly knowledge. No, retorts the Pastor, the true wisdom is to be found "down here" in the humanity of Jesus. Do you want to know the true ways of God? Don't try to crack some genealogical

---

8. Wall, *1 & 2 Timothy and Titus*, 82.
9. Raymond F. Collins, *I & II Timothy and Titus* (Louisville, KY: Westminster John Knox Press, 2002), 61.

code in the Bible hoping to decipher concealed gnosis. Look at the embodied Jesus. Watch where his feet took him, see what he did with his hands, hear what he spoke with his mouth. There you will learn the deepest wisdom and the truth about human life and the paths of God.

"who gave himself a ransom for all"—The emphasis here falls on the phrase "for all," which connects this christological claim with the earlier exhortation to pray for "everyone." The gospel is not the private narrative of some local Roman deity nor is it the abstract answer to some mystical spiritual puzzle. It is a public event, performed by the human being Jesus—visible, embodied, historical, and universal. Jesus Christ "gave himself;" he initiated the saving action as a gift, and his gift was not for some tribe or nation or class of religious elites but for every human being everywhere—for all.

Much mischief has been done by grasping the image too tightly and attempting to turn a single image into a theological system. Many have been vexed by such questions as, if Jesus offered himself as a ransom, to whom was the ransom paid? To Satan? To God? Such speculation overtaxes the metaphor and misses the point. "Ransom" is not so much a theory of atonement as it is an evocative metaphor of salvation. The language of "ransom" had much currency in the Roman world in which there were large numbers of enslaved people, many of whom were prisoners captured in the countless Roman wars. One way to freedom for a slave was through the paying of a ransom on the slave's behalf, and this slave population and by the evocation of the ransom image, the Pastor elevates this means to freedom to "a parable of the whole of humankind."[10] The power of the parable lies not in trying to figure out the mechanics, who paid what to whom, but in announcing its effects. The self-giving of the fully human Jesus Christ has resulted in the liberation of humanity, in setting free all people from that which prevents them from being themselves fully human.

With a few dramatic strokes, then, the Pastor has articulated the gospel and shown how this gospel makes a difference in the practical life of the community—namely, in its worship and prayer

---

10. Jerome D. Quinn and William C. Wacker, *The First and Second Letters to Timothy* (Grand Rapids: Eerdmans, 2000), 187.

The Fathers, reading the gospel text that Christ gave his life as a "ransom for many" (Mark 10:45), asked to whom the ransom had been paid. Since the term "ransom" means the price offered to set a slave free, it could hardly have been paid to God, who was the *one* who was doing the emancipating, and so they concluded it had been paid to the devil. The question was, of course, misdirected in the first place; as in the Old Testament assertion that God had "redeemed" his people from slavery in Egypt, the stress is upon the cost and sacrifice involved in the act of liberation, not upon a commercial transaction. What matters is not *to* whom the price is paid, but *by* whom. . . .

Paul Fiddes, *Past Event and Present Salvation: The Christian Idea of Atonement* (Louisville, KY: Westminster John Knox Press, 1989), 131.

---

life. This gospel and its practices stand in sharp contrast to the illegitimate doctrines of the false teachers. Now, in 2:6–7, the Pastor, speaking in the voice of Paul and alluding to well-known biographical details, underscores the truth of the gospel by highlighting the truthfulness of himself as the teacher and preacher. He describes himself as a "herald" (that is, a preacher), an "apostle" (that is, one appointed by God and sent to do God's work), and a "teacher of the Gentiles in faith and truth" who gave testimony about Christ "at the right time." In other words, the Pastor is underscoring a conviction already held at Ephesus, that the word of this Paul is testimony to be trusted. "I am telling the truth," he says. "I am not lying," implying, of course, that the false teachers are lying through their teeth (see 4:1–2).

2:8–15

Getting the House in Order: Men and Women in the Life of the Church

In this passage, the ice on the lake gets precariously thin. The Pastor enters into a discussion of gender roles in the Christian community, which to contemporary eyes often seems outrageously misogynistic. Some biblical commentators have pointed especially to the Pastor's curious statement that women "will be saved through childbearing" (2:15) and charged that at this point the Pastor's "theology of salvation for women becomes heretical."[11] While, as indicated earlier, I understand this text, indeed all of the material in the Pastoral Epistles, to be a practical response to a very particular churchly crisis, it cannot be denied that this passage has a long and unhappy history as a proof text against women's leadership in the church generally. Even if this text was originally designed as a wrench to repair an emergency problem, we need to face up to the unfortunate fact that it has often been used as a sledgehammer against women.

As is the case with all biblical interpretation, the text is important, but so is understanding the context. The problem, of course, is that we have the text, but about the context we can only do some educated guessing. Putting forward our best estimations, though, here is the contextual framework in which 2:8–15 is best read:

1. Stable World—In contrast to our own day, where social roles and political structures are fairly fluid, the Pastor lived in a time when the world was viewed as relatively fixed and stable. Today, most Westerners are children of revolutionary movements that toppled monarchs, and we live in a time when "tweeted" messages can quickly gather crowds of protesters in the streets. In the Greco-Roman world, however, the political and social realities were more locked in place. As Luke Timothy Johnson has described the prevailing view, "There may be good emperors or bad emperors, but there would always be emperors!"[12] The way society was ordered, including the relations between men and women, was viewed as "natural," which means that these social structurings were woven into the fabric of things, whereas contemporary people tend to see the same orderings as negotiable. The primary ethical question was not "what can we do to change society for the better?" but "given that the world is as it is, how shall we live and what are our duties?"[13]

2. Masculine and Feminine Natures—The Pastor lived in a world where men and women were thought, stereotypically, to possess certain fixed "natures." Anyone who believes that our own culture

11. Carolyn A. Osiek and David L. Balch, *Families in the New Testament World: Households and House Churches* (Louisville, KY: Westminster John Knox Press, 1997), 122.
12. Luke Timothy Johnson, *The First and Second Letters to Timothy*, The Anchor Bible, vol. 35a (New York: Doubleday, 2001), 194.
13. Ibid., 195.

has outgrown this sharp demarcation between the genders needs only to read articles like *The Huffington Post*'s "The Male Brain: What's Really Going On in There?"[14] or the news story in *The Los Angeles Times* that reports that "women exposed to disturbing news stories absorb an emotional blow greater than do men—so much greater that when next exposed to a stressful situation, their stress levels soar, according to a new study."[15] The most popular recent celebration of indelible gender differences was John Gray's runaway 1990s best-seller *Men are from Mars, Women are from Venus*.[16] Gray argued that men and women act, think, and communicate differently because they are inherently different creatures psychologically. Men and women are, as the title suggests, from different planets.

The problem with viewpoints like Gray's is that they aren't true, not scientifically anyway. The best research shows no such neat divisions between the genders. All men aren't alike nor are all women, and any given personality trait is statistically distributed on both sides of the aisle. So if the facts don't support the thesis, why has Gray's book been so wildly popular, selling millions of copies and morphing into a Broadway show and a television series? Why are we constantly treated to news stories probing the differences between pink and blue? It's probably because there is enough cultural difference in men and women to give the stereotypes a bit of credence in the world of ordinary experience. A wife will sometimes shake her head in exasperation over something her husband has done, muttering, "Typical male!" A man will sometimes shrug his shoulders in puzzlement, sighing, "Women." Even though studies show there is no "typical male" or "typical female," there's enough anecdotal evidence out there to cause many people to assume that the genders can be divided into types.

The Pastor, along with many other writers in antiquity, could perhaps have written their own versions of *Men Are from Mars, Women*

14. Carol Mithers, "The Male Brain: What's Really Going On in There?" *The Huffington Post,* July 26, 2013, http://www.huffingtonpost.com/2013/07/26/male-brain-men-and-women-brain-anatomy_n_3645108.html.
15. Melissa Healy, "Toll of Disturbing News Is Greater for Women, Study Says," *The Los Angeles Times,* October 12, 2012, http://articles.latimes.com/2012/oct/12/news/la-heb-stress-news-women-20121011.
16. John Gray, *Men Are from Mars, Women Are from Venus* (New York: HarperCollins, 1992).

Are from Venus. He shared with many others in his day not only the idea that men and women were fundamentally different but also the conviction that these distinctions were grounded in the essential natures of the genders. Aristotle articulated this view when he wrote, "The male is *by nature* fitter for command than the female, just as the elder and full-grown is superior to the younger and more immature. The relation of the male to the female, [which is one of] inequality, is permanent."[17] The view that women were by nature best suited for roles in home and family and not for public leadership was beginning to change in Roman society at the time the Pastoral Epistles were written, but the debate was still over nature. Perhaps, some were suggesting, women did have business acumen and public leadership in their nature after all.

However, because the Pastor is battling against misbehavior in Ephesus, he is more focused on the dark side of human nature, with what he thinks men and women are prone to do when leading from their worst instincts. As for men, at their worst they were naturally aggressive, combative, hot-blooded, and competitive. Women, at their worst, were flighty and easily swayed by emotion. These lesser natures were behind much of the trouble in Ephesus, and, according to the Pastor, the ethical duty for both men and women, then, was to be self-disciplined and to fight against these natural weaknesses, rather than giving in to them.

3. *House Worship*—Christians in places like Ephesus typically worshiped in the public areas of homes (i.e., usually in the atria, the central rooms or courtyards in Roman houses, and not in the more private spaces, the bedrooms, cooking areas, or baths). The manner of worship, therefore, was influenced by two models, one derived from the church's memory and the other from its domestic liturgical location. On the one hand, there was the memory and continuing influence of the synagogue. Synagogue congregations were constituted by quorums, or *minyanim*, of males, who did the praying and the preaching. Females, when present, sat apart from the men, quietly listening. On the other hand, the fact that Christian worship was located in homes and the church understood itself as a

---

17. Aristotle, *Politics*, book 1, chap. 12, emphasis added, trans. Benjamin Jowett (Oxford: Oxford University Press, 1905), 25.

"family of God" tended to relax the strict separation and rigid roles of men and women. In their own homes, wives were not expected to remain silent, and they "had both status and religious obligations."[18] Negotiating between these two models was a source both of liturgical creativity and ecclesial and social stress for early Christian communities.

With this context in mind, we can turn now to the passage at hand. The first instruction given by the Pastor is addressed specifically to males: "men should pray, lifting up holy hands without anger or argument" (2:8). In other words, because the Christian community at Ephesus is being ripped apart by contentious conflict, which is what menfolk do when they allow their lesser nature to rule, the men should worship in a way that exercises self-discipline and tamps down these natural impulses to anger and aggression. Praying with hands open and lifted is a sign of humility and of dependence on God. Men who have their hands open and raised in prayer cannot close their fists in rage.

Several decades later, Tertullian would elaborate the same theme when he urged Christians to pray with uplifted hands and voices of heartfelt praise, but not hands lifted too high nor voices raised too loudly, since the point is embodying modesty before God:

> But we more commend our prayers to God when we pray with modesty and humility, with not even our hands too loftily elevated, but elevated temperately and becomingly; and not even our countenance over-boldly uplifted. . . . The sounds of our voice, likewise, should be subdued; else, if we are to be heard for our noise, how large windpipes should we need! But God is the hearer not of the *voice*, but of the *heart*, just as He is its inspector.[19]

The Pastor brings up the attitude of prayer and worship not merely as a gratuitous warning to the menfolk before getting down to the real problem, the one with the women, but because the false teachers carried with them "a morbid craving for controversy and for disputes about words" (6:4). This is, of course, a pastoral judgment call,

18. Frances Young, *The Theology of the Pastoral Letters* (Cambridge: Cambridge University Press, 1994), 114.
19. Tertullian, "Of Elevated Hands," *On Prayer*, 17, http://www.newadvent.org/fathers/0322.htm.

the kind of discernment that virtually every congregational leader is compelled at some point to make: Is the conflict in this church healthy or destructive? Are we unsettled here because the Spirit is stirring us up or because of petty bickering and selfish ambition? The Pastor here has clearly decided that the conflict in Ephesus was not a prompting of the Spirit but a prevarication of the false teachers and their "morbid craving for controversy." The Pastor begins with worship, the epicenter of the community's life, because when there is peace and humility in worship, there can be peace in the whole life of the community.

Having addressed the men in the community, the Pastor next turns to the women. He focuses on three areas of concern:

(1) Dress—The Pastor urges the women in the community to dress "modestly and decently," which for him means avoiding braided hair, fancy jewelry, and expensive clothes. To contemporary ears, this may sound quaint or repressive. Does the Pastor really think there is some divine dress code posted on a bulletin board in heaven, "(1) No braids, (2) No pearls, (3) No Saint Laurent dresses . . . "? Actually, the Pastor is simply concerned that the dress of women in the church at Ephesus communicated a commitment to personal, economic, and sexual values out of accord with the gospel. He does not invent a new dress code but urges the women at Ephesus to follow the moral norms for women's clothing advocated by a number of ethical philosophers in the Greco-Roman world.

Plutarch, for example, wrote an essay of advice for newlyweds in which he gave the example of an incident that occurred between a certain Sicilian despot and a military hero named Lysander, the commander of the Spartan fleet. The despot tried to curry the favor of Lysander by sending expensive clothes and jewels to his daughters, but Lysander turned the gifts down flat, saying, "These adornments will disgrace my daughters far more than they will adorn them." Plutarch drew out the moral point by adding, "It is not gold or precious stones or scarlet that makes a wife decorous but whatever invests her with that something which betokens dignity, good behavior, and modesty."[20] Just so, the Pastor indicates that the Christian women of

---

20. Plutarch, *Conjugalia Praecepta*, section 26, from *Moralia*, vol. 2, trans. Frank Cole Babbitt, (Cambridge: Harvard University Press, 1928), 318–19.

Ephesus should not attempt to accentuate their sexual attractiveness or to flaunt their wealth but instead to adorn themselves with the clothing that really counts: good works and reverence for God.

When I was about to graduate from seminary, an experienced, older pastor counseled that I should "always wear black shoes in the pulpit, never brown." The idea was that black shoes were a sign of seriousness and reverence and brown shoes, by contrast, communicated a casual and frivolous attitude toward worship. Likewise, I recently spoke with a wise and thoughtful woman, a layperson, who reported that she had just given a private and gentle word of advice to her youthful new associate pastor that her very short dresses communicated many mixed messages and were probably not the best vestments for a worship leader. Today, remembering the advice about shoe color makes me smile and shake my head, and, as for short dresses in worship, there may well come a time in the future when fashions have changed and albs and Geneva gowns will be routinely cut eight inches above the knee. The point is not to make the dress norms of one culture the rule for all time but to recognize that, in all times and cultures, clothes are taken as external markers of internal values and commitments.

Reading this passage about women's proper dress in worship from a Latin American liberation perspective, biblical scholar Elsa Tamez wonders if the main focus is less on modesty and more on class consciousness. When the Pastor expresses concern about women with braided hair, jewelry, and fancy clothes, many readers assume that these women were trying to look sexually alluring, but Tamez believes instead that they were trying to look *rich*. This passage, she thinks, was not addressed to all of the women at Ephesus but only to affluent women, women "who were probably very dominant" and who were dressing in ways that flaunted not their sexuality but their wealth. "This growing tension between the different social classes in the community was aggravated when some members appeared in luxurious clothing alongside those who dressed poorly. For this reason, we insist that the principal critique is ostentation, not indecency."[21]

21. Elsa Tamez, *Struggles for Power in Early Christianity* (Maryknoll, NY: Orbis, 2007), 5–6.

(2) Teaching—In a stern and quite convoluted passage, the Pastor addresses the role of women as teachers. Taken at face value and without the nuance of context, the Pastor appears to say that he does not allow women to teach or lead men in the church and that women are instead to keep quiet and submit to the men. The reason for this position is presented as biblical, coming from the creation story in Genesis. Not only was Adam created first and Eve second, thereby implying a priority of authority for Adam, it was Eve and not Adam who messed up in the garden. She was the one who was deceived, not Adam, and she was, therefore, the transgressor. Women should stick to their role as bearers of children, which is how they will be saved.

In a time when most Christian churches recognize an equality of gifts between women and men and celebrate the leadership and teaching abilities of women—not to mention a time when most would read the story of Adam and Eve quite differently than does the Pastor—this section of the letter probably cannot be completely rescued. Those who have at great cost fled from the poison-gas-filled house of patriarchy will undoubtedly be disinclined to go back inside passages like this one, even to recover valuables they may have left behind.

Even so, the Pastor deserves to be heard in context and on his own grounds. Remember, the Pastor—like many pastors before and since—has a roaring church crisis on his hands. False and destructive teaching is breaking the community apart. It was initiated by men with a thirst for controversy and fighting, but it has been spread through the whispers, gossip, and testimonies of some women in the community. The Pastor is attempting to calm the storm.

A wry observer once said that when children appeal to their parents, saying, "Billy took my toy, make him give it back," they are convinced that their parents are interested in justice. "But parents aren't interested in justice," he quipped. "They're interested in quiet." Something of the same could perhaps be said of the Pastor, except for the Pastor, "quiet" for a church trying to shout each other down actually means "God's peace," and, therefore, justice and quiet are not really different realities.

What does God's peace and quiet mean for the Pastor? It means something like hitting the restart button for the life of the church. Hit restart by going back to sound teaching, not the speculative nonsense that had infected Ephesus. Hit restart by letting the teaching be done by those who know the gospel deeply, not those who are confused by all these "myths and endless genealogies" (1:4). Undeniably, for the Pastor, these reliable teachers are male, but just being male doesn't qualify one as a wise teacher. We've already been introduced to a couple of male fools, Hymenaeus and Alexander, who sailed the ship of faith onto the rocks (1:19–20).

And what does this mean for the women? Again, hit the restart button by calling them to learn the gospel *einai en hēsychia*, which gets translated as "in silence," but, as Luke Timothy Johnson has pointed out, could more literally be rendered as "be in the quiet" as they learn, which "is different in tone if not in meaning."[22] As they abide in the quiet, learning the gospel, they do so "in submission," that is with humble and obedient receptivity, ultimately to the gospel and to God.

Desiring to add some weight to his command to the women of Ephesus, the Pastor appeals to the Bible, specifically to the story of Adam and Eve in Genesis. He makes two points, both of them dubious by contemporary interpretative standards. First, since Adam was created first and then Eve second (2:13), the order of creation establishes males as authoritative teachers over females. Second, Eve was the one deceived by the serpent and was, thus, the transgressor, not Adam (2:14). Therefore Eve, as the prototypical woman, shows how prone to deception women naturally are.

Neither one of these arguments makes much sense to modern ears. The argument that men should wield all the authority because Adam was created first seems less like a logical conclusion from the creation story and more like an ex post facto justification for patriarchy. One could just as easily make the case the other way: women should hold the authority because, in creating Eve second, God was moving from the lesser to the greater. And as for the tendency of women to be beguiled, a clear-eyed reading of the Adam and Eve story (or at least one more influenced by the psychological

---

22. For "to be in quiet," see Johnson, *The First and Second Letters to Timothy*, 201.

categories of our era) finds mutual culpability and plenty of blame to go around. Both the man and the woman disobeyed, and both were punished. Indeed, the word to Eve that "your husband . . . shall rule over you" (3:16) is a part of Eve's punishment, a mark of the creation gone awry.

We may not wish to defend the Pastor's interpretation of Genesis, but we can say that he didn't make it up. This use of the Adam and Eve story is not original with him. He is simply repeating and bringing to the table conventional interpretations of the text. See the same kind of argument about creation in 1 Corinthians 11:8–9. The first-century Jewish philosopher Philo also applies the creation story in a similar, if even harsher, manner when he writes,

> And [Eve], without any inquiry, prompted by an unstable and rash mind, acquiesced in [the serpent's] advice, and ate of the fruit, and gave a portion of it to her husband. And this conduct suddenly changed both of them from innocence and simplicity of character to all kinds of wickedness; at which the Father of all was indignant."[23]

Philo also adds this eyebrow-raising comment on Eve's action, "Woman is accustomed rather to be deceived than to devise anything of importance out of her own head; but with the man the case is just the contrary."[24] So, by citing the Genesis story in this way, the Pastor is employing a well-known trope to bolster his case, in effect reminding his readers, "We all know what the Scripture says about this matter" and then appealing to the default readings of the creation story. The fact that those are not the readings in favor today is important but not, of course, of consequence to the Pastor in his day.

And then, in something of an ungrammatical non sequitur, the Pastor moves oddly to the issue of childbearing, saying "Yet she will be saved through childbearing, provided they continue in faith and love and holiness" (2:15). New Testament commentator William D. Mounce has called this "one of the strangest verses in the

---

23. Philo, *On the Creation*, 156, http://www.earlyjewishwritings.com/text/philo/book1.html.
24. Philo, *Questions and Answers on Genesis* I, 146, http://www.earlychristianwritings.com/yonge/book41.html.

New Testament."[25] Even the syntax of this verse is puzzling, not to mention its theology. Why does it begin with the singular "she" and end in the plural "they"? Who is "she"? Eve? All women? And who are "they"? The women who bear children? The children who result from the childbearing? And how does the idea of salvation through childbirth come about anyway?[26] Throughout the rest of the Pastoral Epistles, the Pastor takes what can best be described as an orthodox Pauline view of salvation by God's grace, through faith, and "not according to our works" (2 Tim. 1:9). If he is here arguing that men are saved by grace but women through childbirth, it would be a bizarre theological departure from Pauline thought, to say the least.

Once again, focusing on the context helps us through the thicket. The Pastor is vigorously combating the false teachers and their followers, and part of their teaching involves a renunciation of embodiment in favor of a more pure spirituality. Ordinary people may be caught in the mind-and-body-numbing grind of everyday life, but the spiritual elite can rise above all that. They taught that marriage and sex were defilements of the soul's purity and that certain forms of food and drink could sully the unblemished life of the spirit (1 Tim. 4:3). In some ways, the real apostle Paul may bear some blame for these distortions of the gospel. This kind of asceticism possibly resulted from twisting and exaggerating some themes that do appear here and there in Paul's writings, for example his wish that everyone could be celibate, as he was (1 Cor. 7:8). In most ways, though, this disdain for sex, food, and drink was an anticipation of some anti-embodiment ideas that would eventually come to full blossom in Gnosticism.

We can catch a glimpse of this development in a mid-to-late second century apocryphal document, *The Acts of Paul and Thecla*. This legendary narrative recounts how Paul supposedly preached in Iconium in the home of a certain Onesiphorus (perhaps drawn from the biblical Onesiphorus, who makes a couple of favorable cameo appearances in 2 Timothy [1:16–18 and 4:19]). According to the

25. William D. Mounce, *Pastoral Epistles,* Word Biblical Commentary (Nashville: Thomas Neslon, 2000), 143.
26. See Stanley E. Porter, "What Does It Mean to Be 'Saved by Childbirth'? (1 Timothy 2:15)," *Journal for the Study of the New Testament* 49 (1993): 87–102.

document, Paul preached "the word of God concerning self-control [i.e., sexual and other bodily forms of abstinence] and the resurrection," including this curious sermon excerpt, which is a slapdash mixture of Jesus' beatitudes, a pinch of authentic Pauline thought, and a great glob of super spiritual, body-denying, world-renouncing asceticism:

> Blessed are the pure in heart, for they will see God.
>
> Blessed are those who have kept the flesh chaste, for they will become a temple of God.
>
> Blessed are those who are self-controlled, for God will speak to them.
>
> Blessed are those who have renounced this world, for they will be pleasing to God.
>
> Blessed are those who have wives as if they did not have them, for they will be the heirs of God.
>
> . . . Blessed are those who have departed from the shell of this world for the love of God, for they will judge angels and be blessed at the right hand of the Father.
>
> . . . Blessed are the bodies of the virgins, for these will be pleasing to God and will not lose the reward for their chastity; for the word of the Father will be an accomplished act of salvation for them on the day of his Son, and they will receive an eternal rest."[27]

According to the story, while Paul was preaching, a young virgin by the name of Thecla was sitting in the window of the house next door and enthusiastically absorbing every word of "what Paul said about chastity."[28] Deeply affected by Paul's message, she became, from that moment on, a devoted and enthralled follower of this ascetic version of Paul, abandoning her parents' home, leaving her servant maids behind in tears, and throwing over her thoroughly bewildered fiancée, Thamyris. What follows is a tall tale, complete

27. From "The Acts of Thecla," trans. Bart D. Ehrman, in Bart D. Ehrman, *Lost Scriptures: Books That Did Not Make It into the New Testament* (New York: Oxford, 2003), 114–15.
28. Ibid., 115.

with Thecla's baptism in a ditch full of vicious seals, a narrow escape from being burned alive, and a miraculous rescue from an arena fully stocked with lions.

Despite the fact that Thecla's bold preaching and defiance of conventional society has made her a feminist hero in some circles, she is perhaps more aptly understood as a comic book "Wonder Woman" character, striking blows on behalf of a Gnosticized version of Christianity. It was precisely this sort of distortion of authentic Pauline thought that the Pastor is determined to address and correct in Ephesus.

Even though *The Acts of Paul and Thecla* postdates 1 Timothy, the Pastor is up against some of the same ideas trumpeting through that document, such as the rejection of marriage, the prizing of a life of perpetual virginity, and the preaching of abstinence from certain foods and drink (see 4:3; 5:14). So what's the Pastor's problem with chastity, the rejection of marriage, and dietary purity? Was it the fact these were all ways in which women were stepping out of line and undermining male domination? Some have certainly argued so, but the deepest reason for the Pastor's concern is theological: he believes that these world-renouncing ideas all amount to a rejection of the goodness of God's creation and a denial of the truth that grace reverberates in the mundane realities of everyday human life and relationships.

In its fully developed form, Gnosticism taught that the world was created by an inferior deity, the Demiurge. The world, there-fore, was evil, and spiritual maturity was achieved by an escape from materiality. As the "Paul" who appears in *The Acts of Paul and Thecla* preached, "Blessed are those who have departed from the shell of this world for the love of God." But as the "Paul" of this letter will say later in the epistle, according to the gospel "everything created by God is good" (4:4), and God "gives life to all things" (6:13).

So the nub of the theological dispute at Ephesus was this: Where is the arena of salvation? Is it in this world or out of this world? Is it located, as the false teachers claimed, in an airy spirituality, in specu-lations about myths and genealogies? Or is to be found, as the Pas-tor insists, in the messy, material, and incarnate relationships of this world? Where is God's redeeming work to be encountered? In the upper ozone of hyper-spirituality, in the escape from fleshly encounters? Or is it in the hard work of making peace in the conflicted relationships of an actual community with real-life problematic people and in the entanglements of life, such as making marriages, making love, and making children?

Bringing a child into the world, raising a child in the complex unfolding of everyday life, involves a commitment to bear another's burdens and, perhaps more, a faith that grace and hope can be both expressed and discovered in that commitment. The Pastor knows well the doctrine of salvation. He knows that salvation is through grace and not through works. He knows that it isn't the act of getting pregnant and having a baby that effects salvation for women. He says later, in the letter to Titus, "For the grace of God has appeared, bringing salvation to all" (Titus 2:11), and this phrase gets to the heart of his understanding of salvation. It is not as if he thinks males are saved by grace and females are somehow saved by stretch marks and labor pains. Childbearing is not, in the Pastor's view, *how* women are saved. Childbearing is, rather, one of the places *where* they are saved. Childbearing is not the means of salvation for women; it is one of the arenas in which salvation occurs.

For the Pastor, saving grace is not some mathematical transaction that takes place in the clouds. Grace enters our lives, our real, embodied lives. God saves us by grace, fully guiding us, confronting us, transforming us, not in some spiritual never-never land, but in the tangles and complications of life in the places and among the relationships where we actually live. If a husband has in some way wronged his wife and the marriage has fallen into a frosty silence, we can coo about grace, reconciliation, and healing until the sun goes down, but grace and forgiveness are not realized until they take on legs and walk around in real life—until, for instance, the wife at last breaks the silence, places her hand on her husband's cheek and says, "I love you, you old clod, and, by the way, it's your turn to clean up the kitchen."

Unlike the thin spirituality preached by the false teachers, childbearing is a place of incarnate density, a place of human obligation and labor, hope and self-giving, a place where faith is tempered, love is intensified, holiness is fashioned, and grace abounds. (The

Pastor's argument cuts both ways, incidentally, toward men as well as women. If the problem at Ephesus had been that men, caught up in the false teaching, were abandoning their families and fleeing into desert hermitages, the better to escape this evil world, the Pastor would no doubt have aimed the same claims at them. "Men are saved," he would likely say, "through fathering and sustaining children, lifting up their hands in humble prayer and teaching the community in faith." Later in the letter, he will tell Timothy that rolling up his sleeves and getting involved in the hard and messy work of teaching and showing love in this difficult community "will save both yourself and your hearers" [4:16].)

The Pastor knew the biblical story. When Eve disobeyed, God told her that the pangs of childbirth would be increased (Gen. 3:16). No one said that childbearing would be easy, but out there east of Eden, where the man and the woman now tilled the ground and made a life together, their first recorded act was to make love and have a child. Eve was the first to speak about it, giving testimony to the sacredness of the event, bearing witness that even outside of Eden she could continue through grace to take part in God's ongoing creation of life: "I have given life to a man with the Lord's help." (Gen. 4:1 CEB).

So here at the end of chapter 2 of the letter, the Pastor, speaking to the women of Ephesus who have been dazzled by the "spiritual but not religious" promptings of the false teachers, reminds them that they share, not the wild tales of spiritual escape told by the spiritualizers, but the human and earthbound story of Eve. This is why the passage moves from singular to plural. It begins with Eve and moves to gather in all who share her story. Like Eve, they have been deceived, but also like her, they have not been abandoned by God. As they turn their hands, in faith, love, holiness, and modesty, to the incarnate tasks of everyday life, including the bearing of children, they, too, will be able to say, "I have given life with the help of the Lord."

Writing in his own time, the Pastor addresses this word about childbearing, as one would expect, to women. In our time, though, as many young fathers have taken a more active role in caring for their children, the Pastor's word could equally be addressed to them.

Recently, the Norwegian writer Karl Ove Knausgaard created a literary sensation by publishing a six-volume, autobiographical novel that describes in candid detail almost every memory and experience the author could retrieve from his life. Even though Knausgaard was only in his mid-forties when he composed this autobiography, the set of volumes rambles on for nearly four thousand pages. As a young father and an aspiring writer, Knuasgaard was what in America is called a "stay-at-home Dad," and he describes the difficulty of trying to write while saddled with the demands of everyday parenting—the diapers that must be changed, the breakfast that must somehow appear on the table, the faces to be washed, the hair to be combed, and the teeth to be brushed. "Time is slipping away from me," he writes,

> . . . running through my fingers like sand while I . . . do what? Clean floors, wash clothes, make dinner, wash up, go shopping, play with children in the play areas, bring them home, undress them, bathe them, look after them until it is bedtime, tuck them in, hang some clothes to dry, fold others, and put them away, tidy up, wipe tables, chairs, and cupboards.[29]

Knausgaard, like many a mother or father in similar circumstances, understandably longs for relief from these daily burdens. He yearns for escape, for a "moment when life will reach the top, when the sluice gates open and life finally moves on."[30] But instead he sees ahead of him the steady march of days. He will soon be forty, then fifty and sixty. "And when I'm sixty, it won't be long before I'm seventy. And that will be that. My epitaph might read: *Here lies a man who grinned and bore it.* . . ."

No one, including the Pastor, would pretend that an endless stream of days filled with diapers and cleaning is a whitewater adventure of boundless joy. But it is the stuff that makes up ordinary life, its loves and commitments. The fabric of all human relationships and responsibilities, whether they be marriages, friendships, the care of institutions, or the raising of children, when it is seen through

---

29. Karl Ove Knausgaard, *My Struggle: Book 1* (New York: Farrar, Straus and Giroux, 2013), 32.
30. Ibid., 30.

a magnifying glass is woven from the threads of a thousand quotidian acts, an interlacing of repeated acts of everyday care.

And everyone, including the Pastor, would understand the appeal of a word that encourages escape and promises freedom from the messy entanglements of living, perhaps none more than parents of young children. But the Pastor knows the gospel, too, and because of that he is bold enough to say that such dreams of escape are finally spiritual fantasies and that bearing children and folding diapers and setting the table with food and going through the heartbreak of helping children grow up and listening on the phone at midnight to a troubled friend and working to make your town a place of greater justice and trying to figure out how to bail your sister-in-law out of yet another financial disaster and going into the voting booth one more time with hope and helping your neighbor paint his house and forgiving the vexing coworker and carrying the multitude of burdens that embodied life sends our way daily—these are not simply duties and responsibilities. Because God became flesh and dwelled among us in flesh and blood, these are places where mercy, grace, and redemption can be found. These are places of salvation.

It is not clear whether the Pastor's next phrase, "The saying is sure" (3:1), is to be taken as the introduction to a new section on bishops that follows in chapter 3 or as a closing statement for chapter 2. Even though the current versification sets the statement as the first word of chapter 3, it probably makes more sense to read it as an "amen" in response to 2:15, the statement just made about women and childbearing.

The Pastor, like a schoolteacher who has returned to her classroom to find the students in an uproar, has attempted to restore order in the house of worship. To stop the bedlam, he has sternly ordered the men and women to separate sides of the room. He has mustered all his authority to command the men to stop the bickering and to pray with hands upraised and to charge the women to cease spreading foolish myths and to listen and learn quietly as the truth of the gospel is taught. His goal is that the community might experience once again the peace of Christ and the truth of the gospel. Contemporary readers are right to wonder about the Pastor's

> Wendell Berry's moving novel *Jayber Crow* is titled after the name of the barber in the small village of Port William, Kentucky. At one point, Jayber expresses bafflement over the preachers in their local church who preach sermons about the evils of the world and the flesh:
>
> > "[T]his religion that scorned the beauty and goodness of this world was a puzzle to me. . . . While the wickedness of the flesh was preached from the pulpit, the young husbands and wives and young courting couples sat thigh to thigh, full of yearning and joy, and the old people thought of the beauty of the children. And when church was over they'd go home to Heavenly dinners of fried chicken, it might be, and creamed new peas and hot biscuits and butter and cherry pie and sweet milk and buttermilk. . . . And the preacher, having just foresworn on behalf of everybody the joys of the flesh, would eat with unconsecrated relish."
>
> Wendell Berry, *Jayber Crow* (Washington, DC: Counterpoint Press, 2000), 161.

methods and to raise questions about his language and arguments. But, approve of him or not, anyone who has been the pastor of an even slightly contentious congregation will almost surely recognize the intent.

1 Timothy 3:1b–16

Having attempted to restore shalom and calm in the arena of worship, the Pastor now turns to the vexed question of church leadership. He will speak specifically to qualities needed in "offices" in the church—bishop (*episkopos*), deacon (*diakonos*), and (in chap. 5 and Titus 1) elder (*presbyteros*). Our picture of church structures and organization in this early period of Christianity is sketchy, and the exact nature of these offices and the distinctions among them are not completely clear. Eventually it appears that "bishop," "elder," and "deacon" came to refer to three distinct roles. In this three-tiered model of leadership, each house church had a leader, called an elder. The elders in a cluster of house churches in a region or large town would have an overseer, called a bishop. Those responsible for the practical work of caring for widows and performing other ministries of mercy carried out by the church were helpers, called deacons.[1]

Some scholars think that by the time of the Pastoral Epistles, church structures had evolved to the point that all three offices—bishop, elder, and deacon—were in place and functioning and that some of the distinctive features of each role can be teased out of the texts of these letters.[2] It seems more likely, though, that the three-tiered structure of leadership comes sometime later and that we have in the Pastorals essentially a two-tier rather than a three-tier

---

1. Some commentators translate *diakonoi* as "assistants" or "helpers" to distinguish the term from the later, more liturgical and hierarchal character of the office of deacon. See Benjamin Fiore, *The Pastoral Epistles: First Timothy, Second Timothy, Titus* (Collegeville, MN: Liturgical Press, 2007), 80–81; Luke Timothy Johnson, *The First and Second Letters to Timothy* (New York: Doubleday, 2010), 226–27.
2. See, for example, Bassler, *1 Timothy, 2 Timothy, Titus*, 186.

structure, with "bishop" and "elder" as terms referring to the same role—the one who leads, teaches, and presides over worship in a house church.

The value of the Pastor's view of church leadership is not in imagining that these offices as they existed in the late-first-century, or the structure of church governance they represented, could or should be imitated today. Indeed, the contemporary offices of bishop, elder, and deacon are defined differently by various church bodies, and they are all quite different from and more sharply defined than those in ancient Ephesus. The continuing value of this section of 1 Timothy lies more in the general ethical and theological expectations placed on Christian leaders than in the details of the various offices. What endures are the two basic trajectories of the Pastor's wisdom about leadership. First, he is concerned with integrity and trustworthiness inside the household of God, and second, he is attentive to the public face of the church, with the church's reputation for virtue among its neighbors.

Hardly anyone dissertates at length about leadership simply because they find the topic inherently inspiring. Rather, intense discussions about what is needed in leaders are usually motivated by a lament over the loss of those very qualities. People start fretting about leadership not when things are going well but when they sense a leadership crisis, when the organization has in some way gone off the rails. So it was with the Pastor, but what was the crisis? What was the underlying problem with the leadership at Ephesus? The main problem being addressed in the letter to this point, as we have seen, is false teaching, the speculations over myths that were divisive in the community and were turning worship into a contentious debating society. But when it came to leadership, the problem was not just doctrinal, but ethical. The Pastor is concerned not only with what the leaders were preaching but also with how they practiced what they preached. Some of the leaders were wrong not only in what they taught but also in how they behaved, particularly in their greed and ambition. Some of the leadership, all male presumably, were spreading the popular false teachings, and they were being rewarded for their instruction with flattery and with fattened stipends, underwritten perhaps by the wealthier widows in the assembly.

3:1b–7
About Bishops

The Pastor begins by describing the qualities necessary in bishops, or "overseers," reminding his readers that those who aspire to be bishops should not be seeking power or status but aspiring to "a noble task." Noble tasks are best served by noble ambitions. Not many years after the writing of 1 Timothy, one of the church's bishops, Polycarp of Smyrna, wrote a letter to the Christians in Philippi in which he, too, addressed the importance of ethical leadership in the Christian community. He specifically brought up the distressing case of a wayward elder (presbyter) named Valens, who had teamed up with his wife in some act of chicanery, probably involving the misuse of funds. Polycarp wrote:

> I am extremely sad for Valens, who was once a presbyter among you, that he should so misunderstand the office that was given him. Thus, I urge you to abstain from love of money and to be pure and truthful. "Abstain from every kind of evil." For if someone cannot control himself in such things, how can he preach self-control to another?[3]

That ethical motto—if someone cannot control his own behavior, how can he preach self-control to another—is the theme of what the Pastor has to say about bishops. In the case of the Pastor, he views bishops as stewards of the household of God, and he asks, "If someone does not know how to manage his own household, how can he take care of God's church?" (3:5).

He provides a list of virtues for those who keep their own house in order, qualities that are not so much distinctively Christian but marks of good character shared widely in Greek culture. First, the bishop should be "blameless" or "above reproach" (3:2), that is, of such stainless moral character as to be utterly reliable inside the church and a moral example to those on the outside. This blamelessness is probably connected to the next item on the list, which the NRSV translates as "married only once." The Greek, however, is

---

3. Polycarp, Philippians 11:2, in Bart D. Ehrman, *The Apostolic Fathers*, vol. 1, *I Clement, II Clement, Ignatius, Polycarp, Didache*, Loeb Classical Library (Cambridge, MA: 2003), 347.

more literally "a man of one woman," which carries a certain ambiguity. It could be addressed to the problem of polygamy ("only one wife, not two or three"), marital infidelity ("only one wife, no mistress on the side"), divorce ("only one wife and not divorced or separated from her"), overemphasized celibacy ("married, not single"), or serial matrimony ("married only one time and not again, even if divorced or widowed," as the NRSV translation would support).[4]

It may be that a combination of two of the above options is the likeliest rendering, namely, "a bishop should definitely be married, but only once, and never again, regardless of the circumstances." Underscoring the importance of marriage would directly counter the ascetic denigration of marriage by the false teachers, and the notion that having only one life partner is a sign of holiness is found elsewhere in ancient Christian writings.[5] For example, the Shepherd of Hermas, in response to a question about whether it is sinful for a widow or widower to marry again, writes, "There is no sin in marrying again . . . but if they remain unmarried, they gain greater honor and glory with the Lord."[6] But deciding among the various translation options is perhaps not nearly as important as recognizing the underlying virtue being held up by the Pastor: a bishop should be one who is committed to living out his faith in the concrete human relationship of marriage and whose marriage radiates steadfastness and fidelity, qualities that make a bishop trustworthy inside the church and above reproach in society.

Next the Pastor turns to the temperament required of a bishop. On the positive side, he should be "temperate, sensible, respectable, hospitable, [and] an apt teacher" (3:2), in other words, a dignified, balanced, wise, and welcoming person. The phrase "apt teacher" includes the element of skill, but the emphasis falls less on technical teaching ability and more on the larger qualities of personality, wisdom, and character that make others say, "He's a *good* teacher."

Having allowed the sun to shine on the positive side of a bishop's temperament, the Pastor now explores the dark side of the moon.

---

4. See the excellent discussion of these possibilities in Luke Timothy Johnson, *The First and Second Letters to Timothy*, 213–14.
5. Bassler, *1 Timothy, 2 Timothy, Titus*, 66.
6. *The Shepherd of Hermas*, Mandate 4 in Alexander Roberts et al., eds., *The Ante-Nicene Fathers*, vol. 2 (Buffalo, NY: Christian Literature Publishing Co., 1885), 22.

On the negative side, a bishop should not be a drunkard, violent, quarrelsome, or a lover of money (3:3). He should not have a family in disarray with rebellious and disrespectful children, because if he can't manage his own children, how can he be a good manager of God's family? (3:4–5—some have quipped that these verses are solid evidence that the Pastor himself was either unmarried or that his own children had not yet become teenagers).

The Pastor lists two more negatives, and they are presented as especially destructive, as indicated by the Pastor's use of "devil" language for both of them. The first of these is that a bishop should not be a new convert. There is nothing immoral, of course, about being a brand new Christian, but for goodness' sake, the Pastor warns, don't make one into a bishop. The reason is that a bishop is supposed to be a wise teacher of the Christian faith and a prudent manager of the household of God, and a new convert cannot possibly have the depth of knowledge or experience necessary. To put a new convert into the bishop's seat of wisdom could easily create the delusion that he actually *had* some seasoned wisdom, an almost certain misconception that is an equally sure path to puffery and conceit. The result is a runaway train: an empty-headed, rookie bishop running around the church teaching nonsense, misleading the flock, stirring up controversy, and running the risk of falling "into the condemnation of the devil" (3:6). This last phrase could mean that a conceited and confused neophyte bishop would be condemned *by* the devil, but given the Pastor's larger theology that judgment belongs to God and not Satan, the phrase more likely means that the misguided bishop would be liable to the same condemnation *as* the devil. In Matthew's telling of the Parable of the Sheep and the Goats, the Son of Man makes a dire pronouncement: "You that are accursed, depart from me into the eternal fire prepared for the devil and his angels" (Matt. 25:41). Callow bishops, warns the Pastor, run the risk of hearing the same verdict. Or to put it more graphically, a pompous and immature bishop who spews myths and folly at God's people instead of the gospel and who blows up the church with contentious mismanagement can "go to hell."

The second strong negative is that a bishop should not live a disgraceful life, thus destroying his public reputation. He should, instead, "be well thought of by outsiders" (3:7). A bishop who wanders off the path of respect runs the danger of getting caught in "the snare of the devil," that is, of wandering blindly into enemy territory and being taken captive to the forces of evil.

Looking over the long list of warnings and negative traits to be avoided in a bishop, one may wonder why this needed to be said at all. Surely it has always gone without saying that the church doesn't need drunk, violent, quarrelsome, greedy, inept, immature, and morally disgraceful bishops! But the list is not an accidental one. The Pastor is, on the one hand, reminding the church at Ephesus, in thrall to false and corrupt leaders, that true leaders are steady, trustworthy, and prudent while at the same time inviting the false teachers at Ephesus to look into the mirror and to see the reflection of their own contentious, confused, and compromised faces.

The list of virtues and vices provided by the Pastor may not, as we noted, constitute a distinctly Christian understanding of ethics. All groups and societies, ancient and contemporary, tend to like their leaders sober and sane. But to this day good, trustworthy church leadership is marked by the kind of gentle, hospitable, faithful, self-giving, dignified spirit described here. Inside, the church grows in faith when nourished by this kind of leadership, and outside, society—even a secularized one—expects moral integrity from the church's leaders and judges the worthiness of its witness accordingly. Responding to the sexual scandals that have rocked the Catholic Church in recent decades, and especially to the attempts by the hierarchy to cover them up, *New York Times* columnist Frank Bruni wrote that he was galled by

> the evil that an entire institution can do, though it supposedly dedicates itself to good . . . [and by] the way that a religious organization can behave almost precisely as a corporation does, with fudged words, twisted logic and a transcendent instinct for self-protection that frequently trump the principled handling of a specific grievance or a particular victim.[7]

7. Frank Bruni, "The Church's Errant Shepherds," *New York Times*, July 6, 2013, http://www.nytimes.com/2013/07/07/opinion/sunday/bruni-the-churchs-errant-shepherds.html.

[If pastors and leaders] are sure in the depths of their being that their center rests in God, and they know how to keep in constant awareness of it, [they] can truly grow into the right kind of love of the people they serve. They will not be afraid of the elderly, the sick, the handicapped, or the dying, and they will insist on a place for them in their congregations. They will care about the poor. They will see folks as they really are and not be judgmental because they will be very sure that God loves all of the congregation infinitely, as God loves the ministers themselves, and they will communicate that love convincingly. They will be anxious to drink deeply of our common Christian resources in Scripture, tradition, and modern theology, and they will be hungry to find ways to share with their congregations in the clearest possible manner the practical, saving insights of those resources. They will not be personally threatened by changes in the world around them, such as the women's movement or an influx of non-English-speaking parishioners, that affect them and their congregation, because they know that their stability is in God, who is ever faithful.

Roberta C. Bondi, "Centered in God," in *What Is Good Ministry?* (Durham, NC: Duke Divinity School, 2003), 37.

The Pastor would shake his head in sad agreement and say once again, "Whoever aspires to the office of bishop desires a noble task."

3:8–13
About Deacons

The use of the word "likewise" (3:8) both introduces a new list of virtues, this time for deacons, and points to the similarity between this list and the one already laid out for bishops. Once again, the Greek ideal for leaders—dignified, self-controlled, of good public reputation—hums in the background. As was the case for bishops, deacons should be serious, sober, and not motivated by greed (3:8). Like the bishops, they should be "married only once" and good managers of their own households (3:12; see comments above on 3:2 and 3:4–5).

Two new phrases, ones that did not appear on the bishops' list, show up in the deacons' list and perhaps open a window onto the everyday role of deacons in the community. The first of these is that deacons "must hold fast to the mystery of the faith with a clear con-science" (3:9). The term "mystery" is used in various ways in the New Testament, but here "mystery of the faith" is first a reference to doctrine, to the essential claims about Christ that form the core of sound teaching (in 3:16, the Pastor will employ a similar phrase— "the mystery of our religion"—to introduce a christological creed).

But the Pastor means more than abstract doctrine. He means instead a creed about Christ that comes to life in the ways deacons (and others) put their faith into practice. So "the mystery of the faith" is tantamount to the whole, embodied Christian life, when it springs out of a true confession of Jesus Christ. The Pastor earlier portrayed how the actions of Christian love come from "a good con-science" (1:5) and how the rejection of conscience caused certain leaders to suffer "shipwreck in the faith" (1:19). When the Pastor urges deacons to "hold fast to the mystery of the faith with a clear conscience," he means not simply purity of belief but also purity of action and integrity in the performance of their ministry. If, as many have argued, the deacons were administrators of the day-to-day operations of the financial care of widows, then this would be a practical place where their true creed would find expression. If they are "greedy for money," then their actions could easily lead to ship-wreck, but if they are lovers of Christ, then the work of their hands as they care for others would be an embodied prayer flowing from a "clean conscience."

They second new phrase in the deacons' list is that deacons should also be "not double-tongued" (3:8). We may have in this phrase another glimpse of deacons in action. If they indeed were the practi-cal helpers in the community, the ones who assisted the elders and bishops in their duties and the ones who did the legwork of running the financial support program for widows, then they would naturally be constantly in and out of homes in the community. If they were people who spoke one way in one home and another way in another, if they were gossips who spread rumors and gave one version of events here and a different version there, or if they were duplicitous flatterers who spoke soothing words of comfort to a widow in need and then whispered about her to the next widow, they could easily spread the contagion of divisiveness.

The proper interpretation of 3:11 presents an exegetical challenge. The Pastor abruptly takes up a new list of virtues, this one also marked off by the word "likewise," and this time it is a list addressed to *gynaikas*, that is, to "women." But to which women? The Greek word could equally mean "wives" as well as "women," and this reading would mean that this is an instruction directed to the wives of the deacons (so reads the KJV). However, the fact that the possessive is lacking (the text does not say "*their* wives," as one usually finds) tends to argue against that understanding. And why was there no parallel passage in the bishops' section about their wives?[8] Some think the Pastor is addressing a certain group of women, namely the mature widows, who are later presented as having a kind of specialized ministry of prayer and good works (see 5:5, 10). It would make sense, then, to have a list of virtues for them like the ones for bishops and deacons. What wouldn't make sense, though, is for the Pastor suddenly to insert this new list into the middle of a section on deacons.

What does make the most sense is that the Pastor is here addressing women deacons.[9] We know that women in the Pauline world had been given that title (see the reference to "our sister Phoebe, a deacon of the church" in Romans 16:1). The office of deacon was not a teaching office; preaching and teaching were done by bishops and elders, so the presence of women in the diaconate was not a conflict with the Pastor's earlier instruction in 2:12–15.

But is the rendering of "women" in 3:11 as meaning "women deacons" simply a product of contemporary readers hoping to find some glimmer of inclusivity in 1 Timothy, a book seemingly untroubled by the oppressive social structures of the ancient world? Hardly so. The great preacher John Chrysostom preached near the end of the fourth century a series of sermons on 1 Timothy. In the one on this passage about women, Chrysostom said, "Some have thought that this is said of women generally, but it is not so, for why should he introduce anything about women to interfere with his subject? He is speaking of those who hold the rank of Deaconesses."[10]

---

8. See Fiore, SJ, *Pastoral Epistles*, 81.
9. There are thoughtful arguments to this effect in Bassler, *1 Timothy, 2 Timothy, Titus*, 70–71 and Johnson, *The First and Second Letters to Timothy*, 228–29.
10. John Chrysostom, "Homily 11 on 1 Timothy," http://www.newadvent.org/fathers/230611.htm.

If the assumption that *gynaikas* in 3:11 means "women deacons" is correct, then the overall flow of 3:8–13 becomes clearer. Verses 8–9 describe virtues that apply to all deacons, male and female. After naming these virtues, the Pastor recommends, in verse 10, that men and women be allowed to serve as deacons only after first being tested, probably meaning a probationary period in which they would be given modest duties, after which they could serve as deacons if they were able to "prove themselves blameless." In the main, the test would consist of whether the candidates for deacon showed the virtues already named. But part of the "test" was gender specific. Women candidates must show that they were not like some of the young women at Ephesus, those who were "gadding about from house to house . . . gossips and busybodies, saying what they should not say," but instead were women who, in the name of prudence and faithfulness, avoided all such slander (3:11). Male candidates, on the other hand, were to be the husband of one wife, married only once, and good managers of their children and households. Those who pass the test and "serve well as deacons" make a bold and worthy showing for themselves "in the faith that is in Christ Jesus" (3:13)

For a church in moral and theological crisis, the Pastor was surely right to insist on leadership—whether in the office of bishop or deacon—that is quietly dignified and socially respectable, leaders with sober spirits and well-ordered households. We should remember, though, that this picture of leadership was constructed in response to a specific crisis of chaos and contention caused by false teaching. Lifted out of context and reified, this picture of a serious-minded, restrained, controlled leadership can itself become deeply antithetical to the gospel. If, as countless sermons have suggested, the father of the prodigal son in Jesus' parable is a figure who can be compared to God, then here we see a parent who was having trouble managing his own household, whose younger son was in full rebellion and whose older son seethed with resentment. And when the wayward prodigal appeared at last on the crest of the road, homeward bound, this father threw all protocols of quiet dignity out the window, hiked up his skirt, and raced with crazy love and unbounded joy toward his lost son.

Maybe this means that God lacks the proper decorum to be a bishop. Or more probably this means the Pastor is right; the church needs wise, quiet, hospitable, irenic, self-disciplined leaders, but leaders whose dignity is rooted not mainly in a catalog of Greek virtues but in the radical gospel. This means leaders, therefore, who are so attuned to the Spirit that, when the right moment comes, restraint is tossed to the winds and the love of God spills out in unchecked, unexpected, and maybe even undignified ways, such as washing the feet of the poor, kissing lepers, lavishly displaying the love of God, dancing with wild abandon when the lost are restored, and welcoming sinners with joy to the feast.

In *Open Secrets: A Memoir of Faith and Discovery*, Richard Lischer's finely crafted book about his early years as a Lutheran pastor in the farm community of Cana, Illinois, he describes the kind of relationship between the church's doctrine and its larger life that good pastoral leadership cultivates. "In Cana," he writes, "we baptized our babies, celebrated marriages, wept over the dead, and received Holy Communion, all by the light of our best window." What Lischer calls "our best window" was a stained glass depiction, in schematic diagram, of no less than the doctrine of the Trinity, set high into the east wall of the sanctuary above the altar.

"Our window's geometric design," observes Lischer, "seemed to say, 'Any questions?'"

Thinking about the relationships between this window, his ministry, and the life of his congregation, Lischer observes,

> We believed that there was a correspondence between the God who was diagramed in that window and our stories of friendship and neighborliness. If we could have fully taken into our community the name Trinity, we would have needed no further revelations and no more religion, for the life of God would have become our life.
>
> An aerial photographer once remarked that from the air you can see paths, like the canals on Mars, that crisscross pastures and fields among the farms where neighbors have trudged for generations, just to visit or help one another in times of need. These, too, are the highways among *Pater, Filius,* and *Spiritus Sanctus* grooved into human relationships. The word "religion"

comes from the same root as "ligaments." These are the ties that bind.[11]

3:14–16

Pilgrims in the Household of God

In some ways, this passage sounds like it could be the ending of the letter. The Pastor has given instructions about worship and has named the qualities desired in bishops and deacons, and now he seems to be winding things up by announcing a possible visit: "I hope to come to you soon . . ." (3:14). But the recipients of this letter (as well as modern readers) know two pertinent facts here. First, Paul, being dead, is of course not actually coming for a visit, and, second, the letter is not actually coming to an end. There are three more chapters to go.

The true function of this passage is not to end the letter but to serve much like the closing of the first movement of a symphony. It may sound like an ending, but there is more to come. In fact 3:14–16 actually works like a hinge between the first half of the letter and the second half. It pivots, first of all between the major themes and issues of the letter—worship, community, and leadership—to the smaller, more closely grained details of congregational life. Second, although the entirety of this letter is ostensibly addressed to "Timothy," the first three chapters speak more generally to the whole congregation, while chapters 4–6 speak more directly to "Timothy" himself as a church leader with particular duties and challenges. In other words, in the first half of the letter, "Timothy" is a symbol for the whole life of the congregation, and in the second half of the letter, "Timothy" is a symbol for its leaders. In fact, the Pastor may have his eye here, in the second part of the letter, on the "elders," the teachers and guides for the house churches.

This concluding passage in chapter 3 consists of two panels: first, a personal word from "Paul," in which, as we have noted, he announces a hoped-for visit (3:14–15), and second, a christological creed

---

11. Richard Lischer, *Open Secrets: A Memoir of Faith and Discovery* (New York: Doubleday, 2001), 81.

Character grounded in one's sense of calling is also an essential attribute of the good leader. The pastoral leader not only does something in and for the church. She or he also is something—a symbol of God's presence and purposes. Although different ecclesial traditions would express it differently, pastoral leaders are bearers of God's mystery as first among equals in a priestly community that itself is also called to bear God's mystery in the world. This is to say that good pastoral leaders . . . exhibit what John Fletcher has called "religious authenticity." They have "head and heart together." Without such authenticity, it is unlikely that leaders will be able to establish the necessary fiduciary bond that makes it possible for them to lead and for laity to trust their leadership. This is especially true when congregational members have to make difficult decisions personally or corporately, when changing circumstances challenge old and well-loved ways of doing things and make change and adaptation imperative.

. . . The good pastoral leader's character is . . . not self-generated, but it is grounded in one's relationship to God, in one's call to ministry. The call is not only a "churchly" call . . . but it is a "secret" call that signifies a deep and abiding relationship with God.

Jackson W. Carroll, "Good Pastoral Leadership for the 21st Century," in *What Is Good Ministry?* (Durham, NC: Duke Divinity School, 2003), 41.

(3:16). In regard to the first panel, since there will, of course, be no actual visit from the real Paul, this curious autobiographical detail serves to reassure the readers that this letter is what Paul, the iconic apostle of Jesus Christ, would have said if he were indeed standing among them at Ephesus that very moment. When they hear "I hope to come to you soon," they can imagine this revered apostle walking into their assembly, taking off his sandals and cloak, and sharing with them tales of missionary adventures, days in prison, and wisdom about the faith. When this imagined Paul goes on to write "if I am delayed, you may know how one ought to behave in the household of God, which is the church . . ." (3:15). The readers know, of course, that he will, in fact, be delayed, permanently. So the message is, "Worry not if I don't show up in person. You have this letter with all the instructions I would have given you were I there myself." If, Paul were to walk through the door, he would tell the Christians in Ephesus all these things himself, but since he is not actually going to be there, they have this letter and its instruction in his stead. It is authoritative and trustworthy, just as if it had come from the very mouth of Paul.

The letter is described as "instructions to you [meaning "Timothy," but also the whole group of believers in Ephesus] so that . . . you may know how one ought to behave in the household of God, which is the church of the living God, the pillar and bulwark of the faith" (3:15). To describe the church as "the household of God" is a particularly fertile metaphor, given the circumstances of this epistle. As we noted in the discussion of chapter 1, the "church" at Ephesus is actually a cluster of house churches, most if not all of them meeting in actual homes. So when the church gathered for worship and teaching, it was one household, "the household of God," meeting in the context of another, a Hellenistic household (see, e.g., Rom. 16:3, 5, where Paul greets Prisca and Aquila as well as "the church in their house").

In this nesting of the household of God into the Greco-Roman household, we can see at work the tension of what church historian Andrew Walls calls the "indigenizing principle" of Christianity versus the "pilgrim principle." On the one hand, the Christian gospel has the capacity to make itself at home in a vast array of markedly different cultures spread across time, and making itself at home means inescapably being shaped and changed by those cultures. This is the "indigenizing principle." The whole of Christian history, Walls argues, is one adaptation of the faith after another to local situations. On the other hand, all Christians share a common core of faith and practice that marks them off from their cultures and joins them with each other and even with their biblical forebears. This is the "pilgrim principle."

So a French Christian in Paris in 1250, an Episcopalian in Chicago in 1895, and a Methodist in São Paulo in our own day experience and articulate the faith in quite different ways. They live in different historical and cultural settings, with all the social markers that come with those locations, and their Christianity is indigenized in their milieus. But if, by some trick of time travel, they were to meet for coffee, they would recognize each other and would become aware that, as vastly different as they are, they nevertheless share a common faith. They would cling to the same biblical story, would understand each other's worship and experiences of the grace and power of Christ. They would not cease, of course, being a medieval European, an industrial age Midwesterner, and a contemporary Brazilian, but they would be aware that they were nonetheless brothers and sisters in the faith, and because of that, pilgrims and sojourners in their own times and places. In other words, the gospel is at home everywhere and truly at home nowhere. As Walls says,

> [With] the indigenizing principle which makes his faith a place to feel at home, the Christian inherits the pilgrim principle, which whispers to him that he has no abiding city and warns him that to be faithful to Christ will put him out of step with his society; for that society never existed, in East or West, ancient time or modern, which could absorb the word of Christ painlessly into its system.[12]

The Pastor applies both the indigenizing and pilgrim principles to the house churches of Ephesus. According to the Pastor, the household of God ought, in some ways, to mirror the virtues and structures of a well-run Hellenistic household. For example, a bishop (also called "elder") who aspires to manage God's household ought to be someone who cares well for his own regular household (3:4–5). In other ways, however, there were striking differences between the household of faith and the domestic household in which it met for worship. The fact that masters and slaves, men and women, rich and poor, old and young gathered together as brothers and sisters for fellowship, learning, and prayer would have created a contrast, if not a tension, with the highly structured households of Greco-Roman society. Everybody had been well-schooled by custom and habit in how to live in a polite Hellenistic household, but in the household of God sometimes the moral rules of culture were in force and sometimes there were new rules. How should one live in God's household? So, here in the middle of the letter, the Pastor is reminding the readers of his chief purpose, namely, to speak not only in "Paul's" voice but also to stimulate their imagination to see "Paul" present

---

12. Andrew Walls, *The Missionary Movement in Christian History: Studies in the Transmission of Faith* (Maryknoll, NY: Orbis Books, 1996), 8.

with them, giving clear teaching about "how one ought to behave in the household of God" (3:14).

When the Pastor uses the phrase "how one ought to behave in the household of God," he means to describe a whole way of Christian life, not just rules of moral conduct. There, meeting in the atria of Roman houses, were these little societies of Christ. The Pastor wants them to be living witnesses to the life of Christ in the world. All around them was the emperor-worshiping, emperor-serving Greco-Roman world. All around them was social strife and ambition, the kind of jockeying for wealth and status common to every human society. But, the Pastor hopes, there in the common spaces of these homes would be these tiny alternative households, God's households, which would be inhabited by faithful Christians who would pray for each other and for the world, who would attend to the gospel, and who would "lead a quiet and peaceable life in all godliness and dignity" (2:2). In these alternative households, God alone would be worshiped, truth alone would be taught, and Christ alone would be served as Lord. Such households would be a light to the nations, leaven in the loaf of culture, a judgment to human strife and vanity, and finally and astonishingly a beacon of hope for the whole world.

This brash idea, the notion that what was happening among small bands of believers meeting in house churches just might be instrumental in God's desire to redeem the whole world, leads the Pastor, here in the second panel of this concluding section of chapter 3, to sing out the words of an old creedal hymn:

> Without any doubt, the mystery of our religion is great:
> He was revealed in flesh,
>   vindicated in spirit,
>   seen by angels,
> proclaimed among Gentiles,
>   believed in throughout the world,
>   taken up in glory.

The opening phrase "the mystery of our religion is great" connects to the Pastor's earlier statement that deacons "should hold fast to the mystery of the faith with a clear conscience" (3:9). When the Pastor reminds them that "the mystery of our religion is great," this is not tantamount to his saying, "The whole thing is one big mystery." To the contrary, what the Pastor is affirming is that the ordinary round of Christian activities—the praying, the singing, the Bible study, the acts of charity and compassion, the care for the widows and orphans, the raising of children, the maintaining the steadfastness of marriage, in short, the Christian life—is more than just ethics. This way of life is infused by the presence, power, and blessing of God. Today we might say it this way, that everything Christians do in the practical living out of their faith is sacramental.

This is what the apostle Paul was getting at when he describes himself as a "steward," or perhaps better, as a "household manager of God's mysteries" (1 Cor. 4:1). A household manager is involved in scores of everyday decisions about the running of the household. The same is true with a household manager in God's house, the church. Somebody has to plan worship, select the hymns, compose the sermons. Someone has to show hospitality to strangers who enter the assembly, and others have to decide what to teach in the educational life of the community and how fairly to distribute the canned goods and money contributed at Christmas. Details, details, details. The life of the church is a thousand often-humdrum details. But the Pastor wants his readers to remember: God is in the details. This presence of God in the everyday activities of the Christian household is the mystery of faith—or, as he puts it in 3:16, "the mystery of our *religion*," to accentuate the practical, lived-out reality involved.

The hymn fragment the Pastor quotes is a poetic version of "the mystery of our religion," of the truth that the divine is mingled with the earthly in the church's life. Jouette Bassler has persuasively argued that, contrary to the NRSV, which sets this hymn as two stanzas of three lines each, the hymn actually consists of three stanzas, each with two lines.[13] In each stanza, one of the lines speaks of an earthly reality and the other line describes a heavenly reality:

Stanza One
(Earth)—He was revealed in flesh (Jesus' earthly life and

13. Bassler, *1 Timothy, 2 Timothy, Titus*, 75–76.

ministry)

(Heaven)—He was vindicated in Spirit (on the earthly side, Jesus was crucified, but God vindicated Jesus' life and death via the resurrection)

Stanza Two

(Heaven)— He was seen by angels (he was a member of the heavenly court, and his true actions were visible to the eyes of heaven)

(Earth)—He was proclaimed to the Gentiles (the hard work of the church engaged in mission)

Stanza Three

(Earth)—He was believed in throughout the world (the spread of the gospel)

(Heaven)—He was taken up in glory (the ultimate victory of Christ)

Bassler's division of the hymn into three stanzas makes good sense, but there is also a case to be made for the NRSV's twofold structure. Read this way, the first stanza describes the ministry of Jesus in an upward arc. He performed his ministry "in the flesh," he was vindicated in spirit in the resurrection, and now, as the ascended Lord, is seen by the heavenly court. The second stanza describes the life of the church in a similarly upward arc. The church preaches the Gospel to all peoples, they are vindicated by the belief in Christ found throughout the world, and they will enjoy the great victory when they are joined in glory with Christ who is all in all.

Regardless of how we parse the hymn, though, the theological import remains the same: the church's life is not simply an endless collection of details about worship and service. It is, rather, a participation in the story and life of God. Therefore, in this creedal affirmation, the pilgrim principle is on full display. These little clusters of Christians gathered in houses around Ephesus may be fully immersed in the culture of the Greco-Roman world, but their true home is in a community of faith that ranges in time from the incarnation to the consummation, in ethnicity from Jew to Gentile, in place from heaven to earth, and in breadth across all nations and peoples. They may be a small assembly of the faithful, gathered for prayer in the atrium of a home in ancient Ephesus, but the Pastor is now leading them in a never-ending hymn reverberating across time and space, a hymn being sung by Paul and the other apostles, by believers in every place and epoch, by the seraphim and the cherubim, by the saints that have gone before and by those who will follow, and by the whole host of heaven.

Over against the false teachers, who promise spiritual fullness through escaping earthly constraints and relationships, the Pastor is affirming that the hassles and details of trying to be faithful in marriages and money, childbearing and loving service to those in need, are the best and deepest way into the life of God. The Christian faith is lived locally and expressed in a thousand daily acts and relationships. But if you know how to look—and know how to sing—this gospel is a great mystery of immense size and scope.

1 Timothy 4:1–16

The great themes of this letter have been set forth in the first three chapters. The Pastor, speaking as Paul, has ended the third chapter with a flourish—a rousing hymn and a promise to visit soon (3:14–16). But just as he is about to seal the envelope, the Pastor pauses with what seems to be a second thought: "In case I happen to be delayed, I have written down some instructions for good behavior in the household of God" (3:15).

"In case I happen to be delayed"—this is obviously a rhetorical device. There will, of course, be no actual visit from Paul, just the conviction that this is what he would have said had he been around to say it personally. The implication of this device is to say, "If something happens to keep me from showing up on time, there are some things I hope to tell you that are so urgent I want to send them in advance in this letter." The effect is to underscore the importance of what follows in chapters 4–6, which are detailed instructions about various pastoral and practical matters in the church. The whole letter presents itself as addressed to Timothy, but, as we saw, the first three chapters really had the whole community in view as readers and hearers. These next three chapters, however, become even more personal in their word to Timothy in his role as pastor, which is almost surely an indication that this section of the letter is intended especially for the leaders of the community.

4:1–5
The Perils of the Last Days

It is one thing to be a leader of the church when all is going well, when the congregation is growing, when the stewardship campaign is over-subscribed, when people love the pastor, the church has a fine reputation in the community, the young couples group is overflowing, and the nursery is filled with babies every Sunday. It is another thing to be a leader when all ecclesiastical hell is breaking loose, when the peace of the church is shattered by rancor, controversy, and malicious gossip, when the structures of the church, so loved and so carefully nurtured, are breaking apart in a windstorm of fear and uncertainty. To be a leader in the Christian community is to be a steward of the house of God, but how to be a steward when the house itself seems to be falling in?

The Pastor has no stars in his eyes, wears no rose-colored glasses. These are no ordinary times, he says, not even the ordinary, expected times of struggle and controversy that all congregations inevitably experience. These are, in fact, stormy, apocalyptic times, the "later times" (4:1), times full of portent and meaning. By this, the Pastor may mean that the final end of the world is at hand, but he more likely means that the congregation is going through one of those critical moments when the tissue becomes thin and the battle between the gospel and the powers of evil is seen in vivid colors. These are times when God's will and presence become even more urgent, when the stakes are high, and when one world is passing away and a new world is being born (see "Further Reflections: The Later Times and the Night of the Living Dead," below). Such times are disorienting, full of smoke and confusion, so the Pastor does not wish to sound an uncertain trumpet. God's word must be heard with clarity and force. So, he begins sharply and without equivocation: "Now the [Holy] Spirit expressly says. . . ."

FURTHER REFLECTIONS
The Later Times and the Night of the Living Dead

In 1968, the social fabric of the United States seemed to be dramatically fraying. In January, the Tet Offensive launched by the Viet Cong and the North Vietnamese disclosed how badly the American war effort was going, both on the battlefield and in political support. In March, President Lyndon Johnson, wearied by conflict and having lost control of his party and the confidence of much of the citizenry, shocked the nation by announcing that he would not run for reelection. The next month, Martin Luther King Jr. was assassinated in Memphis, followed in June by the murder of Robert Kennedy. The year was marked by racial disturbances in several major cities, student protests on campuses across the country, and police violence in the streets outside the Chicago convention of the Democratic Party. The moment felt more than volatile; there was a sense that the time was apocalyptic. In his essay "The Haunting of 1968," Robert Newman says,

> 1968 American culture exploded in violence and excess. . . . American society seemed to be unraveling in pre-millennial chaos. Bob Dylan had proclaimed "the times they are a changin'" and the Jefferson Airplane's anthem "gotta revolution" was to echo through college dorms.[1]

That same year, a poorly financed, independently made film by a then-unknown movie director named George Romero was released, and it eventually changed the history and culture of American cinema. The movie was *Night of the Living Dead*, a film about an army of malevolent corpses rising suddenly and mysteriously from their graves to cannibalize the living. It was the first in what has become a well-stocked genre, the zombie movie, and the film reduced theatergoers to cringing terror and tears. Audiences, schooled on tamer horror fare such as *The Creature from the Black Lagoon*, were simply unprepared for the graphic violence and the terrifying, ghoulish realism of *Night of the Living Dead*. Roger Ebert, who was then a young reviewer for the *Chicago Sun Times* and who saw the movie at a Saturday matinee filled with children, described the response in the theater:

> The kids in the audience were stunned. There was almost complete silence. The movie had stopped being delightfully

---

1. Robert Newman, "The Haunting of 1968," *South Central Review* 16/17 (Winter 1999–Spring 2000): 54.

scary about halfway through, and had become unexpectedly terrifying. There was a little girl across the aisle from me, maybe nine years old, who was sitting very still in her seat and crying.[2]

The movie precipitated outrage. There were appeals for censorship, or at the least for a rating system that would restrict films like this one to adult viewers. In retrospect, however, *Night of the Living Dead* is recognized as a cult classic and one of the most innovative and creative films ever made. Thirty years after it was released, the Library of Congress added *Night of the Living Dead* to the National Film Registry, a list that recognizes the most artistically significant American films.

What turned the critical tide was the awareness of just how perfectly attuned the film was to its historical context. While the zombies in the movie were making war on the living, the movie itself was waging attacks on the American culture shared by the audience, the jingoistic patriotism, the racism, and the bourgeois 1950s model of the American family. The film successfully milked social anxiety and apocalyptic fear, the deep dread that the shaking of the foundations in American life was necessarily a time when evil—unspeakable and humanly invincible—would be released from the realm of the dead. "The film deprives us of any means by which to counter our anxiety," Robert Newman writes. "Like our experience in the shopping mall through which we meander when *Night of the Living Dead* concludes and the lights come up in the multiplex, it consumes us as we consume."[3]

Like *Night of the Living Dead*, the apocalyptic vision of the New Testament exposes the fragmentation and decay in this world, which, despite its boasts of vitality, is actually passing away. The New Testament, with its eye on God's reign, turns its searchlight on what it calls "the present age," revealing all of the posturing and pretense of a world compelled to party deep into the night, showing the reveling to be but a thin cosmetic spread over the loneliness, heartache, and despair it is designed to conceal. But unlike

2. Roger Ebert, "Night of the Living Dead," http://www.rogerebert.com/reviews/the-night-of-the-living-dead-1968.
3. Newman, "The Haunting of 1968," 58.

Night of the Living Dead, the New Testament is no mere attack on bourgeois society. This world, after all, is the world God loves, the world God, in sadness and love, will redeem. For the New Testament writers, if God is shaking the foundations of the present age, it is not simply to destroy but finally to build up, to establish what the human heart, in its deepest yearning and highest hopes, seeks: "the city that has foundations, whose architect and builder is God" (Heb. 11:10).

In his survey of the use of eschatological and apocalyptic language in Scripture, biblical scholar George B. Caird observes that the New Testament writers believed in a literal end of the world, "that the world had had a beginning in the past and would have an end in the future." This world, seemingly permanent and imperishable, will, in fact, come to a dramatic end, yielding to the breaking in of God's new creation. However, Caird goes on to say that these same New Testament writers "regularly used end-of-the-world language metaphorically to refer to that which they well knew was not the end of the world."[4] In other words, when a New Testament writer uses apocalyptic language, he could be talking about the literal end of the world, but not necessarily. He may instead be referring to some dramatic and cataclysmic, but smaller, event in the middle of history, such as the fall of Jerusalem, which is not itself the end of all things but which gives a foretaste of the eschaton. In sum, the New Testament speaks both of the world that will ultimately come to an end and of a world that is always coming to an end, passing away every day.

So when the Pastor who wrote 1 Timothy speaks apocalyptically and calls his own historical moment "the later times" (4:1), what exactly is he talking about? Perhaps he believed himself to be on the edge of history, at that dramatic breakpoint when the world would literally end, when the flow of ordinary time would cease and the world would face its final reckoning. Or maybe the Pastor senses that his own time is one of those smaller apocalypses that punctuate human history, one of those moments like the fall of Jerusalem, or the year 1968, or September 11, 2001, when it is clear to all that

4. George B. Caird, *The Language and Imagery of the Bible* (London: Duckworth, 1980), 256.

the foundations of the world are shaking and the old order is passing away.

His evidence for the fact that he was in the last times is that
people find false teaching ("deceitful spirits and teachings of
demons" [4:1]) more attractive than the gospel. In one sense, the
rising cacophony of human blasphemy and evil is always, for apocalyptic writers, an ominous thunderclap signaling that the mighty
storm of God's judgment is approaching. After all, did not God
flood the world and start over fresh with Noah when "the wickedness of humankind was great in the earth . . ." (Gen. 6:5)? On the
other hand, when has there ever been a moment in history when
a substantial number of people were not more dazzled by some
"deceitful spirit"—Roman imperial power, godless totalitarianism,
self-vaunting racism, greedy consumerism—than by the gospel?
It is always the "last times."

Whether his vision is larger or smaller, ultimate or more proxi-
mate, the Pastor is aware that such times are ripe for the appearance of evil and for the testing of true faith. The crisis of the Pastor's
own day yields lies, deceit, renunciation of the faith, and the spew-
ing of demons (4:1–2), but it also serves as the occasion for renewed
"hope set on the living God, who is the savior of all people" (4:10).
Here is the hope offered by the New Testament, that when this old
world falls apart, as it does, as it always does, as it must, God is right
in the middle of it, not only as judge but also as redeemer, offering,
amid the ruins of the world that once was but is no more, the new
world of life and joy.

In the meantime, the breaking apart of the old world and the
emerging of the new summons people of faith to courageous ethical action. Speaking of how biblical views of apocalypse lead to
striking moral choices, New Testament scholar Brian Blount says,

> Resident within the evil age is the promise of the past cre-
> ation and a hope for a future reclamation. Between those two
> auspicious points, though, there is war. God will play God's
> part; humans must play their part. In fact, apocalyptic escha-
> tology's sense of clarity, striking as it is, presumes to make it
> easier for humans to make a stand about where they belong.
> The eschatological dualism creates a moral dualism where

right and wrong are as clearly differentiated as black and
white. As the Christ-followers in Laodicea learned, there is no
lukewarm gray, no neutral ground (Rev. 3:14–22). A side must
be chosen. Radical choices must be made.[5]

Just so, the Pastor sees the time as fraught, and he urges Timothy
to apocalyptic vigilance and decisiveness: "Pay close attention to
yourself and to your teaching; continue in these things, for in doing
this you will save both yourself and your hearers" (4:16).

The Clear Message of the Spirit—So the Pastor says that the Holy
Spirit speaks unambiguously, but how does the Pastor know so
clearly what the Spirit says? Does the Holy Spirit speak to the Pastor
through Scripture? Through precedent? Directly through personal
revelation? The Pastor does not say, but this firm declaration that the
Spirit speaks expressly is an encouraging claim that, even as the raf-
ters of the church are cracking and the foundations are shaking, even
as the once-peaceful assembly of God is consumed by acrimony and
deceit, the Spirit has not withdrawn into silence and in fact speaks
clearly and directly. The church may be confused, but the Spirit of
God is not confused. The church may be dissolving into rancorous
babble, but the Spirit speaks with a single voice, speaking shalom
into the turmoil.

What does the Spirit "expressly say"?

1. The first word of the Spirit is that the church should not be
surprised that a volcano of contention and controversy has erupted.
The gospel never travels alone but is always accompanied by opposition. The stronger the witness to God's mercy, the Spirit reminds us,
the more some people will "raise hell" to undermine that witness.
The theological idea here is that one sign that God is acting in the
world is that the demons are stirred up in opposition, or, to put it in
more contemporary terms, nothing rouses the powers of evil more
than the redemptive work of God and the teaching of the gospel.

When Jesus preached his first sermon in his hometown synagogue at Nazareth, he quoted Isaiah to the effect that God's Spirit

5. Brian K. Blount, *Invasion of the Dead: Preaching Resurrection* (Louisville, KY: Westminster
John Knox Press, 2014), 3.

The idea that God's redemption stirs up the frenzy of the demonic world
is powerfully expressed in the ancient Easter Homily attributed to St.
John Chrysostom, which is read in many congregations at the Easter Vigil.
The sermon concludes with a crescendo, in which the great victory of the
resurrection arouses the noisy anger of hell:

No one need lament poverty,
for the kingdom is seen as universal.
No one need grieve over sins;
forgiveness has dawned from the tomb.
No one need fear death;
the Savior's death has freed us from it.
While [He was] its captive, He stifled it.
He despoiled Hades as He descended into it;
it was angered when it tasted His flesh.
Foreseeing this, Isaiah proclaimed: "Hades," he
said, "was angered when he met You below."
It was angered because it was abolished
It was angered because it was mocked
It was angered because it was slain.
It was angered because it was shackled.
It received a body and encountered God.
It took earth and came face-to-face with heaven.
It took what I saw and fell by what if could not see.
Death, where is your sting?
Hades, where is your victory?
Christ is risen and you are overthrown.
Christ is risen and demons have fallen.
Christ is risen and angels rejoice.
Christ is risen and life rules.
Christ is risen and not one dead remains in the tomb.
For Christ, having risen from the dead,
has become the first fruits of those that slept.
To Him be the glory and the dominion, forever. Amen.

This translation of the Easter sermon attributed to St. John Chrysostom can be found in "Paschal Sermon of St. John Chrysostom: A 4th-century sermon still preached every Easter in Orthodox churches,"
Reformed Worship (December 1999), http://www.reformedworship.org/article/december-1999/
paschal-sermon-st-john-chrysostom-4th-century-sermon-still-preached-every-east.

had anointed him to "bring good news to the poor, . . . to proclaim
release to the captives and recovery of sight to the blind, . . . to let
the oppressed go free . . ." (Luke 4:18). Who could oppose such a

hopeful, life-giving agenda? The powers of hell, that's who. Just let someone actually try to bring good news to the poor, to urge prison reform, to propose a program of health care for those in need, to work for the liberation of the oppressed, or even to announce such things as the will of God, and the forces of evil, often clothed in respectability, will begin a chorus of howls, protests, and screams. Those working in tune with God's Spirit will be aggressively opposed by tyrants, dismissed as dreamers, denounced as panderers and insurrectionists, and, in dire cases, nailed to crosses. When God and God's people go on the offensive, so do the powers of evil.

2. The second thing that the spirit "expressly says" is that demonic activity in Ephesus has taken a particular and predictable form, namely false teaching—people are wandering away from the truth of the gospel and paying heed instead to "deceitful spirits," the "teachings of demons," and the lies of hypocrites (4:1–2).

This sounds extreme to us. Calling the false teaching "demonic" strikes our ears as odd and perhaps misplaced. Of all the tactics to use in a controversy, demonizing one's opponents usually turns out to be the least effective, and the least ethical. Church history is littered with the wreckage of acrimonious disputes and painful schisms provoked because some people, convinced they were champions of the "truth," declared all their opponents to be children of Satan. Why doesn't the Pastor leave aside the talk of demons, simply admit that he and the other teachers have a sharp disagreement, and then calmly debate the issues?

Part of the challenge here is that we often read 1 Timothy, including this "teachings of demons" language, through the intellectual lens of our own time and thus tend to misread it. In our day, the terms "doctrine" and "Christian teaching" often tend to be viewed as a set of ideas and biblical principles, a collection of free-standing truth claims such as "the Bible is the inspired Word of God" or "Jesus was both human and divine." For more conservative Christians, especially among fundamentalists, these doctrinal assertions have something of the status of scientific claims. To say that "Jesus is Lord" is like saying "water boils at 100 degrees Celsius under standard atmospheric conditions" in the sense that this theological claim is understood to be objectively true. Those who

believe these claims are "right" and those who don't are "wrong,"
maybe tragically so.

Most other Christians, however, especially those of a more pro-
gressive stripe, agree that the gospel is a set of ideas, but not ideas
to be fought over. Christian doctrines, rather, are construed as
creative proposals for spiritual insight and ethical living. As such,
Christian doctrinal ideas are set down in our world amid a thousand
other ideas to be considered and debated. Anyone with access to a
library, a bookstore, or a computer can browse among these ideas—
ideas drawn from philosophy, the many religions of the world, life
coaches, self-help gurus, and from experience—and choose the
ones that seem to have the most personal power and meaning. For
example, some say peace comes through prayer, but others say it
comes through meditation and physical exercise, therapy, or by carrying around crystals in one's pocket. These are all just ideas, after
all, so why not try them out, see which ones work for you, even mix
and match them if you wish?

Sociologist of religion Peter Berger has pointed out that many
Christians in the educated West have become, in a technical sense
and of necessity, "heretics." The term "heresy," Berger reminds us,
comes from the Greek word *hairein*, which means "to choose." In the
ancient world, when every member of a group, clan, or village had
a shared view of life, that view of life was not chosen but inherited,
assumed, breathed in with the air. It was, quite simply, the way things
are, and anyone who differed from that shared view of life made a
choice to step out of the tribal circle. Such persons were "choosers,"
that is to say, quite literally "heretics." It is a mark of contemporary,
technologically developed life, that we are—most of us, anyway—
choosers. Intellectual and moral worldviews have become fragmented, and since there is no comprehensive, coherent, assumed,
universally shared view of life, contemporary people, Berger goes on
to say, are compelled to choose among competitors in the market-
place of ideas. Thus, we are all compelled, as it were, to be "heretics."[6]

In our world, a world of choices (i.e., a world of "heresies") it is
common to encounter plural views of just about everything. For

6. Peter Berger, *The Heretical Imperative: Contemporary Possibilities of Religious Affirmation* (New York: Doubleday, 1980), 25 et passim.

example, someone may say, "In my work with a charity for under-privileged children I have found that Jesus was surely right when he said, 'It is more blessed to give than to receive.'" But someone else may counter, saying, "Well, in my work as a psychotherapist, I have found that the opposite is often true. For some people, the ability to receive from others is more blessed than the need to be constantly giving all the time." So we shrug our shoulders and say, "Well, maybe they're both right in their own ways," or "to each his own," or "live and let live." Hardly anyone would feel the need to declare one right and the other wrong, much less stake out one of these views as heretical, much less as "demonic."

It is important, then, to note that the Pastor of 1 Timothy has a radically different frame of reference regarding doctrine than Christians today, conservative or liberal. The earliest Christians, including the Pastor, did not understand doctrines as truth claims abstracted from practical living, claims that could be judged "right" or "wrong" on external, logical grounds. Christian teachings were not, for them, ideas to be pondered but claims about the nature of reality that were reliable guides for actual living. A doctrinal claim was something like, "There are two roads to Centerville, the high road and the low road, but don't take the low road. The bridge is washed out." Christian teachings were like road maps for traveling along the Christian way. They described ways to live, ways to discern the wise path to follow.

Nor was the gospel of Jesus Christ viewed as a set of ideas placed among other ideas, concepts to be considered, weighed in the balance, and hopefully chosen because they were deemed personally meaningful. In fact, the gospel was not first and foremost an *idea* at all but an *event*, the incarnation of God in the man Jesus of Nazareth, his life, death, and resurrection. The gospel led to ideas, of course, but these were all derivative, growing out of what had happened, what God had done in and through Jesus. Moreover, this event of God was not a philosophy of life but a *saving* event. To place one's trust and to build one's life around the event of Jesus Christ was to be rescued from a life of hopelessness, despair, and self- and other-destructiveness. The gospel was not to these early Christians a collection of opinions about this or that issue but a way of life in the most radical sense, specifically a way of *life* in contrast to the ways of *death*. To put it sharply, these early Christians did not think that God had merely given them some new religious choices or enlightened them with a new spirituality. Instead, God had, through Jesus, snatched them from the snares of death. Indeed, the Pastor has already described his own experience in just such rescue terms ("even though I was formerly a blasphemer, a persecutor, and a man of violence ... I received mercy ..." [1:13]).

Living the Christian life meant walking a narrow pathway, bathed in light, leading up a perilous and darkened mountainside. To follow the gospel path, they believed, would lead to peace and fullness of life. Step off the path, and one risked a terrifying, fatal plunge back into darkness. This is why the false teachers and their teachings were of such concern to the Pastor and other early Christian leaders. These false teachers were not like assistant professors of religion at a community college, trying to expand the minds of their students by suggesting various alternative ways to view some religious truth. Instead, they were reckless, perhaps even malevolent, guides, pointing the innocent and unknowing faithful down paths that led to the fearful abyss. For the Pastor, these teachers were heretics and liars not because he merely disagreed with them about some doctrine and felt the need to demonize their positions, but rather because their counsel destroyed community, damaged real people in significant ways, and even led to despair and death. These teachers had lost their inner moral compass, and their consciences were numb and insensitive (cauterized with a hot iron, 4:2). They were like vandals who, as a malicious prank, remove stop signs from dangerous intersections and turn one-way signs to point in the opposite direction. They were like destructive saboteurs who put a glass of scotch in front of a recovering alcoholic with two years of hard-won sobriety. Their teachings were not a matter of opinion; they were matters of life and death.

Once Again, the False Teachings—What are the false teachings that the Pastor finds to be such a threat to life? We have encountered them earlier in the letter (see comments on 1:3–11), and here the Pastor adds a few more details. The false teachers, he says, "forbid marriage" and "demand abstinence from foods." Abstinence from foods refers not to a hunger strike—people have to eat something to stay alive—but to practices in which certain foods are avoided for spiritual reasons, maybe practices, suggest some commentators, such as fasting, refraining from drinking wine, or vegetarianism.[7]

So what's the problem here? Yes, the false teachers urge their followers not to marry and to be religiously picky about their diet, but so what? Are these teachings really signs of the "later times," demonic lies, and threats to faith and life? The Pastor would say yes, and his alarm arises not just because of the practices themselves but mainly because of the theological worldview in which they are rooted. Their attitudes toward marriage and foods spring from a single source, namely a basic rejection of the goodness of God's creation, and that is a deep threat to one's relationship to God and others. As Jewish theologian Michael Wyschogrod says, "Praise of God is . . . rooted in gratitude and wonder at the complexities and beauty of creation. . . . Praise does not involve measuring God's creation and conduct by external standards and declaring them good because they live up to those standards. Praise is an act of gratitude that is totally focused on God to whom we are grateful."[8]

It is here, then, that we begin to see even more clearly the battle lines of this controversy at Ephesus between the Pastor and the false teachers. It is essentially a battle over whether or not this world is God's good earth or not. It is a battle over whether God calls us to come alive as human beings in this world or by renouncing this world.

Early Christians shared with Jews the Genesis story of creation, the narrative of how God created the heavens and the earth, the seas and the land; the moon, the sun, and the stars; plants, animals, and human beings, and all of this was declared by God to be "very good" (Gen. 1:31). Most contemporary people would agree—the creation is very good indeed. The night sky spangled with stars is awesome, the crested mountains breathtaking, the flashing blue seas impressive. The changing colors of the leaves in the fall, the refreshment of

7. Martin Dibelius and Hans Conzelmann, *The Pastoral Epistles,* Hermeneia (Philadelphia: Fortress Press, 1972), 65.
8. Michael Wyschogrod, *The Body of Faith: God in the People Israel* (Northvale, NJ: Jason Aronson, Inc., 1996), 59.

a spring rainfall, the blanketing of a forest with snow, the rosy glow of a sunset, are all deeply inspiring.

Hardly anyone today would object to the claim that nature is lovely, breathtaking, and "very good." But Christians (and Jews with them) do not stop there, and this is where the trouble starts. Creation is "very good" not simply because it is beautiful but also because it is the place where human beings—interacting with God, others, and nature—come alive with faith, meaning, and purpose. In short, early Christians believed that the creation was "good" not simply because it was a lovely place to live but also because it is the theater of God's salvation. Creation is not merely a garden full of roses and robins, it is the place where humanity is commanded to till and to keep (Gen. 2:15), the place where God comes to meet us in the cool of the day (Gen. 3:8), the place where humanity experiences God's presence, providence, love, and, eventually, judgment and redemption.

This is precisely where the false teachers at Ephesus part ways with the gospel. They rejected the claim that the everyday world of God's creation was the place where human beings achieved religious fulfillment.

They had two main reasons for this rejection of the gospel:

First, God is not material. God is spiritual, and it therefore makes no sense that God would be experienced in and through materiality. The false teachers had a point. Almost every great religious tradition—East and West—agrees that God is a Spirit, not a material thing. God does not have a body, does not live in a cave in the mountains or a chamber in the sea. As the Westminster Confession of Faith of the Reformed tradition bluntly puts it, "There is but one only, living, and true God, who is infinite in being and perfection, a most pure spirit, invisible, without body, parts, or passions." So if God is a Spirit and doesn't have a body, then it stands to reason, does it not, that God would relate to humanity on a purely spiritual plane, that it would be the spiritual essence of human beings that could truly comprehend God, that God would be concerned with human souls more than with human bodies. The more "spiritual" a person is, it stands to reason, the more that person is like God, the more that person pleases God and is in tune with God.

But the biblical witness and the Christian gospel flatly disagree. They stand as counterintuitive testimonies that exactly the opposite is the case. The gospel affirms that God is more concerned with human beings in their full embodiment than with people construed as ethereal spirits. God created the heavens and the earth—soil, water, and flesh—and declared these material realities to be "very good." God's Spirit hovered over the waters, spoke materiality into reality with a Word, and created humanity by breathing into the dust of the ground. When God wished to be present in the world, it was not in the form of an abstract idea, disembodied reason, or an esoteric spirituality; it was in the embodied form of the real people Israel, in the form of Abraham and Sarah, living in the land, trying to get pregnant, trying to make their way forward in life. Israel was called to be holy, because God was holy, and this holiness was not sweet piety or a privatized spirituality but was an embodied holiness, incarnated in the way Israel kept the Sabbath, gleaned its fields, treated its neighbors, and rendered justice in the courts (Lev. 19).

Then, as the gospel affirms, the Word became flesh once again and dwelled among us, in the body and the life and the death of Jesus (John 1:14). He was not a spiritualized presence emanating from never-never land. He was born in Bethlehem and raised in Nazareth. His mother was a woman who had a name, Mary, and, like all other infants, Jesus kicked and moved in his mother's womb (Luke 1:41). As a child, he "grew and became strong, filled with wisdom . . ." (Luke 2:40), and as a man, he became angry and tired, loved and wept and cried out in agony when he died. The incarnation of God in the human being Jesus is an affirmation that salvation occurs in the created, embodied realm, and his resurrection in the body is not a supernatural violation of the so-called laws of nature, but an affirmation that the creation is still "very good," not simply as the backdrop for picture postcards but as the very arena of God's sacred deeds of redemption.

A central claim of the gospel, then, is that God came in embodied form, moved among us not in some gaseous, generalized way, but in Galilee and Judea, touching the bodies of the sick, raising the bodies of the dead, and that God continues to save us in and through the material, created order. But this central claim has been in trouble from the beginning. For example, Celsus, a second-century Greek philosopher who wrote a major attack on Christianity, found the whole idea that God would be born in bodily form among Jews in some backwater Judean village to be ridiculous. He reminded his Christian targets of a well-known comic scene in Roman drama in which the great Jupiter, king of the gods and chief god of the empire, awoke from a deep sleep and, in his drowsiness, thoughtlessly dispatched his courier Mercury with a message for the towns of Athens and Sparta. The sight of mighty Jupiter sending a divine word to a couple of local burgs instead of to the whole earth and the entire sweep of humanity made him look foolish and small, a two-bit deity, and evidently left Roman theatergoers rolling in the aisles. But what Jupiter did was nothing compared to the God of Christians, claimed Celsus. This so-called God supposedly showed up in a feed stall in Bethlehem. "If God, like Jupiter in the comedy," he wrote,

> . . . should, on awaking from a lengthened slumber, desire to rescue the human race from evil, why did He send this Spirit of which you speak into one corner (of the earth)? He ought to have breathed it alike into many bodies, and have sent them out into all the world. . . . Do not you think that you have made the Son of God more ridiculous in sending him to the Jews?[9]

The false teachers at Ephesus agree with Celsus. The idea of searching for a spiritual God in some corner of a material world seemed absurd. But these teachers had a second reason for rejecting the claim that the everyday world of God's creation was the place where human beings achieved religious fulfillment.

Second, the world is a mess. Here again, the false teachers of Ephesus had a point. If we look out at the world, it is clear that we do not live in Disneyland where every vista has a rainbow and every landscape is filled with bluebirds, butterflies, and marigolds. We live in a world where the sea, blue and calm one moment, rises suddenly and violently to dash ships and devastate the land with tsunamis the next. The natural world has butterflies, and it has cancer and tuberculosis, too. Nature has its loveliness, but also its red claw, and the messiness of creation extends to human relationships. Marriage, which begins

9. Origen, *Contra Celsus,* book VI, chap. 78, http://www.newadvent.org/fathers/04166.htm.

in a romantic glow, soon devolves into the hard work of making a life, adjusting expectations, and mending constantly broken places. Children grow in jagged spurts, loving and defying, staying and leaving, as much a mixture of joy and disappointment to their parents as their parents are to them. Finally they, and we, die, and hearts are broken. Even in our most sacred communities, even in the church of Jesus Christ, sometimes *especially* in the church, the world is often too much with us. People are people, and our pettiness, petulance, and pomposities, our weaknesses and outright wickedness, often overwhelm any sense of sanctity. And the false teachers of Ephesus lifted their voices to say what millions have said since, "Surely true religion is more spiritual than this!"

"Surely true religion is more spiritual than this!" The dispute boiled down to this. Everybody agreed that human life, set down in a messy world, was infused with tragedy. Human beings have bodies, are in fact limited to bodies, and this means that humanity is subject to the change and decay of creation. Look in the mirror and see the truth that the frail body changes, suffers, ages, and decays. For the false teachers, this embodiment is the reality from which we need to be delivered. For the gospel teachers, this embodiment is the reality in which and by which we will be delivered.

For the false teachers, the goal was escape—escape from the body, escape from messy relationships, escape from materiality, escape into spirituality. This is why they shunned marriage and fussed over their diets; they were avoiding what they considered the crude vulgarity of material life. For the gospel teachers, to the contrary, the goal was to enter more deeply into embodiment, to trust that human relationships by the grace of the incarnate Christ are holy places, that putting one foot in front of the other in the faithful living of our everyday embodied lives is the way to salvation, that humanity is most alive in the palpable experience of Christ in the bread and the wine and by living as Christ's very own body in the world. Two paths lay before humanity, life and death. The dispute at Ephesus, plainly put, was over which was which.

It is no wonder, then, that one of the fault lines between the Pastor and the false teachers ran through the Old Testament (see comments on 1:3–11). As Jewish theologian Michael Wyschogrod has pointed out, the Hebrew Scriptures, in Jewish understanding, emphasize the material and carnal as the location of God's encounter with humanity. God's creation of Israel, he maintains, was the establishment of a people that would serve God "in the totality of its human being and not just in its moral and spiritual existence." This embodied service is evidence of the fact that "Israel's symbol of the covenant is circumcision, a searing of the covenant into the flesh of Israel and not only, or perhaps not even primarily, into its spirit."[10]

But since the rallying cry of the false teachers is, "Surely true religion is more spiritual than this!" they stepped around straightforward Old Testament interpretation in favor of presumably deeper, hidden, more spiritual "myths and . . . speculations" (1:4) "The difficulty with this spiritualization of the God-man relationship," writes Wyschogrod, "is that it is untrue to man's nature, which is largely carnal." It is not even accurate, he goes on to say, to think of human beings as a blending of the fleshly and the spiritual:

> This unity must not be conceived as a coupling of the spiritual and the material because any coupling presupposes an original separation, which is simply not warranted. Man is not a coupling of the spiritual and material but a creature who thinks and runs, grieves and cries, is amused and laughs. He is, in short, what he is: a being with an identity and a world in which he lives. Here, again, God could have played a godly role, interested in certain features of human existence, the spiritual, but not in others, the material. He could even have assigned man the task of wrenching himself out of the material so as to assume his spiritual identity, which is just what so many religions believe he did. Instead, the God of Israel confirms man as he created him to live in the material cosmos. There is therefore no possibility of a divine requirement for the discarding of a part of human existence. Instead, there is a requirement for the sanctification of human existence in all of its aspects.[11]

The Goodness of Creation—Having pointed out what the Spirit says about the false teachers, the Pastor goes on to proclaim the gospel

10. Wyschogrod, *The Body of Faith*, 67.
11. Ibid., 66.

about creation. Since "everything created by God is good" (4:4), it is not to be shunned but to be "received with thanksgiving." When the Pastor adds that everything created by God is good because it is "sanctified by God's word and by prayer" (4:5), he means, in the broadest sense, that the Christian assembly affirmed, in their reading of Scripture and in their prayers, that the whole of creation is holy because it is gathered up into the providential and redemptive activity of God.

But there is almost surely a more focused liturgical connection here. The phrase "sanctified by God's word and by prayer" is an echo of their observance of the Lord's Supper. Not long after the Pastor wrote 1 Timothy, Justin Martyr wrote his *First Apology*, in which he tried to explain Christian faith and practice to a suspicious Roman culture. Among other practices, Justin describes Sunday worship, recounting how Christians gather from far and near for the reading of Scripture, a sermon, prayers, and the Lord's Supper, followed by an offering of alms for the widows and orphans. At one point, he focuses his attention on the Lord's Supper, and his language is similar to the Pastor's:

> For we do not receive these things as common bread or common drink; but as Jesus Christ our Savior, being incarnate by the Word of God, took flesh and blood for our salvation, so also have we been taught that the food, "eucharistized" [i.e., blessed and consecrated with thanksgiving] by the formula of prayer that comes from Him [i.e., Jesus], and from which our flesh and blood are nourished by transformation, is the flesh and blood of that incarnate Jesus.[12]

What Justin is describing here is the church's practice, established very early, of speaking a prayer of thanksgiving over the bread and wine of Holy Communion, following the formula of Jesus' own prayer in which he "gave thanks" at the Last Supper. This prayer is connected to the conviction that, in the Eucharist, the bread and wine become the body and blood of Jesus Christ, thus more than

---

12. Justin Martyr, *The First Apology*, 66. The translation is by Bard Thompson, based on the critical text of Prudent Maran. Thompson's translation is found in *Liturgies of the Western Church* (Philadelphia: Fortress Press, 1980), 8–9.

ordinary food. The Pastor's word about food, "for it is sanctified by word and prayer," is a clear reverberation of this liturgical formula.

So the Pastor is challenging the false teachers' rejection of food in two theological directions: creational and soteriological. First, the goodness of food is a truth that radiates forward from the very beginning. God created all things, including food, and declared all created things "very good." Like all else in creation, then, food has been "very good" from the beginning. How dare the false teachers claim that avoiding the good gifts of God is somehow more spiritual than embracing these gifts? Second, food—bread and wine—are given to us by the risen Christ at the banquet table of the kingdom. The goodness of food is a truth that radiates back to us in the present from the end of all things, when Christ will be all in all. At the table the church prays a prayer of thanksgiving, just as Jesus prayed, in the faith that the bread and wine would become instruments of salvation and that this table would be a foretaste of the great heavenly banquet. In sum, food, which has been "very good" from the beginning of creation is also good in another way, as a means of grace. Christians experience the saving power of God not by abstaining from food but by gathering with others around the table and eating and drinking with the risen Christ with glad and generous hearts, proclaiming "the Lord's death until he comes" (1 Cor. 11:26). In food, in an ordinary loaf of bread and an ordinary cup of wine, providence and salvation, creation and eschatology, blessing and hope come together.

FURTHER REFLECTIONS
Food and Sex: Keeping It between the Navigational Markers

It is not all that surprising that the early Christians were confused about sex, marriage, food, and drink. These human realities, wrapped up as they are in bodily appetites and desires, are perennially confusing anyway, regardless of religious orientation. But there were also mixed signals in Scripture and in Christian teaching that contributed to the perplexity.

First, there was the tendency of the apostle Paul to talk about marriage and sex in ways that tended to scatter the troops. For example, the Corinthian Christians seem to have become fond of the moral maxim: "It is well for a man not to touch a woman" (1 Cor. 7:1). In other words, sex is to be avoided and abstaining from marriage is a good, morally superior state. Paul spends a whole chapter of his first letter to the Corinthians essentially undermining this maxim, but not in the direct and straightforward way of the "Paul" of 1 Timothy. He seems at first to zig in one direction, giving for the sake of argument a little credence to the maxim, but then he zags in the other, reminding the Corinthians that human beings, after all, do have sexual urges. So, "because of cases of sexuality immorality," marriage and its accompanying and mutual "conjugal rights" are actually good things (1 Cor. 7:2–4). But then he appears to change directions once more, allowing that a time of sexual abstinence between married couples for "spiritual reasons," namely, prayer, might be desirable, only to come around again to say that this abstinence should not last too long, lest Satan take advantage of the situation (1 Cor. 7:5). He then seems to throw up his hands and wish for the whole issue to go away when he says that it would really be best if everybody were like him, unmarried (1 Cor. 7:7). The bottom line is that Paul affirms marriage and sexuality, but he takes a roundabout path to do so.

Paul engages in a similar pattern of open-field running on the issue of food, particularly on the question of whether or not it is permissible to eat food that had been offered to idols. His answer is finally a combination of "yes" and "it depends" (see 1 Cor. 8 and 1:23–33). As for Jesus on the issue of food, he had, after all, "declared all foods clean" (Mark 7:19), and Peter had a vision of God telling him via a heavenly voice to eat previously forbidden foods. "What God has made clean," the voice tells him, "you must not call profane" (Acts 10:15). But the food freedom of Jesus and Peter became a political problem in the delicate relationships between early Gentile Christians, who had no proscriptions on food, and Jewish Christians, who had all their lives avoided nonkosher foods.

Jewish-Christian relations have often been negotiated along the fraught border of food. In his memoir, *The Search for God at Harvard*, Ari Goldman, a religion journalist who spent a year's leave studying

at Harvard Divinity School, recalled the first time he ever heard—
in a New Testament class—the story of Peter and the voice from
heaven encouraging him not to call profane what God has made
clean (Acts 10:9–16). The story provoked a strong reaction in Goldman, an Orthodox Jew, one for whom food rituals are a strict marker
of his own religious commitments:

> With that, Peter had his first *traif* [nonkosher] meal. My reac-
> tion to his vision, however, was quite different. "Yet another
> reason to keep Kosher!" I scrawled in the margin of my Bible.
> For me, keeping Kosher is more than a Jewish observance, it
> is a daily, tangible declaration that the Mosaic covenant was
> *not* superseded by Jesus. Keeping Kosher is my way of saying
> no to Christianity.[13]

In the first century, the Council of Jerusalem struck a compromise: Gentile Christians should not be hindered or burdened in
any way in their freedom to love as both Christians and Gentiles,
but they should nevertheless be encouraged "to abstain only from
things polluted by idols and from fornication and from whatever
has been strangled and from blood" (Acts 15:20). This memo evidently did not make it to the church at Pergamum, who, according
to the book of Revelation, had the full wind of freedom blowing
though their hair as evidenced by the fact that they ran roughshod
over the Jerusalem compromise and would "eat food sacrificed to
idols and practice fornication" (Rev. 2:14).

So early Christians were all over the charts on matters of food
and sex. Some were turning on the hedonistic party lights in the
name of Christian freedom, others were rejoicing in Christ but
remaining chaste and keeping a kosher table, and still others were
finding spiritual fulfillment in celibacy, austere diets, and the renunciation of the flesh. In the midst of all this, the Pastor of 1 Timothy is
attempting to sail down the middle of the channel. To one side lay
a sinful self-indulgence, and to the other side lay a foolish and misguided spirituality of worldly renunciation. In the middle there was
room for Christians to view all that God had given as joyful gifts—all

---

13. Ari L. Goldman, *The Search for God at Harvard* (New York: Ballantine Books, 1992),
256–57.

food, all drink, sexuality and marriage—and, in modesty and moderation, to receive these gifts with blessing and thanksgiving.

4:6–16
The Response of a Good Minister

It is said that the fourth-century desert father Arsenius once prayed, "Lord, guide me so that I may be saved." The response he heard was, "Flee from humans, and you will be saved." When he withdrew from community, a brother Christian asked him, "Why do you flee from us?" "God knows that I love you," replied Arsenius, "but I cannot be both with God and with humans."[14]

It is precisely the opposite advice that the Pastor gives to Timothy (and, through "Timothy," to the leaders of the church at Ephesus). Being with God means being with others, in all the messiness that entails. Christians are not to flee from the brothers and sisters in the church but to invest in them, work alongside them, labor to repair the broken places in the community. Salvation is to be found not in the lonely desert but in rolling up their sleeves and doing good ministry in and for and with the church. This section of the letter, which consists of a set of instructions for action in the midst of the faith crisis of the congregation, is very practical, but it is not merely a matter of church management; it is how church leaders participate in the saving work of Jesus Christ. "Continue in these things," writes the Pastor, "for in doing this you will save both yourself and your hearers" (4:16).

Given the crisis at Ephesus precipitated by conflict and false teaching, the Pastor names four strategic patterns of good ministry:

1. When the people are being fed spiritual junk food, give them something solid (4:6–7a). Leaders, the Pastor urges, are to nourish the people with "the words of the faith and the sound teaching that you have followed" (4:6) instead of the dog's breakfast of "profane myths and old wives' tales" (4:7) served up by the false teachers. The false

---

14. Kallistos Ware, "The Way of the Ascetics: Negative or Affirmative?," in Vincent L. Wimbush and Richard Valentasis, eds., *Asceticism* (New York: Oxford University Press, 2002), 4–5.

teachers would, of course, object to such a dismissal of their message and could well respond, "But what we teach is more exciting, more fulfilling, and more spiritual."

What keeps this from being a stalemate is that this is not merely a matter of dueling pedagogies, Timothy's ideas about the faith versus the false teachers'. Timothy is being urged to present the gospel to the brothers and sisters, and the gospel has several distinct advantages over the false teaching.

First, there is the manner in which the gospel is to be taught. The verb used here in 4:6 (*hypotithemenos*) can be translated several ways in the phrase—"put these instructions before the brothers and sisters" (as in the NRSV); "point these things out" (in the NIV); "put the brethren in remembrance of these things" (as reads the KJV); or even, "suggest these things," "recommend these things," or "remind the brothers and sisters about these things"—but the tone is clearly about a way of teaching that is open and congenial, not disciplinary.[15] The false teachers themselves are to be confronted and chastised, but not the brothers and sisters, who are to be gently refreshed in the good news.

Second, unlike the false teaching, the gospel is not speculative wisdom (1:4) but is instead firmly anchored in the event of Jesus Christ. It is the event of God incarnate in Jesus from which the truth of the teaching and good ministry spring. To teach this gospel is more than being an effective religious teacher; it is to be "a good servant of Jesus Christ" (4:6).

Third, even though 1 Timothy appears relatively early in Christian history, there is already a growing sense that the gospel forms a "tradition," that is to say that the gospel has been taught, pastor to congregation, parent to child, strong to the weak, mature to the young, over the years. It has been tested, can be trusted, and is more than the provisional religious expression of the present moment. The word translated "nourished" in the NRSV (*entrephomenos*) can also be translated "to be reared by," as in the raising of a child.[16] The gospel is a tradition that Timothy and all other Christians have been "reared by" and "nourished by," a tradition that connects them to

15. Philip H. Towner, *The Letters to Timothy and Titus* (Grand Rapids: Eerdmans, 2006), 303.
16. Dibelius and Conzelmann, *The Pastoral Epistles*, 68.

the faith of those who have gone before them and to those who will come in generations to follow. Timothy is not being urged to make up some innovative and clever retort to the false teachers. Instead he is being encouraged to do as Paul himself did: to hand on as of first importance the gospel that he had received (1 Cor. 15:3).

To love God, in the sense of placing trust and hope in the One identified in scriptural traditions and attested in the ongoing life of the church as the Lord, is at the same time to refuse to trust and hope in what the writers of Scripture in their distinctive ways refer to as idols, false gods, false prophets, unclean spirits, or even as the Anti-Christ. Scripturally this refusal to give allegiance to that which is not of God is presented as a faithful act. To believe in God is at once to disbelieve what is not of God. Faith in God, we are led to conclude, is not only believing; it is a disbelieving as well.

Christopher Morse, *Not Every Spirit: A Dogmatics of Christian Disbelief,* 2nd ed. (New York and London: T. & T. Clark, 2009), 5.

When the great church historian Jaroslav Pelikan was interviewed by Krista Tippett on her public radio program, *On Being,* the topic was the value of creeds as emblems of the Christian tradition. Tippett voiced some nervousness about fixed creeds from the past, such as the Nicene Creed, wondering if people in a postmodern culture could just as well do without creeds or, perhaps, should create new creeds for a new day.

"It's a plausible suggestion," replied Pelikan, noting that Tippett, by desiring to be free of the weight of creedal tradition, was in agreement with many Americans, including the notable Ralph Waldo Emerson. The conversation continued:

> Pelikan: Emerson was a graduate of Harvard Divinity School
> and was a Unitarian minister, so he was quite prepared
> to believe that everyone should compose a creed
> different from the tradition. He said to the Divinity
> School students at Harvard in 1838, "You must be
> yourself a newborn bard of the Holy Spirit and sing
> it out." The trouble with that is, you do it and then
> you do it a little bit more, and pretty soon you have to
> teach your children something, and so the best you

can do is to teach them what you have, and you do
that a generation or two, and all of a sudden, there you
have . . .

Tippett: . . . a new creed.
Pelikan: . . . a new creed.
Tippett: All right.
Pelikan: And the only alternative to tradition is bad tradition.[17]

*2. Train yourself in the same life of faith and discipleship that you expect
of the rest of the community (4:7b–10).* The Pastor, like a lot of other
Greco-Roman writers, employs an athletic metaphor to describe
the development of virtue. He urges them "to train yourself in godliness," that is, to have daily "work outs" for faithful living. The word
for "to train" is *gumnase,* from which we get "gymnasium."

He knows that he needs to be careful in using this exercise image.
On the one hand, he does not intend this metaphor literally. Physical exercise does not in and of itself produce godliness; sports, in
other words, do not automatically build character. As the Pastor
puts it, "Physical training is of *some* value," (4:8) but it isn't the only
thing or the main thing. On the other hand, he does not want his
language spiritualized, either, as if he were speaking only of body
exercises associated with asceticism or with purely mystical "soul
exercises" implying an escape from embodiment. That would play
into the hands of the "false teachers" with their emphasis on spiritual
release from ordinary fleshly concerns. No, when the Pastor talks
about training in godliness, he is talking about activities that engage
the whole self—mind, body, and spirit.

But what are these activities? What is this "training in godliness"
that the Pastor has in mind? We have three clues. The first is that the
"godliness" described by the Pastor is certainly counter to the teaching of the "false teachers." It is godliness, therefore, on the ground,
godliness that affirms the goodness of creation and of life in this
world rather than being hyper-spiritualized and world-denying. In
the Pastor's day, he possibly saw godliness in such everyday activities
as tending lovingly to the relationships with spouse and children,

17. Transcript of Jaroslav Pelikan, "The Need for Creeds," October 22, 2009, *On Being with
Krista Tippett,* public radio program, http://www.onbeing.org/program/need-creeds/
transcript/1291.

to the faithful enjoyment of sexuality, to the just management of one's house, to making peace with one's neighbors, and to lifting up prayers for the world. In our day, such godliness might also take the form of ecological concern, tending with care to the creation as the gift of God.

The second clue comes from the similar reference to "divine training" in 1:4–5, in which the aim is "love that comes from a pure heart, a good conscience, and sincere faith." Putting this together with 4:7, we emerge with the idea that Christians go to the theological gym to do curls, crunches, and run laps to train themselves not to run a marathon but in order to be people of love. It is one thing, of course, to love the lovable, but when the call is to love those who are vexing and contentious, those who do not or cannot love us in return, even to love those who hate and persecute us—then that takes *practice*.

The National Civil Rights Museum is located in the old Lorraine Motel in Memphis. It was on the balcony of the Lorraine that Dr. Martin Luther King Jr. was assassinated. One of the more striking exhibits in the museum is a bank of screens, some of them showing videos of civil rights workers in the 1960s receiving training in nonviolence. There they are, sitting patiently at mock lunch counters while the trainers scream curses and insults at them and threaten them physically. The other screens show these same workers in real-life situations, sitting in at all-white lunch counters while people spit on them, revile them, and push them to the ground. All the while, they remain true to their training. They do not repay evil with evil but respond with peace and nonviolence, refusing to dehumanize their persecutors even as they are themselves being dehumanized, that is, responding with what the Pastor would call "love that comes from a pure heart, a good conscience, and sincere faith." This is not sentimental love; this is love that takes active and embodied form. This is not a love that springs naturally from the human heart, especially when surrounded by hatred. It comes instead from "training in godliness."

The third clue comes when the Pastor describes the godliness resulting from this training as "valuable in every way, holding promise for both the present life and the life to come" (4:8). In other words, godliness is an enduring set of virtues. It is not a virtue like physical fitness or the ability to make money, which will eventually pass away, but it is more like love or hope, which matters now as well as in the life to come.

When Albert Schweitzer died at age ninety in the hospital that he had built in the African jungle, the *New York Times* obituary said of him,

> As a person, Schweitzer was a curious mixture. Widely hon-
> ored with degrees, citations, scrolls, medals, special stamps,
> even the Nobel Prize for Peace in 1952, he seemed oblivious
> to panoply. . . . He seemed to many observers to be a simple,
> almost rustic man, who dressed in rumpled clothing, suffered
> fools gladly, stated fundamental verities patiently and pater-
> nally and worked unobtrusively.
>   . . . He took the search for the good life seriously. For him
> it had profound religious implications. "Anyone can rescue his
> human life," he once said, "who seizes every opportunity of
> being a man by means of personal action, however unpretend-
> ing, for the good of fellow men who need the help of a fellow
> man." He sought to exemplify the idea that man, through good
> works, can be in the world and in God at one and the same
> time.[18]

But this commitment to live today in ways that last eternally cuts in the other direction as well. Not only is godliness a quality that begins now and is carried into God's future, it is also a quality that comes into the present *from* God's future. To be "godly" is to live today, in this world, as one who already belongs to God's eternal kingdom.

Some years ago, when the church was first beginning to address the question of gender inclusive language in prayers, hymns, and Scripture, there was, of course, resistance to these new patterns of speech in worship. Some pushed forward, saying that the use of gen-der inclusive language was a justice issue; it was only fair to speak of women and men equally—and they were right. Others pushed forward on pastoral care grounds, saying that people should not be made to feel excluded by the church's language—and they were right

---

18. "Albert Schweitzer, 90, Dies at His Hospital," *New York Times*, September 6, 1965, http://www.nytimes.com/learning/general/onthisday/bday/0114.html.

too. But the deepest reason for the church's language of inclusion is eschatological: the church is trying to practice today, here and now, including the way it speaks, the way of life it *will* practice in the communion at the Great Banquet table of Christ. To speak inclusively, then, is a matter not only of justice and care but also of godliness, a quality not grounded entirely in present reality but instead serving as an advance down payment on the life to come.

In 4:9, the Pastor recites for the third and last time in the letter the formula "the saying is sure and worthy of full acceptance" (see 1:15 and 3:1), which is probably a sign that the language of verse 8, "the present life and the life to come," comes from the liturgy at Ephesus and is a time-honored and trusted expression. It is surely a way for the Pastor to indicate that this discussion about godliness is standing on solid ground, unlike the will-o'-the-wisp speculations of the false teachers.

The Pastor rounds out this portion of the letter by providing a theological reason for going to "God's gym." We do all this "toil and struggle," he says, because of "our hope set on the living God." The Christian way of life makes little sense apart from hope. The rest of the world—from hedge fund managers to trial lawyers to real estate developers to tennis players—works out to get strong enough to flatten the opposition and to win at whatever game is being played. The followers of Christ, however, are in training to turn the other cheek, to practice forgiveness instead of revenge, to make peace, and to love even those who revile and persecute them. Viewed with the cold eye of reality, it appears to be a game plan for losers. Only in the light of hope is the way of Christ revealed as the path that leads to life.

The last phrases of 4:10 are curious. It almost seems as if the Pastor forgets himself in a moment of jubilant hymn-singing, exulting that "God . . . is the savior of all people," only to catch himself mid-air and to make a midcourse doctrinal correction, "Actually, what I mean is that God saves those who believe."[19] By this ambiguity, the Pastor puts us in the middle of an agonized theological debate over

---

19. Jouette Bassler, citing T. C. Skeat's work on the Greek word *malista* (translated as "especially" in the NRSV of 1 Tim. 4:10), says there is evidence that the word "means in this context something like 'that is to say'. . . ." (Bassler, *1 Timothy, 2 Timothy, Titus*, 85).

Society will still have the Fortune 500 for profits, and non-profits for service and day care centers for children and the Elks Club for socializing and Starbucks for overpriced coffee and many other things we may not ever be. But we should never judge ourselves as the church according to these things because you know what the culture around us will NEVER do? Preach the Gospel, administer the sacraments and proclaim forgiveness of sins. You know why? That's OUR job. That's our *main* job and while we are free as the church, to participate in any number of other activities in the world that seem bigger and more impressive let's remember: We are those who have been, and continue to be, entrusted with nothing less than the Gospel.

If in your congregation, regardless of size, prestige or property, if the Word is preached and the Eucharist shared and water poured and forgiveness of sins received, then congratulations, your congregation is a success. So when the numbers crunchers and church consultants say the church is dying . . . may I suggest that we only say this when we forget what the definition of church is.

And when we forgot *whose* the church is. Because as the prophet Isaiah said, the Word will do that for which God purposes it and people. . . . God will continue to send for the Word which God has always sent forth. So let us step back from the worry of how the church is dying, because long after we have gone, the WORD will remain. . . . The church will not be dead because people will continue to gather in the name of the Triune God, hold up bread, say it is Jesus and that it is for the forgiveness of sins. Just as we will do here tonight so will it forever be done until the time in which we gather around the throne of the Lamb.

Nadia Bolz-Weber, "Stop Saying the Church Is Dying (sermon, Rocky Mountain Synod Assembly, May 10, 2014), http://www.patheos.com/blogs/nadiabolzweber/2014/05/stop-saying-the-church-is -dying-a-sermon-for-the-rocky-mountain-synod-assembly/.

the breadth of God's salvation. Does God save "all" or only "those who believe?"

The evidence throughout Scripture is unclear. As theologian Paul Dafydd Jones states,

> Straightaway one must acknowledge that scripture does not provide a clear answer to queries about the scope of salvation. In fact, the Bible admits of diverse and sometimes conflicting interpretations. An appeal to Colossians 1:19 ("through him God was pleased to reconcile to himself all things") can be set against an appeal to Romans 9:15 ("I will have mercy on whom I will have mercy"; see also Exodus 33:19). An appeal

to Romans 5:18 ("just as one man's trespass led to condemnation for all, so one man's act of righteousness leads to justification and life for all") can be countered by an appeal to John
6:44 ("No one can come to me unless drawn by the Father
who sent me").[20]

Actually, the Pastor's stutter step here may be instructive for us
as we think through this question. His first impulse, born out of his
view of hope and the mercy of God, is toward universalism. "God is
the savior of all," he sings. It is in the very character of God to be merciful to all. It is the truth of the cross that God was in Christ forging
reconciliation with the world. And it is a faithful act of the Christian
imagination to hope for the redemption of the whole of creation,
including all of God's creatures.

But then there is the second more hesitant step—"actually those
who believe." For the Pastor, indeed for Christian theology more
generally, salvation is not merely an abstract idea, a decision about
humanity hidden in the recesses of the mind of God. Salvation matters in human life and takes shape in human community. Salvation
is not a free-floating concept; it is a way of life. God's saving act cre-
ates a community of belief and action, and salvation forms a people
who embody God's saving work in the world: in sum, God's saving
intentionality is most visible and palpable in the form of the church,
the body of Christ. In fact, the whole of 1 Timothy is an attempt to
restore the community at Ephesus to its proper shape as a church
fashioned by God's saving action in Christ. Therefore, what they
believe, and how they live together, and how they act in and toward
the world matters. What is more, the Pastor is keenly aware that not
everyone believes this gospel, not everyone participates in this way
of salvation.

So the Pastor does what all Christians must do at this point—
he stutters. Or, to put it another way, he sings two hymns simulta-
neously: "There's a Wideness in God's Mercy" and "The Church's
One Foundation." Between the hope in a God who saves all and
the reality of a believing community that includes only some, there
is a breadth of mystery and a depth of divine freedom over which

20. Paul Dafydd Jones, "A Hopeful Universalism," *The Christian Century* 129/13 (June 27,
2012): 25.

our minds cannot travel. So we live the Christian life, caring for the earth, tending to our relationships of love, putting one foot in front of the other in daily vocation, traveling down the pathway toward a horizon of God's mercy greater and brighter than our frail minds can imagine. As the sign on the door of an old English church reads:

> This is God's House. Be welcome to this House, whosoever you are—whether of this household or of another way, or wanderers or deserters—be welcome here. But you who are of the household, pray for us now, for us and for all sinners here or departed, that mercy draws us all one little pace nearer to Love's unveiled and dazzling face.

3. *Set a public example in the way you speak and the way you live (4:11–12).* The Pastor calls on "Timothy," as a leader, to let his own life be a public example, in word and deed, of Christian love, faith, and purity. The reference to letting "no one despise your youth" (4:12) reflects a common problem of leadership in the early church. The leaders of house churches, that is, bishops, were sometimes

---

In Georgia Congressman John Lewis's memoir of his experiences in the civil rights movement, *Walking with the Wind,* he remembers his time in Mississippi in the early 1960s as an organizer with the Student Nonviolent Coordinating Committee. He describes his work with the local people as a kind of ministry, a ministry not unlike the kind the Pastor urges in Timothy. Lewis writes:

> There was a great deal of faith involved in this. We were venturing out on our own, becoming missionaries in a sense. But not missionaries in a traditional sense because we were meeting the people on *their* terms, not ours. If they were out in the fields picking cotton, we would go out in that field and pick with them. If they were planting squash, we planted, too. Whatever the people were doing, we were there with them, *really* there. We lived with them in their homes, held hands and prayed with them, shared their food, shared their beds, shared their worries and their hopes. We listened to them. Before we got around to sharing what we had to say, we *listened.* And in the process, we built up both their trust in us and their confidence in themselves. Essentially we were out to spread faith and courage, and naturally we had to find those things in ourselves first.

John Lewis, *Walking with the Wind: A Memoir of the Movement,* with Michael D'Orso (New York: Simon and Schuster, 1998), 187.

younger than some of the other members of the community, which put their authority in question in a society where the young were always expected to defer to their elders. In one of Ignatius of Antioch's letters (probably dating from just shortly after 1 Timothy), he urges a congregation not to become disrespectful or overly familiar with their bishop because of his "youthful appearance," but instead to submit to him and, by doing so, to submit to "Jesus Christ, the bishop of us all."[21]

The encouragement to Timothy to set a good example and not to let his youth trump his leadership frames the discussion that follows in chapter 5, which raises matters of practical ministry with older folks—older men, older women, widows, and others in leadership role (the "elders"),[22] but it also prompts a more general question about leadership in the church. Those who are called to positions of authority can almost always find some reason for self-disqualification: "I'm too young." "I'm too old." "I don't know enough." "I can't pray in public." "Others have more experience." There are always reasons to duck the responsibility, but the Pastor reminds Timothy, and all in such positions, that when the Spirit calls us forth to lead, to hide behind youth or any other excuse is to "neglect the gift that is in you" (4:14).

4. Focus on the central realities of the church's life: worship and formation (4:13–16). Over against the false teachers, with their fancy word games with Scripture, their esoteric diets, and their enticing escape-from-the-flesh acrobatics, the Pastor urges "Timothy" to focus on the basics: reading Scripture, preaching ("exhorting"), and teaching. No need to put on a tutu, wave sparklers, and dance around the altar to keep people's attention. Instead, strengthen the community by giving them a diet of solid food: read the Bible publicly, preach the Word faithfully, and teach the people soundly.

As the Pastor closes this section of the letter, he beautifully evokes the ceremony of ordination (4:14). We know from other references that the earliest church designated its leaders, set them apart for service, by praying over them and laying hands on them (e.g., Acts 6:6;

21. Ignatius of Antioch, *Letter to the Magnesians*, 3.1.
22. Bassler, *1 Timothy, 2 Timothy, Titus*, 86.

> When public radio host Krista Tippett asked the legendary church historian
> Jaroslav Pelikan how it could be possible for a fixed and historic Christian
> creed to be reconciled with a faith that is honest, intellectually rigorous, open
> to new truth, and not locked into rigid certainty, Pelikan responded that this is
> precisely the point of the great creeds:
>
>> My faith life, like that of everyone else, fluctuates. There are ups and
>> downs and hot spots and cold spots and boredom and ennui and all the
>> rest can be there. And so I'm not asked on a Sunday morning, "As of 9:20,
>> what do you believe?" And then you sit down with a three-by-five index
>> card saying, "Now let's see. What do I believe today?" No, that's not what
>> they're asking me. They're asking me, "Are you a member of a community
>> which now, for a millennium and a half, has said, we believe in one God?"
>
> Pelikan and Tippett, "The Need for Creeds."

13:2–3). The laying on of hands was a sign both that the Spirit had
chosen this person for this ministry and that the church recognized
this calling of the Spirit and blessed and authorized the one called.
The Pastor reminds Timothy, and all others in his role, that his leadership in the community comes not because he successfully managed some power grab, but instead because the Spirit summoned
him. The church recognized this when they gathered for worship,
named out loud what they discerned the Spirit to be saying (proph-
ecy), and the elders gathered around him and laid hands on him.

The laying on of hands hearkens back, of course, to the
anointing and blessing of baptism. It serves as a reminder of the
blessing and call of God on every life. Pastoral theologian Paul
Pruyser once observed that, when a therapist and a patient are
meeting for a "therapeutic hour," there is almost always a moment
of awkwardness at the end. Neither patient nor therapist know
exactly what to say, so they mumble out something like, "Well,
we've done some good work today. I'll see you next Thursday."
But, says Pruyser, what both are hungering for is a moment of
blessing, a hand placed tenderly on a head in benediction.[23]

---

23. Paul Pruyser, "The Master's Hand: Psychological Notes on Pastoral Blessing," in William B.
Oglesby Jr., ed., *The New Shape of Pastoral Theology* (Nashville: Abingdon, 1969), 364.

1 Timothy 5:1–6:2a

In much of chapter 4, the Pastor instructs "Timothy," that is to say the leadership at Ephesus, in how to be a worthy minister, "a good servant of Christ Jesus" (4:6). As we have seen, the Pastor uses a physical exercise analogy. Getting ready to do good ministry is like working out in the gym in order to be a fine athlete A leader must train in godliness and discipline oneself to be a good example of the gospel. So, if chapter 4 is a manual of exercises to be done by church leaders in "God's gym," then, in this next section of the letter, it's "game time." The moment has come to go out onto the field of contest.

The Pastor provides specific advice on doing ministry with six groups in the church—older men, younger men, older women, younger women, widows, and slaves—but in terms of space and energy, there is a special emphasis on widows. Why isn't the list longer? Why no instructions for dealing with orphans or children or unbelievers? Why the underscoring of the situation with the widows and not with the other groups? Probably because the Pastor is aiming a laser beam at the current hot spots in the life of the church. What we have here is not a general, comprehensive manual on ministry to all of the types of people found in a congregation but specific instructions on ministry to the current problem areas in the congregation's life. Just as today we might find an article on "ministry to the twenty-somethings," not because the sixty-, seventy-, and eighty-somethings aren't important, but because the twenty-somethings constitute an urgent challenge at this point in the church's life.

It is important to keep this narrower window in mind as we make our way through this section of the letter. This letter is indeed the church's Scripture, but it is not a universal description of the church's ministry. We are looking through a window in time and catching a moment in the life of the church at Ephesus. The church is troubled and the leaders are now being charged to enter the fray, to get in there and to do good, corrective ministry—ministry, as it turns out, with specific groups in the community. These are not the only people worthy of ministry, and these forms of ministry are not the only actions of ministry needed by these people. It is as if we had walked into an eighth-grade classroom just as a student is struggling with an algebra problem. The teacher has to intervene with *this* student and about *this* problem. It's a valuable pedagogical moment to observe, but it is not the totality of good teaching.

In sum, moving through this section of 1 Timothy is not like reading a polished essay on good leadership in the Christian community. It's more like reading the minutes of the officers' meeting after a particular difficult conversation.

5:1–2

The Tone of Pastoral Guidance

Even though prescriptions are given for ministry to several separate constituencies in the congregation, we are really dealing with only one, complex problem. It is, of course, the problem we have encountered all through this letter, the false teachers and their negative impact on the whole body of the church. Because the teaching has gone sour, the leadership has become infected by a misuse of power, the mission of the congregation has gone awry, and the communication patterns in the church have become deceptive. Almost every adult in the congregation is affected, even implicated, in some way, and so men and women, older and younger, need to be corrected. But how?

If they had simply employed the social protocols of the ancient world, the leaders of the church would have deferred to the older folk, especially the men, and would have had the right to pull rank on the younger folk, especially the women. But the Pastor articulates a different standard of leadership: treat everyone, young and old, male and female, as family. If the older men[1] need to be disciplined, don't upbraid them harshly like a Roman officer would speak to a wayward soldier; speak to them instead as one would speak to one's father. Likewise, if any of the older women need pastoral guidance, speak to them as if they were your mother, to younger men as brothers and to younger women as sisters. When it comes to younger women, the Pastor adds the phrase "with absolute purity," which almost surely signifies sexual purity. Whether this implies that the church was experiencing actual sexual misconduct involving some younger women or whether sexuality is simply in the air because of the false teachers' polemic against marriage is not clear. Later in this chapter (5:14) and contra the false teachers, the Pastor is going to urge the leaders at Ephesus to encourage young widows to, in effect, become sexually active ("marry, bear children"), and it is of crucial importance that this encouragement remain within the bounds of marriage and propriety.

This use of familial language underscores the Pastor's image of the church as the household of God (see comments on chap. 3, especially 3:14–16 on pp. 97–104). But even though the Pastor's advice is to speak to everyone in familial ways, this does not mean merely warm and fuzzy affirmation. The context is still one of pastoral correction. Things have gone astray, and it is the responsibility of the leadership to guide the sheep back into the fold, albeit with gentleness and affection. The leaders are to speak to the men and women of the church with love and respect, just as they would speak to a member of their family, but also with strength and a desire to set things right.

This stands over against the often timid, excuse me, pastoral leadership sometimes found among more psychologically oriented pastors today. In his memoir *Open Secrets*, Richard Lischer, quoting Stanley Hauerwas, bemoans the fact that ministers have too often become nothing more than a "quivering mass of availability."[2] One

---

1. The term "elder men" (NRSV alternative reading) is ambiguous. It could simply mean men in the church who are older, or it could mean "elders," that is to say those who hold the office of "elder," a group mentioned in 4:14. The rhythm of the passage—older men, older women, younger men, younger women—points to the former.
2. Richard Lischer, *Open Secrets: A Memoir of Faith and Discovery* (New York: Doubleday, 2001), 67.

Episcopal priest, on reading this, responded, "That seems about right. We like to do the easy bits, but we priests don't always want to do the hard things, and we sometimes don't want to challenge people. As I've said before, we need to do this work. The church is about salvation, not just self-improvement."[3]

The church is . . . always a body that has built into its very structure a twofold measure of its honesty and fidelity, a twofold means of self-questioning and self-criticism, Bible and public ministry. The Church is never left to reimagine itself or reshape itself according to its own priorities of the moment; for it to be itself, it has received those gifts that express and determine its essential self as a place where the eternal self-giving of Christ is happening in such a way as to heal and change lives. . . . Ministry is one of the things that renders every local community in its witness and worship responsible to the creative source of the Church's life.

Rowan Williams, "The Christian Priest Today," in Douglas Bales et al., eds., *Glory Descending: Michael Ramsey and His Writings* (Grand Rapids: Eerdmans, 2005), 165–66.

5:3–16
The Problem of "Widows"

This section is a longish, twisted wrestling with what was one of the major issues in the congregation at Ephesus: the question of the care of widows (see comments on 1:3–11). The basic principle is expressed in the first two words of the passage: "Honor widows. . . ." The church has a basic responsibility to honor widows in its midst, and here "honor" does not merely mean "make a fuss over" or "show respect to," like a church might do on Mother's Day, but something much more costly and concrete: namely, take care of widows socially and financially.

The word "honor" here is used in the same way that it is employed in the commandment "Honor your father and mother . . ."(Exod. 20:12; Deut. 5:16), where it means to care for one's parents financially, materially, and otherwise in their old age. The Christian church learned, also from its Jewish roots, to extend this commandment

---

3. Scott A. Gunn, "What Is a Priest?," *Seven Whole Days* (blog), May 29, 2008, http://www.sevenwholedays.org/2008/05/29/what-is-a-priest/.

about honoring parents to include an ethical responsibility toward widows and orphans (see Deut. 24:19; Jer. 7:6). And caring for widows was a characteristic part of the church's missional life from the very beginning (see Acts 6:1–6).

But by the time 1 Timothy was written, though, we are now many decades into the church's history, and the broad injunction "honor widows" no longer covers all the wrinkles and complications that have developed. At this point in the church's life, there are widows and there are "widows," that is to say women wealthy enough to care for themselves financially or young enough to be marriageable, and a single strategy for ministry to them no longer suffices. A congregation where my family and I worship experienced something of the same complication regarding ministry to the homeless. It is a downtown church in a large city, a church with a strong commitment to social justice. At first, the zeal to "care for the homeless" was guidance enough. But gradually the monolithic category "homeless" began to be nuanced and refined. Some of the "homeless" were people who slept on the sidewalk outside of the church, often people who were chronically mentally ill. Others of the homeless came in off the street and joined in worship with the congregation, sometimes becoming vital members of the congregation. Others were temporarily homeless, women pushed out of their homes by abusive husbands or men who had been financially self-sufficient but found themselves suddenly unemployed and with no financial reserves. Still others of the homeless were wandering beggars, making their way from church to church and agency to agency seeking handouts, often telling the same fabricated stories of need. "Caring for the homeless" was no less urgent in all of these situations, but it could no longer be a unified approach. There were the homeless, and there were the "homeless," and ministry took different forms in different situations.

5:4–8 *Naming the "Real" Widows*

As the Pastor of 1 Timothy talks about the need to "honor widows," we are listening in on one side of the conversation, and it is difficult to tell with certainty exactly what the social and theological circumstances were on the other side of the exchange. But an educated guess goes like this: In the earliest church, there were among the believers some widows. Since, for the most part, women of the first century did not have employment for pay, widowhood often meant financial distress, and the ethical call was clear: care for these widows financially. Those who had financial means among the believers shared with those who were in need, and needy widows were provided with food and money.

Over time, however, this ministry to widows changed. First, it became more organized. Already in the Book of Acts we can see that the ministry to widows was time-consuming and administratively challenging (see Acts 6:1–6). By the time of 1 Timothy, many congregations kept a formal "widows roll," listing the names of the widows who were to be given financial support, and some of the believers were given supervisory responsibility over this ministry.

Second, the category "widow" became at once more defined and more variegated. On the one hand, "widow" gradually developed to be more than just a circumstance of life but a valuable role in the church. Most widows were women of a relatively mature age whose husbands had died. The fact that they had no money was not viewed as a moral flaw but, in a sense, as a spiritual virtue. These widows were visibly and utterly dependent on God, and they were, therefore, living symbols of what is finally theologically true about all human beings. Their very condition taught them, in the context of Christian community, to give thanks for mercy and to be students of prayer and humility. As they learned these lessons, they became equipped to serve as role models for other Christians, especially for younger women. These widows received financial support from the church, and in return they were expected to live their lives as examples of the faith. They were, in some ways, like "mothers of the church" in some African American church traditions today, wise women who serve as mentors for others. Their sufferings and their losses in life had taught them hard lessons about the need to trust in God, and they were teachers of those lessons to others.

On the other hand, the category "widow" became more diverse. Not all women who were widows fit into this mature female mentor role. Some women had lost their husbands, true, and they were, therefore, technically "widows," but they had children of financial means. In the ancient world, children did not go to college and then move to San Francisco, Des Moines, or Rome, leaving their parents behind. Extended households mostly stayed together, and these widows were, thus, not financially desperate because their children were around to support them. Still other widows were quite young, having lost their husbands at a youthful age. Not only were they too youthful to serve as spiritual examples of mature discipleship, they were also young enough to be marriageable again, and, in the best case scenarios, this meant that they would only temporarily be on the widows list. In still other cases, there is some evidence that the term "widow" was occasionally applied to women who weren't widows at all. They were, in our vernacular, "single" women who were, for whatever reason, outside of their parent's household and care but not yet married. In such cases, this could mean poverty, so sometimes the church enrolled them on the widows list simply as a matter of practical pastoral care.

The term "widow," then, described a lot of different women in many different circumstances. So what happens to the injunction "care for the widows" when the term "widow" now covers so much diverse territory? That is precisely what the Pastor seeks to sort out in this section. The first move the Pastor makes is to carve out a sub-category: "real widows" as opposed to those who are not. When the pastor says, "Honor widows who are really widows" (5:3), he means that the church should financially support some of the widows but not all of them. But who are these "real widows"? As the passage develops, it becomes clearer that the Pastor has in mind the widows who have three characteristics: they are mature in age, devoted to the Christian life, and truly financially needy.

The category "real widows," then, does not include widows with children or grandchildren around who can support them. The sentences in the passage dealing with this exception (5:4–8) get a bit convoluted and are interrupted by digressions, but essentially the Pastor observes that the younger generation should take care of their families, including their widowed mothers or grandmothers. To do so is "pleasing in God's sight," and any children or grandchildren who are tempted to shirk their financial responsibility by saying, "Why don't we keep our money and just let the church take care of grandmother" need to be reminded that caring for one's parents and grandparents is more than a social obligation; it is a profound religious duty, one that goes all the way back to the Ten Commandments.

In his own ministry, Jesus confronted some religious folk who mouthed pious affirmation of the commandment to "honor your father and your mother" but who had figured out clever ways to avoid actually forking over the cash to support their parents (Mark 7:9–13). In other words, they recited the commandment, but they didn't actually keep it, and Jesus said that such people were "making void the word of God" (Mark 7:13). The Pastor agrees. So important are the bonds of social responsibility in the family that not to honor one's parents and grandparents in tangible and financial ways is, says the Pastor, in effect to deny the faith (5:8).

Also excluded from the category "real widows" is any widow who "lives for pleasure" (5:6) instead of living a life of devotion. The word *spatalōsa* is rendered as "lives for pleasure" in the NRSV but is perhaps better translated by the RSV as "self-indulgent." This makes it clear that the Pastor is not talking about widows who live joyfully and with a zest for life but rather widows who live self-centered lives. Commentator Luke Timothy Johnson prefers the RSV here because it conveys that the passage has in mind both moral and financial concerns. The Pastor is talking about widows who "can afford a life of luxury and idleness"[4] and who, in fact, selfishly choose that life. Such widows look for all the world as if they are living the carefree good life, but they are really dead in terms of the life promised in the gospel. These widows are, therefore, doubly to be excluded from the church's roll of widows. Their bank accounts are flush, so they don't need the church's support. Their moral lives are bankrupt, so they don't deserve the support.

Having pared away the widows who, in the Pastor's view, do not merit inclusion on the widow's roll, we can now see in clear relief what a "real widow" is: she is "left alone" and "has set her hope on God" (5:5). In other words, she is by herself, with no family or treasure to depend on, and she trusts in God alone to preserve her

4. Luke Timothy Johnson, *The First and Second Letters to Timothy*, The Anchor Bible, vol. 35a (New York: Doubleday, 2001), 262.

life. Her life, then, is one of constancy in prayer, crying out to God "night and day" (5:5; see Ps. 88; 1 Thess. 3:10). The supplications and prayers of these women are more than simply a sign of their piety. This is their vocation, their ministry on behalf of the whole community. By praying night and day, they undergird the worship life of the congregation (see 2:1), and through living example they teach the nature of the faith to those who are just learning it.

> **A true follower of the lamb. Having even in the days of her youth dedicated herself to the service of her maker, she grew in grace and in the knowledge of Jesus, proving by her daily walk and conversation that hers was indeed a "life hid with Christ in God."**
>
> A plaque on the wall of a country church, dedicated to the memory of a widow in the congregation.

5:9–10 Getting Even More Specific about "Real Widows"

As an experienced minister, the Pastor anticipates what the next question from the leadership of the church will be. Having beautifully portrayed the "real widows" as mature women of deep devotion and prayer, the Pastor knows that someone around the table will raise a hand and say, "Well fine, fine, that's a lovely description of a real widow, but we need a clear policy here. Whom do we put on the widows roll and whom do we not?"

So the Pastor gets even more specific. "OK, first of all, no widow under sixty years of age goes on the roll." In our day, of course, a sixty-year-old widow could be still quite vibrant and active, playing tennis in the morning, taking dance lessons in the afternoon, and having dinner in the evening with someone met on the seniors dating Web site. But in the ancient world, sixty was a ripe age indeed, and a sixty-year-old widow was almost surely no longer a candidate for remarriage. Setting the bar at sixty also had a practical value, of course. It trimmed the widows roll considerably and limited the church's financial responsibility. But the Pastor is not just being practical about the budget. He has a deeper goal in setting the cut-off at sixty. He thinks of "real widowhood" as a revered role, a kind of office, in the church, a position of honor and responsibility like the office of deacon (see the discussion of 3:8–13), and a sixty-year-old widow has a reasonable chance at being steady and constant in this role. She was not going to be a widow this week only to cast this position aside the next week because she's a newlywed and off on a honeymoon cruise to the Greek Isles.

To the criterion of age, the Pastor adds a second requirement: she must "have been married only once" (5:9). With this, it is even clearer that the Pastor has in mind widowhood as a church office, since this is exactly the same requirement set forth for bishops and deacons (3:2, 12). Again, it is technically ambiguous what the phrase "married only once" might mean (no bigamy? no lover on the side? married and not single? married once and never again? [see the discussion of 3:2 on pp. 86–92]). But here, as was the case for bishop and deacon, it likely means married only once and not remarried after the death of the spouse. Again, as we saw in the discussion of the marital status of bishops and deacons, the document known as the *Shepherd of Hermas* probably names the principle at work here: "There is no sin in marrying again . . . but if they remain unmarried, they gain greater honor and glory with the Lord."[5]

There is one more practical requirement a widow must have to earn a place on the widows roll: she must have a proven track record of good works in the community. Interestingly, raising children is listed as the first of those good works (5:10). Anyone who has raised children can certainly understand how it would be viewed as a "work," even as a "good work." But the Pastor puts it first among a series of good works, probably because raising children is inevitably an embodied act, the very thing so distasteful to the false teachers. There is no way for a woman to raise a child without nourishing the child at her breasts, changing diapers, scrubbing dirt off the child's face, making sure the child is clothed, wiping tears away when the child is hurt. It a deep commitment to the fleshly needs of another, and it is in these embodied actions that the grace of God is both found and expressed. This is why the Pastor said earlier that women are "saved through childbearing" (2:15). The Pastor knows full well that both men and women are saved by God, "who saved us and

5. *The Shepherd of Hermas*, mandate 4, in Alexander Roberts et al., eds., *The Ante-Nicene Fathers*, vol. 2 (Buffalo, NY: Christian Literature Publishing Co., 1885), 22.

called us with a holy calling, not according to our works but according to his own purpose and grace" (2 Tim. 1:9). But it is here in the raising of children, in the fleshly entanglements with the needs of another that the incarnational reality of the gospel comes alive. These widows, who have raised their children, are living counter-testimony to the false teachers' claims that true spirituality is to be found in virginity and in escape from the world of flesh and necessity. No, true spirituality is in rolling up one's sleeves as a mother and doing what is necessary to see that your child grows up strong and full of faith and hope.

To child-raising, the Pastor adds two more specific items to the list of good works. First, these "real widows" are full of hospitality. Hospitality was a social virtue widely honored in the ancient Mideast, but in the Christian context it was also a theological value. To welcome guests, even strangers and outsiders, was not only to make a gracious space for others, it was also to welcome the presence of God. "Do not neglect to show hospitality to strangers," says Hebrews, "for by doing that some have entertained angels without knowing it" (Heb. 13:2).

Not only are they hospitable, these widows also "washed the saints' feet [and] helped the afflicted" (1 Tim. 5:10). Washing someone's feet was a sign of humility, a willingness to be in service to another. The Pastor may be literal here—widows could well have washed the feet of the believers as they gathered for worship—but this is more likely a symbol for an attitude of humble service seen in many ways, including ministering to the afflicted, distressed, and needy. In sum, "real widows" are known in the community for "doing good in every way" (5:10).

5:11–15 Younger Widows

All that is true about the mature "real widows" stands in contrast to the situation of "younger widows." Since the Pastor thinks of the role of the widow in much the same way that he thinks of bishop or deacon, as a holy office, a ministry, in the church, widows become qualified to hold this office by virtue of age, wisdom, piety, and good works. They are no longer a part of a natural household, so the church agrees to be their household and to provide financial support. In return, they vow—perhaps a literal vow made in worship but probably a symbolic vow signified by their willing commitment to the household of faith—to be in constant prayer and to serve as a living example of hospitality and service.

Younger widows are not qualified to serve in this way and, therefore, the Pastor says, should not be put on the widows roll (5:11). Why? Because, says the Pastor, they are young and want to get married and have sex, and this alienates them from Christ. Here is one of those places where the Pastor, were he to have known that his letter would end up in the Bible and were he to have known how his words would sound to readers today, would probably have asked for the privilege of a rewrite, because his words come across as something quite different than what he really means. It sounds as if he is saying, "Real Christian women aren't interested in sex, real Christian women aren't concerned about marriage, and all this passion for sex and marriage alienates them from Christ." Actually nothing could be further from his actual intent. In fact, just a few lines later (5:14), he is going to urge these young women to get married and to have children, which of course means having sex.

So what's the concern here? For the Pastor, a real widow, since her days of marriage and parenting are behind her now, is free to move to a new and different kind of commitment. Her "household" is Christ's church, her "husband" is Christ, and her "children" are the brothers and sisters in the church. Younger women, being young, are quite understandably still open to the possibility of human husbands and biological children. This is fine and good and natural, but it is not automatically compatible with the role and service of a "widow" in the church. The Pastor does not want a younger widow making an ill-considered vow to live out the lifelong role of a widow in the church only to find that vow at war with her quite natural desire to be married again and to raise a family. In other words, younger widows should not be put in the position of promising Christ one good thing—to serve the church in the office of "widow"—only to find that their hearts and desires lead them to want another good thing— a husband and a family. It is in this way, and only this way, that these younger women would be alienated from Christ and be under "condemnation for having violated their first pledge" (5:12).

The Pastor does not scold these younger widows for desiring marriage and sex. To the contrary, he encourages them to seek these things: "marry, have children, and manage [your] household" (5:14). This advice has both theological and practical value. Theologically, marriage, sex, children, and living out a life together as a family are all good gifts of the creator God—despite what the false teachers may say—and human beings are called to receive these gifts with gratitude. On the practical side, a young widow who remarries is no longer financially unstable, and the church can focus its resources on those widows who have no other means for support.

The Pastor has another reason why these young widows should not be put on the widows roll; the damage their behavior does in the church. Here again, the Pastor might wish for a chance to rewrite, because he sounds misogynistic. These younger widows, he says, are not spiritually qualified to be "real widows" because "they learn to be idle, gadding about from house to house; and they are not merely idle, but also gossips and busybodies, saying what they should not say" (5:13). More dramatically, he claims that some of these women have "turned away to follow Satan" (5:15), which does not mean that they have joined a satanic cult but that these women are behaving in ways that aid the enemy of Christ instead of the cause of Christ. From a contemporary perspective, the Pastor here seems to be churning out a mishmash of male biases. "Gadding about?" "Gossips and busybodies?" "Followers of Satan?" What are these but stereotypes of female character and behavior?

To be sure, we would hope that a pastor today, describing women in the congregation, would find other descriptors than "gossips, busybodies, and agents of Satan." And, if the Pastor is expressing a negative essentialism in his description, namely that all women, by nature, are weak in character ("well, you know how women are, all their gadding about and gossiping"), then the informed contemporary reader will simply have to part company with the Pastor here. We should preach against this passage, not from it. But if we can look through this language and see this text in its own context, it is possible to discern the outline not merely of male prejudice but also of a genuine and practical problem in the church.

We must first imagine the social situation of these younger widows in ancient Mideastern culture. Many of them were no doubt teenagers. As females, they would likely not be afforded the opportunity for formal education. Their "school," where they learned how to be mature adults, was in the relationships of home and family—first in the home of their parents and then in their own households. It was here that most women grew up, experienced accountability, and learned responsibility and wisdom. But these young women were widowed, and widowed too early. A young widow in our society would likely seek out a network of friendships and a career, but this was not a strong option for a woman in the ancient world. So here they are, just getting started in terms of emotional and social development, and they are set adrift socially and financially with little chance of education, income, or community support. Such circumstances, whether they occur in the ancient Mideast or in the inner city, in suburbs, or small towns today, to males or to females, can be a recipe for disaster.

So what were these women going to do? What should the church do in response to their plight? The Pastor sees two basic alternatives. One, the church could wink and pretend that these young women were more mature than they actually were, mature enough to take on the role of widow, of "mothers of the church," of spiritual guides and examples to the faithful. If the church closed its eyes to the fact that these young widows were not yet ready for such a role and proceeded to put them on the widows list, then that would at least take care of their financial distress.

This is probably what the church at Ephesus decided to do, and the Pastor is trying to point out what a costly and unfortunate decision this was. Not only were these young women put in the untenable position of being asked to make a vow of perpetual widowhood that they would almost surely want to break, these young women were also in over their heads and were failing at the responsibility of being spiritual mentors.

These young widows, therefore, were between a rock and a hard place. If they dropped the guise of "real widowhood" and decided to remarry, the society around the church (not to mention "the adversary," that is, Satan [see 5:14]) could point fingers and cry, "Hypocrites! You make vows to your so-called Lord but then break them because of fleshly passions." If, on the other hand, they stuck it out and remained as widows, trying to emulate the mature ministry of the "real widows," they would miss the pleasures of marriage and family and would be imprisoned in a role they were not seasoned enough to pull off.

"Real widows" would go from house to house in the church, bringing a lifetime of Christian discipleship with them in the form of prayer, hospitality, and good works. But when the younger widows went from house to house, they often had little spiritual wisdom to bring. Instead, they brought what they had, which was sometimes news from the last house they'd visited. That is to say, they brought the gossip, and this flawed form of communication no doubt exacerbated the divisions and loss of communion in the church. We may wish that the Pastor had not called them "busybodies," but he is almost certainly pointing to a real problem, a broken practice in the life of the church at Ephesus. Even today, an unwise pastor or church worker—male or female—who lacks discretion in communication about pastoral concerns can hurt many people and divide a congregation.

Given the options available in that culture, the Pastor, therefore, recommends alternative number 2: that these young widows not be thrust into a role they could not play but should instead remarry and find their true vocation in their households and with their spouses and children. This path probably meant that the church found temporary ways to support these young women, but nothing so permanent as rostering them on the widows roll.

5:16 An Exceptional Case

The section closes with an unusual situation. What if, among the faithful, there are some women who have independent financial means (an exceptional, but not unheard of, circumstance), and these women happen to be kin to other women in the church who are "real widows?" The Pastor says that these financially resourceful women should voluntarily take care of their relatives. This would allow these "real widows" to function in the role, but it would enable the church to take them off the assistance list and to allocate its meager resources to those truly in need.

All of this fussing over who is a "real widow" and what to do with "younger widows" may seem remote from the concerns of today's Christian communities. But we see here church leadership wrestling with how best to use limited resources to care for those in need. We see a Pastor trying to find ways to enable Christian believers to discover their true vocations in Christ and to employ their gifts in ways and relationships that build faith and give life. On the surface, these ripples in the life of the church may not be beautiful. They look for all the world like arm-wrestling over policy and bureaucracy, and sometimes it may seem as though the false teachers had it right all along; the church is too institutional and too leaden to be the home of the Spirit. Why not break loose from the encumbrances of the church and head out into the wide open spaces of free-range spirituality?

But the Pastor knows a truth that is still ours to discover: that the Christian faith is a wager that it is here, right here, in this too, too solid flesh of Christians trying to live together in house and church and marriage, washing each other's feet, trying to be good stewards of resources that seem too small to be stretched over all the needs, showing hospitality when one is bone weary, minding carefully how one speaks about brothers and sisters in the congregation, and caring for the afflicted when one is already drained, that it is here that the Spirit is to be found, and it is here where the incarnate Christ has chosen to dwell.

5:17–25

Miscellaneous Practical Matters

In this section, it is almost as if the Pastor says, "Now that we have addressed the thorny problem of what to do about widows in the congregation, let's scratch off some other items on your leadership problem list." What follows is practical advice about a cluster of concerns.

5:17–18 *Stipends for Elders*

As we saw in chapter 3, the congregation at Ephesus is arranged as a constellation of house churches, and each of these house churches is led by an elder (a "presbyter," in Greek, a *presbuteros*). These elders are not only the leaders of the house church units, they are also usually the main leaders of worship and teachers of the Christian faith, and, like the "real widows," they receive a stipend in return for their service.

One of the problems at Ephesus is that the false teachers, some of them anyway, have discovered that their alternative view of the Christian faith is marketable. These teachers have a following, some of the followers have money, and the false teachers have figured a way to pry some of this money loose in terms of fatter stipends for their popular teaching. The Pastor will address this problem directly in 6:2b–10, but here he does a preventative strike by defending the practice of paying elders. He is perhaps anticipating that his criticism of the greed of the false teachers will be countered by the charge, "Well, the teachers you think are good are being paid too. What's the difference?"

The difference, according to the Pastor, is that these elders, who teach the truth and exercise the kind of ministry already described in 4:6–16, "rule well" (5:17). Because they rule well, they are justified in receiving what the Pastor calls "double honor." This may mean receiving twice as much money as widows receive (according to 5:3, widows are to be honored and here good elders are to be doubly honored), or that they are to be honored in two senses of the word: esteem and financial compensation.

To support the argument that good elders are worthy of being paid for their work, the Pastor (like the historical Paul before him [see 1 Cor. 9:9]) quotes Deuteronomy 25:4: "You shall not muzzle an ox while it is treading out grain." This idea, that an ox doing the labor of harvesting grain needs to eat some of that grain to keep on laboring, is applied metaphorically to elders doing the labor of preaching, teaching, and guiding. To this is added a word that Jesus said when he sent missionaries out to do ministry: the missionaries, said Jesus, should eat and drink what people offer them on the road, because "the laborer deserves to be paid" (Luke 10:7).

The practical point here is that it is perfectly acceptable to pay an elder. The theological point is that this pay is justified not because ministry is for sale, but instead it is needed to honor good ministry and to keep the labor of good ministry going. Later in the letter, these reasons will serve as a stark contrast to the financial motivations of the false teachers.

5:19–22 Public Charges against Elders

If we needed further evidence of trouble at Ephesus, we could certainly find it in this somewhat convoluted passage about elders being accused of sinning. We have to piece together what lies behind this section of the letter, but it is apparently some kind of tangled mess involving rumors about some of the elders, the leaders of the house churches. Some of the elders, as we have seen in the previous passage, are "good elders," and others of them, as we have seen throughout the letter, are "false teachers." There may even be some who vacillate between these two camps. Rumors and gossip swirl around the congregation (often spread, says the Pastor, by the younger widows as they move from house to house [5:13]). Some of the false teachers probably have mounted a whisper campaign against the other elders. There is finger-pointing in every direction, and charges and countercharges are flying.

So the Pastor is here attempting to calm the churning sea of recrimination. He does so with four measures:

1. He invokes the standard specified in the Torah for charges against another. In Deuteronomy 19:15, a lone accuser does not have the right to make allegations. It takes two or three witnesses against someone before charges are seriously considered. Thus, the Pastor instructs the leadership not even to consider a charge against an elder unless two or three witnesses are willing to step forward (5:19), which weeds out a lot of spite and personal vendetta.

2. He instructs that, if the charges made by these witnesses turn out to be true, then the elder involved should be publically corrected ("rebuked"). It is not specified here who does the rebuking. In later church development, the term "bishop" describes a supervisory office; a bishop guides a group of elders. But at this point, the rebuking would probably be the responsibility of the wayward elder's peers, or perhaps an elder with seniority (see Titus 1:9).[6] The emphasis in this text, though, falls not on who does the rebuking but on where and how the rebuking is done—in public, out in the sunshine, where everybody can see it and where the discipline can serve as a deterrent to sin among the others (5:20).

3. The Pastor, in his most solemn and liturgical voice ("In the presence of God and of Christ Jesus and of the elect angels . . ."), warns those in charge of these proceedings to be impartial and evenhanded (5:21). He phrases this in oath-like language because of its urgency. Nothing would undermine the trustworthiness of a disciplinary process more than bias on the part of those administering it.

4. Finally, the Pastor instructs the leadership to be more careful in selecting elders in the first place. The leaders should not rush to ordain but instead allow enough time to get to know a person's character before thrusting them into a position of leadership. Those in charge of the selection process should remain above the fray, not getting entangled in the intramural squabbles, deceptions, and misdeeds ("the sins of others") and keep themselves "pure" (5:22).

We are not told in this passage exactly what the "sins" of the elders might be. These unspecified sins are almost surely connected to the false teachings being promulgated by some of the elders, since that is the pervading concern of the whole letter. But beyond this, the fact that this passage occurs in the context of a discussion about young widows and monetary stipends, and that it includes a warning to "stay pure," may well indicate that we are dealing here with the age-old problems of sexual misconduct and financial impropriety.[7]

The underlying theme here is to restore confidence in the life of

6. Jouette M. Bassler, *1 Timothy, 2 Timothy, Titus* (Nashville: Abingdon Press, 1996), 101.
7. Johnson, *The First and Second Letters to Timothy*, 281.

the community and in the integrity of its leadership. This is to be done by dragging the whole nasty business of charges and counter-charges, accusations and abuse of power out of the shadows and into the light of public witness and accountability. This is more than a matter of good management. Restoring health in the church and among its leaders happens in the presence of God, Christ, and the angels (5:21). This apocalyptic framing of the matter means that truthfulness and reliability in the life of the Christian community is one of those manifestations of godliness that has value and promise both now and in the life to come (4:8). Or to put it another way, when the faithful can trust their leaders to exercise power with love, care, and mercy, it is a foretaste of the kingdom of God.

5:23 "Medical" Advice

At first blush, this is a very puzzling verse. Right in the middle of a discussion about leadership, ordination of elders, and sin, the Pastor gives "Timothy" a little medical advice, namely to get off the water-only regimen and to drink a little wine for stomach problems and other ailments. This sudden piece of folk medicine is odd enough in its own right, but it is especially bewildering as a seeming non sequitur, a stick thrown at random into a flowing river.

The mystery clears a bit when we look more closely at the structure of the verse. If the Pastor had been concerned in a literal sense only about "Timothy's" stomach distress, he would probably have simply said, "When your stomach is bothering you, my son, take a cup of wine." But instead he makes a point of saying first, "No longer drink only water." In other words, he wants "Timothy" to *stop* doing something (drinking only water) and to *start* doing something else (drinking a little wine). In the ancient world, a water-only regimen was not simply a diet choice; it was an element in an ascetic lifestyle, the very way of living advocated by the false teachers.

A contemporary of the Pastor, the Stoic philosopher Epictetus, advises his followers occasionally to drink only water and to abstain from food and even from desire. The goal was to take a break from the usual flood of food and drink and to discipline one's desires and appetites so that one would "desire well."[8] Seemingly harmless advice there from Epictetus, maybe even beneficial—except for the fact that at Ephesus the false teachers also urged their followers toward abstinence as a means to escape the pollutions of the fleshly life and to elevate their spirituality to a higher level (see 4:3). The Pastor is not impressed, and he calls it like he sees it. He does not view this renunciation of food and drink as spiritual enlightenment; he sees it as self-righteous ingratitude to the God who gives us daily the gifts of a good creation (see 4:3–5). For the Pastor, the godly life is in the world, not in retreat from it.

So when, midstream in a discussion about good and bad leadership, the Pastor dispenses medical advice, urging "Timothy" to knock off the water-only routine and to take a little wine, it is more than likely clever code for, "Spare me, please, leaders in the church who consider themselves religious virtuosi and who delude themselves and others into thinking that they can achieve spiritual elitism through silly diets and fleshly renunciation. Give me instead leaders who wisely and in moderation embrace food and wine and their own bodies and the bodies of their spouses and all the other delights of this good creation with joy and thanksgiving and prayer as the gracious gifts of God. It will make your stomach feel better, and the body of Christ will be healthier as well."

So, for the pastor, taking a little wine is not just a home medical remedy; it's almost an ordination standard. Obviously, given the seriousness of alcoholism, drinking wine is not to be taken as a requirement for Christian living. It stands here as a symbol for something larger: the full affirmation of the goodness of God's creation.

5:24–25 Sins and Virtues Cannot Be Hidden Forever

Here the Pastor puts the finishing touches on his discussion of sin among the church leaders. Sometimes a person's sins, the Pastor says, "are conspicuous" and out there for everyone to see, but sometimes sins are hidden. We look at the sweet-faced woman working in the church office, the one with a cheerful word for all who pass by,

---

8. Epictetus, *Discourses*, 3.13.21, http://classics.mit.edu/Epictetus/discourses.3.three.html.

and never imagine that she's embezzled a fortune from the church's bank account. She may go to her grave undiscovered, but the Pastor warns that her sins will follow her to the grave, and the all-searching light of the judgment will disclose the truth.

Likewise with good works. Some people are publicly celebrated for their virtues and good deeds, but not everyone. There is the woman who taught the third-grade church school class almost all of her adult life, doing things every week like with one hand showing the children a picture of Jesus healing the leper while, with the other hand, putting Neosporin and a Band-Aid on a little boy's skinned knee and drying his tears with her handkerchief. She received no medals of honor; there is no brass plaque on the wall of the church to remember her deeds. But be assured, says the Pastor, even when good works are not conspicuous and publicly recognized, on judgment day "they cannot remain hidden."

The Pastor, of course, is most concerned here with the sins and virtues of the leaders, the good elders and the bad ones, the faithful teachers and the false teachers. Commentator Benjamin Fiore puts well the Pastor's theological conviction that those who work evil in the community of faith cannot hide forever:

> The secrecy of false teachers who sneak into homes will be exposed, as will their victims. . . . The widows who are enjoying an overindulgent life are as good as dead (1 Tim. 5:6), despite appearances to the contrary, and the rich who are immersed in greed are on their way to ruin (1 Tim. 6:9), whether they or others know it or not.[9]

Thinking theologically about what the Pastor says here about sin, virtue, and judgment, we may be troubled by an apparent omission of a theology of grace. The Pastor seems to think that some people do good and some people do evil, and, regardless of whether these deeds are public or concealed in this life, in the final judgment all will be revealed. There will be an accounting, a tallying up, and the good will be rewarded and sinners unraveled. Left out there by itself, the Pastor's view seems to be a theology of salvation by works.

9. Benjamin Fiore, SJ, *The Pastoral Epistles: First Timothy, Second Timothy, Titus*, Sacra Pagina Series, ed. Daniel J. Harrington (Collegeville, MN: Liturgical Press, 2009), 12:113.

Two considerations, however, push against boxing up the Pastor's position this way. First, when the Pastor writes on the theological topic of salvation itself, it is clear that his is no works righteousness view. His comments are scattered throughout the letters, but nowhere is he more transparent than in Titus 3:4–8:

> But when the goodness and loving kindness of God our Savior appeared, he saved us, not because of any works of righteousness that we had done, but according to his mercy, through the water of rebirth and renewal by the Holy Spirit. This Spirit he poured out on us richly through Jesus Christ our Savior, so that, having been justified by his grace, we might become heirs according to the hope of eternal life.

Second, the function of his remarks about sin and goodness in 1 Tim. 6 is not to carve out a systematic theology of salvation and judgment but to restore trustworthy teaching, faithful leadership, and wholesome relationships in the congregation at Ephesus. The warning that deeds evil and good will be disclosed in the judgment is there to encourage moral self-assessment on the part of all of the leaders at Ephesus to the end that wayward elders might come to their true selves and be restored to sound and humble leadership. The moral question on the table for these elder-teachers is not whether they get *caught*, but whether the believers get properly *taught*.

So we should not picture the judgment as a nightmare scenario where sinners who have "gotten away with it" on earth will stand before the judgment seat of God and have the Book of Deeds opened to their homepage, revealing a nasty, damning, and shaming list of secret sins. Rather, the judgment is the full revelation of the life of God, a bright light in which all can see clearly what truly matters, what really counts, what surely endures. To anticipate the judgment in our lives here and now is to shine the light of God's life over our little lives and to ask ourselves, "When I get to the end of all things, will I want to say, 'Gee, I wish I'd spent more time at the Xerox machine, or gossiping on the phone about my neighbor, or undermining the ministry of Rev. Smith, or trying to squeeze another ten grand out of the real estate deal?" Or will I be glad to be able to say instead, "I decided to give myself to doing justice, loving mercy, and walking in humility with God?'" The judgment of God is not about punishment; it is about God's love setting all relationships right, restoring all things. As Paul Ricoeur said, "Without doubt there is still a long way to go in order to understand or guess that the Wrath of God is only the sadness of love."[10]

6:1–2a

Slaves in the Household of God

It is almost impossible for contemporary readers, especially in North America, to encounter these verses, with their injunction for slaves to "regard their masters as worthy of all honor," and not to interpret them in the light of the history of slavery in the Americas. If the Pastor's injunction is lifted out of his context and placed in nineteenth-century America, and the Pastor is, thus, heard to be commanding slaves under the lash in an Alabama cotton field to "honor your masters," then the text becomes toxic, thoroughly offensive, and worthy only of being discarded.

Is there any other ethical and responsible way to read these verses? Some commentators have attempted to rescue these New Testament slave texts for at least a more sympathetic reading by comparing slavery in ancient Roman society favorably with the terrible conditions of chattel slavery in America. As biblical scholar John Byron noted, "From the early 1970s until the early 1990s, New Testament scholars tended to portray slavery in the Greco-Roman world as a benign form of mass employment for the under classes as well as an effective means of integrating foreigners."[11] Scholars of this period pointed out that slavery was usually a temporary status, that most slaves could expect to be freed by age thirty, and that some people actually sold themselves into slavery as a means of acquiring societal security and as a stepping stool toward higher social status. The implication was that, all things considered, first-century slavery was not as monstrous as we might imagine.

10. Paul Ricoeur, *The Symbolism of Evil* (New York: Harper and Row, 1967), 67.
11. John Byron, "Paul and the Background of Slavery: The *Status Quaestionis* in New Testament Scholarship," *Currents in Biblical Research* 3/1 (2004): 116.

In more recent scholarship, however, the pendulum has swung in the other direction. A growing consensus of biblical scholars now considers slavery in Greco-Roman society to have been not benign at all but a harsh, dehumanizing, and often viciously cruel reality.[12] This change in perspective is the result both of improved data and a shifting interpretive stance regarding the social context of biblical texts. Still other scholars have sought to find a sort of compromise position, namely that slavery, in whatever era, is by definition a system of domination, a treating of human beings as less than human. Within this demeaning system, however, the actual living conditions of particular slaves differed dramatically, and it mattered very much for a slave whose slave he was. Byron says that biblical scholar "[John] Barclay seems to have found the middle ground when he concludes that: 'during the first century . . . slaves could expect a combination of protection, provision, abuse and exploitation.'"[13]

But regardless of any distinctions we may make between slavery in one time and place and slavery in another, slavery is still slavery. Ethically, it is unacceptable to attempt to make this passage more palatable by somehow putting a pretty face on Greco-Roman slavery. Even under the mildest of conditions, slavery was a matter of the powerful stealing the agency and freedom of the weak, or, to put it theologically, a terrible social and personal sin. It is perfectly understandable that those who bear today much of the burden of slavery's legacy have little patience with this text, or any of the similar slavery biblical texts. New Testament scholar Mitzi J. Smith, writing in *True to Our Native Land: An African American New Testament Commentary*, says,

> African Americans have historically considered as offensive and unconscionable Pauline and deuteropauline texts mandating slaves to be content and servile in their legal status. African Americans have reinterpreted, trumped, and rejected such oppressive texts and the oppressive hermeneutical maneuvers that have relied on such texts.[14]

12. Ibid., 119–21.
13. Ibid., 134. Byron quotes John M. G. Barclay, "'Paul, Philemon and the Dilemma of Christian Slave-Ownership," *New Testament Studies*, 37/2 (April, 1991), 167.
14. Mitzi J. Smith, "Slavery in the Early Church," in *True to Our Native Land: An African American New Testament Commentary*, Brian K. Blount, ed. (Minneapolis: Fortress, 2007), 19.

So, mindful of "oppressive hermeneutical maneuvers" and eager not to approach this passage with willful blindness, we can still discover in what the Pastor says a word more complex and nuanced than a mere reinforcement of the tyranny of slavery. We will, as always, need to be mindful of the Pastor's context, and two aspects of this context deserve to be named:

1. Social Imagination. Today, morally alert readers of 1 Timothy cannot imagine a world in which slavery of any kind would be viewed as anything but a detestable social evil, one that should be abolished as quickly and thoroughly as possible. Christian readers in particular know that the gospel played a crucial historical role in inspiring abolition movements, and it is clear to us that when the gospel is set down in the reality of slavery, it works untiringly to eliminate it.

But the Pastor did not live in our world. He lived instead in a world where certain social realities, slavery being one, were like the weather—givens and not subject to change through political efforts. One expert in ancient slave societies, the Jamaican-born sociologist Orlando Patterson, says this about Paul the apostle (and it applies to the Pastor as well):

> The truth of the matter is that Paul neither defended nor condemned the system of slavery, for the simple reason that in the first-century Roman imperial world in which he lived the abolition of slavery was intellectually inconceivable, and socially, politically and economically impossible.[15]

Patterson goes on to argue that our modern idea that the gospel calls us to political action toward dramatic and large-scale changes in society is a very recent development, taking root in our imagination only in the last part of the eighteenth century in Western Europe and America. Up to that point, Patterson says, Christians believed that they had a wide choice in how they related to others in their personal lives, including how they viewed and treated slaves, "but

---

15. Orlando Patterson, "Paul, Slavery and Freedom: Personal and Socio-Historical Reflections," *Semeia,* 83–84 (1998): 266.

virtually no room for moral or conceptual doubt about the institution of slavery or slave society where it existed."[16]

This shift in social understanding should not be underestimated. Even though we are aware that times change—for example, from the industrial age, to the information age, to the digital age—we still tend naively to assume that people in all ages see the world essentially the same and, thus, have the same choices before them. But such is not the case.

Philosopher James K. A. Smith points out a shift in the social imagination that has occurred between the medieval world and our world today. Most Christians in the twenty-first century, Smith observes, are well aware that we live in a world where atheism is not simply an option but is an attractive and persuasive worldview for many people. Advocates of atheism such as Richard Dawkins and the late Christopher Hitchens have written wildly popular books ridiculing religion, and on television, in magazines, and in online blogs many people freely, even proudly, proclaim themselves to be atheists. But in the medieval world, says Smith, "atheism is pretty much unthinkable,"[17] and when Smith says "unthinkable," he means it. It is not that medieval people were simply more religious than we are and, therefore, considered atheism to be an unacceptable choice. It was, rather, that for people in the medieval world there was no such choice to be made; a creation charged with the presence of God was the water in the fish tank. It was simply assumed, and unlike all of us today, medieval people couldn't conceive of a world without God. It wasn't that people were reluctant to be atheists; it was that they literally couldn't imagine being so. "No one," Smith says, "has yet dreamed of Nietzsche or Christopher Hitchens."[18]

From our vantage point, then, not only can we imagine a world without the oppressive social structures of patriarchy and slavery, we also cannot fathom any other acceptable moral view than opposing those structures. We are understandably troubled when Paul, the

16. Ibid., 267.
17. James K. A. Smith, *How (Not) to be Secular: Reading Charles Taylor* (Grand Rapids: Eerdmans, 2014), 27. Smith's book is a commentary on Charles Taylor's magisterial *A Secular Age* (Cambridge: Harvard University Press, 2007). Taylor makes the same point about the unthinkability of atheism before the rise of modernity.
18. Ibid.

Pastor, and other New Testament writers miss or, in our view, *avoid* opportunities to advocate for major changes in those structures, especially when we can see the seeds of those very changes scattered here and there in the very Scriptures they composed. They frustrate us when they step over the macro issues and settle instead for the micro changes, adjustments within the systems rather than revolutionary overthrowing of the systems themselves.

But if Patterson is correct, it wasn't that the Pastor missed or stubbornly avoided a chance to advocate for the abolition of slavery; it was, rather, that it was impossible for him to imagine it. He wasn't for slavery and he wasn't against it, in the same way he wasn't for or against a world with an emperor in it or for or against male-female marriage. These issues were not yet even on the table. Given his historical moment, this was the way the world was, period. What other world could there be? In the kingdom of God, Christ was Lord, and Christ was Lord even now in the lives and hearts of believers, but this had to be lived out in a world where there was a Caesar and would be a Caesar until that Great Day. The Pastor could no more envision a society this side of heaven in which there was no slavery than those of us raised in the 1950s and 1960s could imagine the digital world we now inhabit.

Some commentators, nevertheless, operate as if the Pastor had before him two main choices, liberal and conservative. He could have been a liberal and gone after the oppressive macro structures of his society, in particular patriarchy and slavery, but sadly and consistently he contented himself with the narrower conservative option, suggesting only micro calibrations within the prevailing systems.[19] There may be a measure of truth here regarding patriarchy, since changes in the status of women in Roman society were happening around him, altering the social imaginary, but even there, to think that the Pastor could conceive of what later followers of Christ have embraced with joy, a world of fully liberated and empowered women, stretches the possibilities to the breaking point.

This leaves us, it seems, with an ironic text. The Pastor cannot

---

19. For example, the statement in Jouette Bassler's otherwise marvelous commentary: "The author of the Pastoral Letters consistently chooses a conservative social route." *1 Timothy, 2 Timothy, Titus,* 107.

imagine a world without slavery in it. But he *can* imagine a world in which what can be seen about people in the light of Jesus Christ matters far more than how they might be defined in the frail and corrupt structures of this present age. He *can* imagine a world in which every person and thing created by God is declared "good" (1 Tim. 4:4), a world in which God wishes to give to all "the life that is really life" (1 Tim. 6:19), a world in which Christ is the only judge and is the one ready to give to all who yearn faithfully for God's reign the "crown of righteousness" (2 Tim. 4:8). The irony in these letters, then, is that the Pastor's theological imagination bears witness to a world much larger than his limited social imagination, a world in which, by the grace of Jesus Christ, the Pastor's own time-bound counsel—slaves honor your masters—will thankfully pass away.

2. *The Household within the Household.* So the focus of the Pastor's concern in this text is not with the institution of slavery per se, but instead with the question of how Christians in the congregation at Ephesus who are a part of that institution should live together.

As we have discussed, the congregation at Ephesus was a cluster of house churches, and these house churches often met for worship and study in the atrium or in a large room inside of a Roman house. There was, in other words, the household of God meeting in the context of a domestic Greco-Roman household—a household within a household.

Sometimes the rules that prevailed for good behavior in the Roman house were applied, with only slight modification, to the household of the church. We find evidence for this in the so-called household codes, which occasionally appear in the letters of the New Testament. Churches today who have "covered-dish suppers" might well frown on anyone who broke in line because they wanted to eat first or who piled their plates high with all the best pieces of the fried chicken, mindless of the needs of others. Such rules of conduct, however, aren't distinctively Christian, of course, but are instead the rules of etiquette that may be followed by the church but which are borrowed from society generally. Just so, the earliest Christians sometimes advocated in the house of God codes of behavior that made sense to them but that also prevailed in the Roman household.

But at other points, there was a tension between life in the church house and life in the Roman house, and the slave-master relationship was one of those points. In the Roman house, the master was the dominant figure and the slave was to be utterly subservient. In the church house, masters and slaves were brothers and sisters in Christ. They prayed together, shared the Lord's Supper together, labored together on behalf of the gospel, and held in common their faith and hope.

To use an example far less drastic than slavery, we can still catch a glimpse of the tensions here by imagining a Marine recruit in basic training at Parris Island who, on Sunday, worships at the base chapel beside his drill instructor. During the week, the drill instructor snarls and snaps and curses at the recruit, demanding complete obeisance. On Sunday, they pass the bread and wine to each other and grasp each other's hands saying, "The peace of the Lord Jesus Christ be with you." There is an obvious disconnection here. What is the true relationship between drill master and recruit, and how should they negotiate their interaction when there is conflict between the ethics expected in the "two houses"?

The Pastor, then, is addressing this tension between the two houses: the Roman house where certain standards are in force governing masters and slaves, and the household of God, where other standards obtain. He does not simply pluck this issue out of thin air. The fact that he includes it on the list of miscellaneous topics to address indicates that this has become a problem at Ephesus. In Colossians 3:22–4:1, the historical Paul addressed both slaves and masters regarding their relationship, but the Pastor addresses only the slaves, which probably means that he considers them, in this place and at this moment, to be the source of the current distress in community life.

The problem, as the Pastor sees it, appears to be that slaves who are members of the church desire that they be treated the same way in the workplace, that is, in the Roman house, as they are treated in the church house. They are brothers and sisters around the Lord's table, and they want to be brothers and sisters at the master's table.

We don't know the forms of expression this desire took in the workplace—perhaps insubordination, maybe special pleading, perhaps simply a desire to be treated with respect and dignity, or maybe a refusal to serve as a slave at all. We don't know. It is important to note, though, that these slaves in the church at Ephesus and the Pastor, even though they are in different places about what should be done, are basically on the same page theologically. Both parties agree that the gospel breaks down the distinctions between slaves and masters and makes of them brothers and sisters in Christ. Neither party imagines that slavery itself will be abolished. The question is what kind of interpersonal relationships will prevail between master and slave—will they be like brothers and sisters, as they are in God's house, or will they still relate as master and slave, as is the norm in the Roman house?

The slaves' answer to the question, clearly, is that the equality of God's house be translated somehow into the workplace. The Pastor thinks that this is impossible, that it will result only in conflict and unrest that would be viewed negatively in society and could bring scorn to God and to the faith. The Pastor believes that these slaves should indeed view themselves as belonging to Jesus Christ, which should lead them to be even more diligent in their service to others, especially if their master is a beloved brother in Christ.

The irony is that the slaves, whatever their behavior, were operating out of a more truthful vision of themselves, especially when we think about the issue as more than just a practical problem at Ephesus. The gospel had revealed who they really were, not someone's property but children of the heavenly king. The double irony is that the theology affirmation that all people, regardless of social status, belong to Jesus Christ as his brothers and sisters, which both the slaves and the Pastor held, would end up transforming society in ways neither the slaves at Ephesus nor the Pastor could have ever imagined. It would be many centuries before this vision found political expression in Christian abolitionist movements, but the time-bomb that would bring down slavery was already triggered in these house church gatherings of believers.

1 Timothy 6:2b–21

Here the Pastor concludes the letter with an appeal to the leadership to be steady in teaching and guiding the church and content with their own lives. Almost everything about this final section of the letter signals that the Pastor is winding things up. The closing music is playing, the credits are rolling. Only once does the Pastor get distracted from the task of closing up shop, of summarizing and concluding the already stated themes of the letter. A remark about wealth seems to remind him of a question he overlooked earlier: What about members of the congregation who are already wealthy? How should they live, given the fact that they are currently rich? So there is a brief, "oh yeah, one more thing" passage in which that issue is addressed (6:17–19).

6:2b–10
Godliness and Contentment

The Pastor refers to the whole of the previous letter and to all of the counsel he has provided when he says succinctly, "Teach and urge these duties" (6:2b). But, of course, it isn't that simple. First Timothy is not a set of instructions in a cardboard box for assembling a barbecue grill. It is a complex word of encouragement aimed at generating able pastoral leadership in a troubled Christian community, and the Pastor knows that the sort of stabilizing leadership needed here is not merely a matter of following orders and executing policies. It involves leadership that grows out of a quality of life and faith.

It's not just about doing things in logical steps—1, 2, 3—it's about being a certain kind of person whose leadership endures and can be trusted.

The nineteenth-century Quaker minister William Hicks created a series of well-known paintings, based on Isaiah 11:6–9 ("The wolf shall live with the lamb, the leopard shall lie down with the kid . . ."). He called them "The Peaceable Kingdom," and they depicted beautiful scenes of wild animals, normally tooth-and-claw enemies, resting peacefully together. In some of the paintings, Hicks included a vignette of Quaker founder William Penn creating a peace treaty with the Indians. The theme of these paintings is the dream of God's great *shalom*, the reign of peace when "the earth will be full of the knowledge of the Lord as waters cover the sea" (Isa. 11:9). Hicks, like many other Quakers, saw the religious life as one of participating as fully as possible, here and now, in that *shalom*.

In like manner, the Pastor conceives of good pastoral leadership in the church as growing not out of clever technique or entrepreneurial savvy but instead out of a truly peaceful life, a life of godliness floating on the calm sea of contentment (6:6).

"There are two ways of getting rich . . . ," William Sloane Coffin, pastor of New York City's Riverside Church, liked to say. "One is to have lots of money, the other is to have few needs. Try the latter. . . ."[1] In a sermon, Coffin told a tale from the Jewish writer Sholem Aleichem. The story was about a Job-like man who experienced almost every possible misfortune. He lost his wife, his children were inattentive to him, his house burned down, his job was taken away from him, and on and on. But no matter what befell him, this man received life with gratitude and good cheer, never repaying evil for evil. Finally the old man died and went to heaven's gate. His goodness was of such renown, even the angels and the Lord gathered to greet his arrival. Coffin continues,

> And when he arrived and stood with downcast eyes, the prosecuting angel arose and for the first time in the memory of heaven said, "There are no charges." Then the angel for the defense arose and after he had rehearsed all the hardships

---

1. William Sloane Coffin, *Letters to a Young Doubter* (Louisville, KY: Westminster John Knox Press, 2005), 146.

and recounted how in all these circumstances the old man always remained cheerful, always returning good for evil, the Lord said, "Not since Job have we heard of a life such as this one." Turning to the man, he said, "Ask, and it shall be given unto you."

The old man raised his eyes from the ground and said, "If I could start every day with a hot buttered roll . . ." And at that the Lord and all the angels wept.[2]

"We don't need all things to enjoy life," Coffin concludes, "because we have been given life to enjoy all things." The Pastor agrees. "We brought nothing into the world, so that we can take nothing out of it; but if we have food and clothing, we will be content with these" (6:7). On the other hand, those who are discontented with what they have in life, if they should fall into the role of minister or lay leader, will inevitably try to make a profit off of religion, to imagine that "godliness is a means of [financial] gain" (6:5).

And that, of course, brings us back to the nasty problem that has vexed the Pastor all the way through this letter, the false teachers who have traded the "sound words of our Lord Jesus Christ and teaching that leads to godliness" for a vacuous, ascetic spirituality, which they have parlayed into fattened stipends for their teaching. These people "want to be rich"—no surprise there, wanting to be rich is an ancient symptom of the disease of discontentment—and their lust for wealth causes them to step right into a snare. They "are trapped by many senseless and harmful desires" (6:9). In case we missed the point, the Pastor has a few more adjectives to pile on: such people are conceited, ignorant, and itching for a fight over silly and inconsequential matters. And a major symptom of their illness is discontentment and a love for money, which is "the root of all kinds of evil" (6:10). Their teaching poisons the well, creating a church that is anything but "the peaceable kingdom," but is, instead, full of envy, suspicion, malicious gossip, and vicious infighting (6:4–5).

It was once said of a certain ruthless and violent king that he had a terrible disease, but unfortunately it was a disease fatal only to others. Not so with the false teachers. Yes, they have created their victims,

---

2. William Sloane Coffin, *The Collected Sermons of William Sloane Coffin*, vol.1, *The Riverside Years: 1977–1982* (Louisville, KY: Westminster John Knox Press, 2008), 196–97.

fragile and unsuspecting Christians who have been cheated out of good teaching and, therefore, deprived of the fullness of life promised in the gospel. But in a rare moment when the Pastor turns the eye of compassion toward the false teachers, he recognizes that the saddest victims of the mess at Ephesus are perhaps the false teachers themselves. They have listened to the siren song of wealth and wandered away from the truth. In a yearning for possessions, they have, therefore, lost their most precious possession, their own faith, and they have stabbed themselves ("pierced themselves," 6:10) over and over again. The false teachers are wounded people, and their wounds are all self-inflicted.

The warning here is not simply about greedy ministers but about all forms of ministry that grow out of discontent. Good ministry nourishes the people and meets their needs; discontented ministry uses the people to meet the needs of the ministers—whether those needs be about money or recognition or psychological compensation. Discontented ministry sells "godliness" for some kind of personal profit; good ministry encourages godliness as an end, not a means, and sees godliness as profitable in its own right.

6:11–16

Remember Your Ordination and Be Emboldened

In 2 Timothy, the young "Timothy" is encouraged to recapture the fire for ministry that was there at his ordination, to "rekindle the gift of God that is within you through the laying on of hands" (2 Tim. 2:6). In this passage, too, the experience of ordination is evoked to put a spring in "Timothy's" step and some iron in his spine as he does ministry in Ephesus.

Although we are not certain exactly what a service of ordination would have been like in the late first century, it is possible to see in this text certain key elements that have been essential in ordinations ever since. First, "Timothy" is addressed as "man of God" (3:11), and in this context this is almost surely a reference to the sense of transformation that comes over anyone who has experienced ordination. By baptism, all Christians are "ordained," called to a holy vocation. But to be ordained, as "Timothy" was, to the specific role of pastor, to be set apart for this form of leadership, means that one has become a focal point—or perhaps a lightning rod—for the identity of the whole church and the church's role of somehow embodying God in the world.

The irony of ordination is that one kneels for the laying on of hands, and the person who kneels is a person who bears all the bruises and flaws of everyone else, the same shortness of temper, the same tendency toward cynicism, the same proneness to lose heart. And then, when the laying on of hands happens and the prayer is prayed, that person stands—still the same, but unmistakably different, too. There are still the same bent places in one's personality and moral life, one's tennis backhand is still lousy, but there is an awareness that one has taken on a burden and a new identity. From now on, this person has the responsibility to body forth God into the world, to "fight the good fight of the faith" (6:12) with virtues that will be hard to learn and impossible to master—as the Pastor says to "Timothy," with "righteousness, godliness, faith, love, endurance, and gentleness" (6:11) People will look at this man or woman differently, will think of him or her – in ways both empowering and discomforting—as a "woman of God," a "man of God."

Peter Gomes, who was for many years the pastor of the Memorial Church at Harvard, described his own ordination this way:

> My local church . . . was determined to ordain me, and when I offered what I thought was conscientious resistance to the notion, my old pastor roared at me: "How dare you resist God's call and the call of God's people? Who do you think you are?" It was reassuring to later hear him say that I was called to the ministry not because I was good but because God was gracious."[3]

The Pastor tells "Timothy" that, as a man of God, he should "take hold of the eternal life to which you were called and for which you were made" (6:12), which is often taken to mean that faithfulness in ministry leads to the reward of eternal life at the end of all things. But

---

3. Peter Gomes, foreword to Lilian Daniel and Martin B. Copenhaver, *This Odd and Wonderful Calling: The Public and Private Lives of Two Ministers* (Grand Rapids: Eerdmans, 2009), xi–xii.

in this context, the Pastor seems to be speaking not of the afterlife but of something that a minister does in the midst of fighting the good fight, that is, in the middle of performing one's ministry. Perhaps we can glimpse something of what the Pastor means in Episcopal priest Barbara Brown Taylor's description of ministry as a participation in Christ's ministry, a partnership with the eternal:

> The first thing to say is that a priest is a representative person—a *parson*—who walks the shifting boundary between heaven and earth, representing God to humankind, representing humankind to God, and serving each other in the other's name. It is not possible to exercise such priesthood without participating in Christ's own, which means there are no entrepreneurs in ministry, only partners.[4]

The partnership with Christ theme is strengthened by the Pastor's reference to "the good confession" which "Timothy" made "in the presence of many witnesses." In an ordination ceremony, before the laying on of hands, those who are to be ordained confess their faith and take vows of obedience. The Pastor points out that Jesus himself made his own confession "in his testimony before Pontius Pilate . . ." (6:13). This linking of "Timothy's" confession at his ordination with Jesus' confession is additional confirmation of the idea of the ministry of church leaders as a participation in Jesus' own ministry. Martin B. Copenhaver, a United Church of Christ minister, wrote about his ordination and the experience of Jesus' presence during the laying on of hands:

> Before I closed my eyes for the prayer, I took a glance around me to see who was standing immediately behind me. But once my eyes were closed, in most instances I couldn't tell whose hands I was feeling on my head or my body. I thought, ". . . The hand that is shaking: whose is that? And that hand on my head that feels particularly heavy, is that my father's? Or on second thought, is that Jesus' hand? After all, his presence has been invoked several times in the service already. About time he showed up."[5]

4. Barbara Brown Taylor, *The Preaching Life* (Plymouth, UK: Cowley, 1993), 32.
5. Copenhaver, *This Odd and Wonderful Calling*, 138.

People who are being ordained make their confession, says the Pastor, "in the presence of many witnesses" in the church, but Jesus made his "before Pontius Pilate" (6:13). This prompts the question: When leaders confess their faith and make vows at the time of their ordination, before whom is this done? The obvious answer is that ministers and other leaders make their vows before the church, but the connection to the story of Jesus before Pilate suggests another face among those many witnesses. Old Pontius Pilate shows up for the ordination too, just as he was there at Jesus' ordination. The church asks its ordination questions, but Pilate asks the new ministers and leaders his old question as well—what is truth? The church tests new ministers for doctrinal soundness, but Pilate, the local representative of the powers that be, flings at them his old threat—do you not know that I have the power to crucify you? It is only in the strength of "God, who gives life to all things" and Jesus, who faced down Pilate and made this "good confession" (6:13), that new ministers and leaders have the courage to take up this ministry and "to keep the commandment without spot or blame until the manifestation of our Lord Jesus Christ" (6:14).

The Pastor concludes this passage with a lyrical description of Jesus Christ, "who alone has immortality and dwells in unapproachable light" (6:16). It would not be farfetched to think that the Pastor is here quoting from the climax of the ordination liturgy—perhaps a hymn or a prayer—and, quotation or not, the effect is to create a soaring crescendo, a rousing reminder to "Timothy" of the day he was ordained, an invigorating reinforcement of his identity as a "man of God."

In his autobiography, *With Head and Heart*, the preacher and theologian Howard Thurman describes how the memory of his own ordination had the power to do just what the Pastor hopes for in this passage, to revive his commitment to ministry in times of struggle and doubt. When he was a young church worker, he decided that he wanted to be ordained as a minister, but he told his mentor in ministry that he had no interest in, in fact a distaste for, the laying on of hands as a part of the ritual. "This custom was altogether too old-fashioned, I argued, with all the arrogance of youth." But his mentor balked, saying "There will be the laying on of hands or there will be no ordination." And so there was. Thurman writes,

> The ceremony of ordination was held at eight o'clock in the evening, and the moment of transcendent glory was for me the laying on of hands, which I had so strongly resisted. During the performance of this ancient and beautiful ritual "the heavens opened and the spirit descended like a dove." Ever since, when it seems that I am deserted by the Voice that called me forth, I know that if I can find my way back to that moment, the clouds will lift and the path before me will be once again clear and beckoning.[6]

6:17–19

As for the Rich

Many commentators find the closing sections of 1 Timothy to be choppy and somewhat disorganized. For some, the choppy part is the passage just discussed (6:11–16). The "man of God ... fight the good fight" encouragement to "Timothy" (6:11–16) seems to interrupt the flow of a long discussion about wealth. The Pastor was saying that "the love of money is a root of all kinds of evil" (6:10), and now, six verses later, he appears to pick up that conversation again: "As for those who in the present age are rich ..." (6:17).

However, as we saw in the commentary on 1 Timothy 6:2b–10, this is actually a passage primarily about the false teachers, and the material about money appears almost by the way. The Pastor was criticizing the false teachers for several faults, including "imagining that godliness is a means of gain," that is, masquerading as teachers of righteousness only to make money. But then the Pastor realizes that his statement about godliness and gain could be misunderstood, so he clarifies that, "of course, there is great gain in godliness" (6:6), but the gain is not a fortune but a contented life. That leads him to do a riff on the false teachers again, who aren't contented but who have a yearning for money that leads them to do mischief in

---

6. Howard Thurman, *With Head and Heart: The Autobiography of Howard Thurman* (New York: Harcourt Brace, 1979), 57–58.

their leadership. In short, the Pastor's focus isn't on money; it's on the false teachers, who happen to have a weakness for money, and one thing leads to another in the discussion.

Now, in the passage at hand, the Pastor takes quite another angle. He's not talking about the false teachers here, and he's not talking about discontented people who frantically run around trying to satisfy their greed for money. He is talking, rather, about people who are already rich in the things of this world, by whatever means. If there is a choppy interruption in this chapter, it may be this passage. The Pastor had taken "Timothy" to the mountaintop in 6:11–16, recalling his ordination and urging him to "take hold of eternal life." The letter seemed to be soaring to grand close, and now it seems that the Pastor, riding off into the sunset, turns back to say, "Oh yeah, one thing I forgot. As for those who are rich . . ."

Then again, there may be more logic in this structure than is evident at first glance. If the Pastor is ending the letter by exhorting "Timothy," the leaders at Ephesus, and all who read this epistle to "take hold of eternal life," it would naturally occur to him to speak a word to those who might say, "I have no need to take hold of eternal life since I have a nice foothold in this life." A defining theme of Christian faith is hope, hope for the appearing of Christ's kingdom, bringing healing to the nations, hope for the disinherited, consolation to the brokenhearted, and justice to the disposed. It is simply a fact that when Christians become wealthy, we lose our edge on hope. In fact, we begin to "hope not"—"I hope we don't have another recession, I hope the market doesn't go down."

So a special word needs to be spoken to "those who in the present age are rich," and the Pastor has three words of counsel:

1. *Do not be haughty.* When the house churches at Ephesus met for worship and teaching, rich and poor were gathered into the same room. It would be tempting for the rich to use their wealth to intimidate the poor by the way they carry themselves, treat those who are poor, and dress (the Pastor has already had a word to say about "gold, pearls, [and] expensive clothes" to worship in 2:9). The Pastor instructs the rich that this kind of class leverage undermines the Christian life and the fellowship of believers.

2. *Do not rest your hope on transitory wealth, but on God.* The

Pastor has already reminded the readers that you can't take it with you (6:7), and here he goes even further: money is uncertain and temporary, and it forms marshy land on which to build one's hope. When people are interviewed on television after a tornado has swept through their community, they often say, quite understandably and tragically, "We've lost everything we have." The Pastor is saying that, if we rest our complete hope on the wealth of this age, we will all be in the position eventually of saying, "I've lost everything I have."

Instead of resting hope on the portfolio, the Pastor urges the rich to rest their hope on God, "who richly provides us with everything for our enjoyment." We call stocks and bonds "securities," but, of course, they give no lasting security. The Pastor is attempting to change the frame on wealth. Instead of looking to riches as a means to provide security for the present and hope for the future—which leads naturally to a life spent jealously hoarding and guarding—look at the things of this world as free gifts from the abundance of God. Seen that way, they relax our grip on them. We can receive them as means for joy, and we can open our hands in generosity toward others, which is the next word of the Pastor.

3. *Be rich in good works and be ready to share with others.* Wealth here becomes an opportunity to be about the work of the kingdom, showing the kind of compassion and generosity that not only marks a disciple of Christ but produces the joy and contentment human beings deeply seek.

All through this section, the Pastor has employed a wordplay on variations of the word "rich"—they are rich, God gives richly, allowing them to become truly rich, "rich in good works" (6:18).[7]

To follow the Pastor's counsel enables the rich to build up an account that really matters, "a good foundation for the future," or what Jesus called "treasure in heaven" (see Matt. 6:20). And then the Pastor adds a beautiful phrase: "so that they may take hold of the life that is really life" (6:19). By using this phrase, the Pastor slices away one popular misunderstanding of this discussion on riches. The Pastor is not talking merely about wealthy people doing good

7. Johnson, *The First and Second Letters to Timothy*, 309.

with their money and becoming charitable. It is quite possible, of course, for wealthy people to set up foundations, endow programs for social improvement, and make lavish contributions to charity but to leave their real lives and fortunes and ways of life untouched in the process. The Pastor is not speaking of rich people simply giving assistance; he is talking about the rich being converted to a new way of seeing and living, of the freeing, joyful, life-giving experience of seeing their wealth as not their own but as a river of God's grace to all humanity that just happens to flow through their yard. Then, and only then, can they "take hold of eternal life," which is "the life that is really life."

6:20–21

Farewell

The letter ends tersely, especially for a one that presents itself as a personal letter. What the Pastor says, though, aptly summarizes everything that has been said in the whole epistle. "Timothy" and all the good leaders at Ephesus are told to "guard what has been entrusted" to them—their faith, the teaching of the church, their hope—and to avoid everything that the false teachers stand for, which is no more than "profane chatter . . . falsely called knowledge."

Come to think of it, that about sums it up. The final word echoes the greeting at the beginning of the letter, and now it has become a benediction: "Grace be with you."

2 TIMOTHY

2 Timothy 1:1–18

In his first letter to Timothy, the Pastor addressed a laundry list of issues and problems in the church at Ephesus—the proper manner of worship, qualifications of leaders, how to manage the widows roll, dealing with accusations against elders, and so on—all connected in one way or another to the main crisis: the false teachers and their departure from the gospel.

This second letter to Timothy, however, has a quite different tone and feel. This letter is much more personal, marked more by affirmation than by detailed instruction and problem solving. The first letter was about troubleshooting a broken church; this second letter is about celebrating and strengthening a warm relationship between an older and younger pastor that is like father and son. The Pastor, speaking in the voice of Paul, talks about his life and about his death, and, with gratitude and encouragement, he passes the mantle of his ministry on to his prize student, "Timothy."

Some commentators see this letter as a kind of farewell discourse, a literary form that portrays someone facing death speaking his or her last words, the finality of the moment thus underscoring the urgency and importance of what is said (the elders at Ephesus had already received one such farewell address from Paul [see Acts 20:17–38]). Others see 2 Timothy more as a kind of last will and testament[1] in which an inheritance is transferred from one generation to the next. In the farewell discourse, the emphasis falls on the one who is dying, that is, on *who* is passing on. In the last will and

---

1. See, e.g., Benjamin Fiore, *The Pastoral Epistles,* Sacra Pagina Series, ed. Daniel J. Harrington, (Collegeville, MN: Liturgical Press, 2009), 12:8.

testament, the emphasis falls on the inheritance, that is, on *what* is being passed on.

There are elements of both forms in 2 Timothy, and the two purposes finally converge. On the side of the "farewell discourse," "Paul" is portrayed in this letter as nearing the end of his life. He has fought the good fight, run the race well, and the finish line is now in sight. This is no time for idle chatter. In the first letter, "Paul" interrupted the flow of a discussion about leadership to give "Timothy" a health tip, urging him to take a little wine for his stomach (1 Tim. 6:23). But not in this letter. There is no small talk here. The rhetoric is more dramatic. Paul speaks in serious, sometimes solemn, tones. There is theme music in the background. Paul's life is being poured out like wine from a cup even as he speaks, and he has matters that need to be addressed before he departs this life.

But, on the side of the last will and testament, what "Paul" has to say is less about himself as a personality and more about himself as the bearer of a faith and ministry now being passed on to "Timothy." It is here that the farewell speech and the reading of the will and testament overlap. "Timothy" is being given a ministry; it's the substance of the ministry that is being passed on to him. But "Paul's" own body is the vessel in which that ministry has been stored and persevered. It is the ministry itself that is being transferred to "Timothy," but that ministry is now inseparable from its most vivid form of expression, the life of "Paul" himself.

In Jean Anouilh's play *Becket,* Thomas Becket has become the Archbishop of Canterbury. In his younger days, he was a drinking buddy of the man who is now King Henry II of England. The king quite naturally believes that his old carousing pal will surely cooperate with his plan to bring the Church of England under royal control. But to the king's astonishment and rage, Thomas resists him, even risking his life to do so. Henry reminds Thomas of their younger days—at the hunt, in brothels, frolicking all night—and complains that this word of resistance "isn't like you."

"Perhaps," Becket replies, "I am no longer like myself." When Henry presses him to explain what he means, Thomas says,

> I felt for the first time that I was being entrusted with some-
> thing, that's all — there in that empty cathedral somewhere

in France, that day when you ordered me to take up this burden. I was a man without honor. And suddenly I found it—
one I never imagined would ever become mine—the honor
of God.[2]

Here, then, is the overarching theme of 2 Timothy: the young
minister is "being entrusted with something," namely faith in the
gospel and the call to serve the church with strength and love, a faith
and a call seen profoundly in "Paul's" own life.

As we have stated, however, we are taking the position that the
Pastoral Epistles, including 2 Timothy, were written around the turn
of the first century. Paul and Timothy are both almost surely dead.
The author of 2 Timothy (we refer to him as "the Pastor") is writing in the voice of Paul to a symbolic "Timothy," as was the case in
the first letter as well. We are surmising that the letters were sent to
the church at Ephesus (although naming the place is not critical to
understanding the letter), and the intended recipients are the "good
leaders" of this church, probably elders, that is, the people who lead
and instruct the house church clusters in the community. Their leadership has been challenged, and in some aspects undermined, by a
cadre of false teachers, also probably elders. In the letter, these good
leaders are supposed to identify with "Timothy." They imagine him
as young, a bit timid, sometimes feeling overmatched by the older
and more aggressive personalities in the church. So when the Pastor writes as if it were Paul encouraging his young protégé Timothy,
these good elders are to find themselves addressed. It's as if Paul were
writing to the "Timothy" in them, building them up for ministry.

1:1–2

The Letter Opens

2 Timothy opens with all of the expected initial parts of an ancient
letter: signature, addressee, and greeting (see comments on 1 Tim.
1:1–2). The Pastor who writes this letter once again identifies himself

2. Jean Anouilh, *Becket, or the Honor of God* (New York: Coward, McCann, and Geoghegan, 1960), 112.

as "Paul, an apostle of Christ Jesus," writing once more to "Timothy," but as stated above, we are viewing this as the Pastor addressing the leaders of Ephesus. There are other possibilities concerning authorship, of course. Some recent commentators, employing new data and sophisticated arguments, have urged the renewal of an older view: that all three Pastoral Epistles, including this one, are authentic letters of Paul. Others wonder if the letters are pseudonymous, written in Paul's voice by a later author, but the recipients were not aware of this. Maybe the recipients believed they were reading a letter the real Paul wrote to the real Timothy many years before, but the letter seemed astonishingly fresh with meaning, almost as if Paul had anticipated the very problems they were facing. There are other theories, but in some ways, questions about authorship and historicity dim in importance when we ask the more urgent question, What might these ancient letters say to our faithful imaginations now? New Testament scholar Luke Timothy Johnson puts it well:

> Most readers of 2 Timothy . . . read this [letter] not as a distinct historical puzzle, but as part of a biblical witness. They must struggle, therefore, with the implicit authority it bears because of its canonical status. For such readers, the issue of Pauline authorship is not really paramount. . . . Such readers are correctly less concerned with the consistency of "Pauline theology" than with the truthfulness—and, therefore, the reliability—of this biblical witness for the present-day struggle to live before God faithfully as disciples of Jesus.[3]

The Pastor signs on as "Paul, an apostle of Christ Jesus . . ." (1:1), a designation borrowed from other Pauline letters (see 1 Cor. 1:1; 2 Cor. 1:1; Col. 1:1; Eph. 1:1). In the first letter, this apostleship was by God's "command" (1 Tim. 1:1), but this time it is by "the will of God." The "command of God" and "the will of God" are, in some ways, synonymous, but in other ways there is a slight color variation in meaning. God's command is the instrument by which one is summoned to service; God's will is the network of divine purpose in which human service is embedded. God's command is how ministry

---

3. Luke Timothy Johnson, *The First and Second Letters to Timothy,* The Anchor Bible, vol. 35a (New York: Doubleday, 2001), 329.

starts. God's will is how ministry is sustained and what it means to have performed it.

To see one's identity and vocation, theologically, as a part of God's will is more nuanced and profound than the message sometimes seen on church signs: "God has a plan for your life." It is not as if God has some tightly written plan, some rigid and secret script for each person's life, and faithful discipleship means somehow cracking the code on what God has designed for us. It is rather to have one's life and work be gathered up into what God is doing—what God "wills"—for the whole creation. The Pastor will say later that Christ Jesus "abolished death and brought life and immortality to light through the gospel" (1:10). This life-giving work of salvation and re-creation is what God's will is all about, and if the shards and fragments of one's own little life can be somehow used by God in this saving action, then one's ministry can be said to be "by the will of God" and "for the sake of the promise of life that is in Christ Jesus."

Each person is called by God not simply to progress through fixed stages of life, nor to fashion a career entirely under his or her own control, but to set out on a journey, which—because it is governed by the providence of a God who is always free—must have a course whose ending cannot be seen, though it may be believed. Thus, the Church prays in the liturgy of evening prayer: "Lord God, you have called your servants to ventures of which we cannot see the ending, by paths as yet untrodden, through perils unknown. Give us faith to go out with good courage, not knowing where we go, but only that your hand is leading us and your love supporting us."

Gilbert Meilaender, "A Complete Life: The 2011 Erasmus Lecture," *First Things*, 219 (Jan. 12, 2012): 30.

1:3–18

Strong, Loving, and Wise

The good leaders at Ephesus are indeed "good," but the Pastor fears they are far too timid, or, as he phrases it, they have "a spirit of cowardice" (1:7). And it is certainly understandable why they might be shrinking violets. The good leaders (and from the perspective of this letter, that means the leadership in the Pauline tradition as symbolized by the figure of "Timothy") are in a battle for the soul of the church with the false teachers, so aptly described in 1 Timothy, and the deck seems stacked in favor of the bad guys.

To begin with, the false teachers are offering a glitzier gospel. They preach an attractive, freeform spirituality with an air of adventure and a dash of escape from mundane reality thrown in as a bonus. The good leaders, on the other hand, have a messier gospel, an incarnational gospel bound to flesh and blood and earth, a gospel that proclaims that God's redemption is to be found in such labor-intensive activities as raising children, keeping marriages strong, and trying to build a church fellowship of trust and support out of the often-contentious and conflicted lives of real human beings. The false teachers have fancier interpretation of Scripture, with their secret codes, exhilarating myths, and mind-boggling spiritual truths hidden beneath the surface of the biblical texts where only the elite can ferret them out. The good teachers have only the plain witness of Scripture and the traditional confessions and doctrines. The false teachers adore controversy, have great debate skills, and love to make the good teachers look backward and dull. Not to mention that the hyper-spiritual leaders are fattening their wallets with the swollen honoraria from rich members of the community, while the Pauline style of ministry seems to have left Paul basically broke and doing a lot of prison time. In the face of such turbocharged opposition, small wonder that the good teachers have become gun shy.

So the Pastor goes to work in this letter to build up some confidence in "Timothy," that is, in the church leaders at Ephesus. God did not instill cowardice in leaders, the Pastor insists, but instead gives the gift of the spirit enabling to be strong, loving, and wise (1:7).[4] The letter flows for the next several verses in a highly personal, somewhat rambling style, but by the time it has wandered around the garden to get to the point, the Pastor has managed to name four different reasons why the good leaders at Ephesus should be bold and confident:

4. "Strong, loving, and wise" is a translation of 2 Tim. 1:7 made popular by liturgical scholar Robert Hovda, who wrote a book on presiding in worship by the same name: Robert W. Hovda, *Strong, Loving, and Wise: Presiding in Liturgy* (Collegeville, MN: The Liturgical Conference, 1976). The NRSV renders the phrase, "a spirit of power and of love and of self-discipline."

1:3–5 Reason 1: A Theological Tradition That Is Older and Deeper Than the Religious Impulses of the Present Moment

"Timothy" did not become a Christian at a weekend conference in Malibu. His faith was shaped in him over the years by his mother, Eunice, and her faith in turn was nurtured by her mother, Lois. "Timothy's" faith is no fleeting fancy; it has been preserved and passed on through the generations.

It should be noted that this picture of two women—Lois and Eunice—playing vital roles in "Timothy's" faith formation stands in some tension with the "I permit no woman to teach . . . a man" command in 1 Timothy 2:12, even when we take into account the fact that here the Pastor is talking about Timothy's childhood formation. This portrait of a mother and grandmother as nurturers of the gospel, combined with the Pastor's high view of the role of older widows as mentors, means, at the very least, that the Pastor's position on women as teachers of the faith is more complex than any single text might disclose.

The Pastor also presents "Paul" as standing in a long faith tradition. Unlike the false teachers, Paul does not create de novo worship "experiences" blown about by this or that spiritual breeze. No, he has worshiped "as my ancestors did" (1:3), and he has done so "with a clear conscience," which could perhaps best be translated as "with single-minded devotion."[5]

The main purpose of these references to the faith being passed down through the generations is to rally the good leaders to the bulwarks in their battle against the false teachers and their distortions. The Pastor is reminding his readers that they are the heirs to the true faith, passed on from grandparent to parent to child, that they are the ones who have been entrusted with the crown jewels of the gospel. The false teachers, on the other hand, are enchanters who lure people off the path with costume jewelry bracelets of glass beads and rhinestones, slapped together the day before yesterday.

In our time, however, the passage also works in the opposite direction, exposing the failures of today's church to pass the faith

---

5. Or "with undivided attention" as in Raymond F. Collins, *I & II Timothy and Titus* (Louisville, KY: Westminster John Knox Press, 2002), 191.

on to our children. The chain from Lois to Eunice to Timothy has, in many places and ways, broken down. Two decades ago, a team of sociologists studied the attitudes toward Christianity of the Baby Boomer generation, who were at that point in the parenting phase of life.[6] If the Pastor who wrote 2 Timothy described Timothy's faith as his precious birthright, something nourished in him by his mother and grandmother, the Baby Boomers saw their religion as simply an "accident of birth." They just happened to be born in a Christian household, and it could have easily been otherwise. "Consequently," wrote the sociologists, "it would be presumptuous of them to stand on their accidental birthright and make claims on others' faith."[7] Many of these Baby Boomer parents held the view that their children should be raised uncontaminated by any religious expectation or pressure and that they should arrive at adulthood free to make their own choices—Christian or not, religious or not. For these parents, the researchers found, whatever their children choose about religion will be fine, "as long as they are happy" and basically good people.[8]

So what happened religiously to the children raised by these Boomers? An extensive study of the religious views of this group found a fuzzy theological worldview in place, what some of the researchers called "moralistic therapeutic deism."[9] In this view, there is a god who created the world and watches over it, but one interacts with this god only when one has a problem that needs to be solved. Otherwise, this god stays in the wings, wishing only for people to "be good, nice, and fair" to others, to be happy, and to feel good about themselves.

These are broad findings, to be sure, and there are many exceptions, but the Pastor would look over these results and probably say that the false teachers at Ephesus had won the day and that it was high time for the Loises and Eunices of the church to get back on the job of forming Christian faith in our children. Kenda Creasy Dean,

---

6. Donald A. Luidens, Dean R. Hoge, and Benton Johnson, "The Emergence of Lay Liberalism among Baby Boomers," *Theology Today,* 51/2 (July 1994): 249–55.

7. Ibid., 253–54.

8. Ibid., 253.

9. Christian Smith with Melina Lundquist Denton, *Soul Searching: The Religious and Spiritual Lives of American Teenagers* (New York: Oxford University Press, 2005), 162–63 et passim.

who is a specialist in the Christian education of youth, picks up the spirit of 2 Timothy when she says,

> What Christian adults know that teenagers are still discovering is that every one of them is an amazing child of God. Their humanity is embedded in their souls as well as their DNA. Their family is the church, their vocation is a grateful response for the chance to participate in the divine plan of salvation, their hope lies in the fact Christ has claimed them and secured the future for them. If we, the church, lived alongside young people as though this were true— if we lived alongside anybody as though this were true— we would be the community that Christ calls us to be.[10]

The most obvious way to learn a language is to hang around somebody who speaks it. There are people in our congregations who speak a faith language. So we need to identify who they are and hang out with them! I'm thinking of a couple in a church my husband and I attended when we lived in Pennsylvania who were at least 25 years older than us, and they'd die if they knew we thought of them as spiritual directors—they don't even know what that term means— but in fact they functioned that way for our family. And part of the reason was that they had a very explicit language of prayer. They spoke about prayer as though it were just a normal part of their lives, because for them, it was! By spending time with Bud and Norma, we learned to talk about our lives in those terms too, because they created this framework in which that was possible.

Remarks of Kenda Creasy Dean in Debra Arca Mooney, "Almost Christian: An Interview with Kenda Creasy Dean," Patheos.com, June 22, 2010, http://www.patheos.com/Resources/Additional -Resources/Almost-Christian-Kenda-Creasy-Dean?offset=3&max=1.

1:6–7 Reason 2: The Empowerment of Ordination as a Sign of the Holy Spirit

As he did in 1 Timothy 4:14, the Pastor once again evokes the ritual of "Timothy's" ordination by naming "the laying on of hands." But this was no mere ceremony. The laying on of hands expressed in action what was taking place theologically, the receiving, naming, and blessing of the inner gifts needed by Timothy and other leaders for service.

10. Kenda Creasy Dean, "Faith, Nice and Easy: The Almost-Christian Formation of Teams," *The Christian Century*, 127/16 (August 10, 2010): 27.

For the leaders at Ephesus to recall their ordination was both empowering and humbling. On the one hand, it reminded them of their high calling and strong responsibility to call the community to be formed in the authentic Christian faith. Just as the gospel was passed from Lois to Eunice to Timothy, so the responsibility for leading and guiding the faithful was passed, through the laying on of hands, from Jesus to the apostles to the leaders at Ephesus. As *Baptism, Eucharist, and Ministry,* an ecumenical statement of the World Council of Churches, puts it,

> As Christ chose and sent the apostles, Christ continues through the Holy Spirit to choose and call persons into the ordained ministry. As heralds and ambassadors, ordained ministers are representatives of Jesus Christ to the community, and proclaim his message of reconciliation. As leaders and teachers they call the community to submit to the authority of Jesus Christ, the teacher and prophet, in whom law and prophets were fulfilled. As pastors, under Jesus Christ the chief shepherd, they assemble and guide the dispersed people of God, in anticipation of the coming Kingdom.[11]

On the other hand, ordination reminds these leaders that the strength and effectiveness of their ministry do not grow out of their cleverness or intrinsic personal charisma but out of the power of the Holy Spirit. Again as *Baptism, Eucharist, and Ministry* states: "Since ordination is essentially a setting apart with prayer for the gift of the Holy Spirit, the authority of the ordained ministry is not to be understood as the possession of the ordained person but as a gift for the continuing edification of the body in and for which the minister has been ordained."[12] In other words, ministry involves charisma, but it is the *charism* of the Spirit, not the charm of the leader. This affirmation should finally have the effect of calming the leaders, who should be reassured by the word, "It's not about you. It's about what the Spirit is doing through you."

---

11. *Baptism, Eucharist, and Ministry: Faith and Order Paper No. 111* (Geneva: World Council of Churches, 1982), para. 11, p. 18.
12. Ibid., para. 15, p. 19.

1:8–14 Reason 3: "Paul's" Own Ministry as an Example

The Pastor wants to counter the negative influence of the false teachers by calling on the "good leaders" at Ephesus to be the kind of teachers, preachers, and leaders that the apostle Paul himself was. One obvious flaw in this plan is the fact that Paul's leadership style seemed to have landed him in prison more times than many church leaders would find acceptable. Beckoning people to "imitate me" while wearing shackles has a certain deterrent effect.

But here the Pastor turns this negative image of Paul in prison on its head. Writing as "Paul," he reminds "Timothy" of the intimacy of their relationship, indicates that he prays for "Timothy" night and day, remembers that "Timothy wept" when he last visited (because of Paul's suffering in prison?), indicates that he yearns for a visit from "Timothy" that would fill him with joy (1:4). Then, drawing on this close and trusting relationship, "Paul" urges "Timothy," "Do not be ashamed, then, of the testimony about our Lord or of me his prisoner, but join with me in suffering for the gospel . . ." (1:8).

The Pastor is, in effect, asking the leadership at Ephesus to look at a ministry like Paul's but then to look again, this time with a squint, in order to see what it really is. At first glance, all one sees is a weak, incarcerated man—reviled, suffering, and in chains. But look again, urges the Pastor, and one sees a different picture—a man endowed with the power of God; called to a high calling by the grace of Jesus Christ; a herald, apostle, and teacher of the eternal gospel (1:9–11).

The theology undergirding this is an eschatological wager. It risks everything on the hope that, at the last day, when Christ will be all in all and the glory of God will fill creation, what seems lowly and despised in the dim light of this present world will be revealed for the ministry of God's grace and power that it truly is and will shine like the sun.

Right now it seems like the false teachers have chosen the path of wisdom. There they are taking magical mystery tours with young widows into spiritual never-never land, while "Paul" sits on the dirt floor of a Roman prison, scraping his rations out of the bottom of a tin cup. Even so, "Paul" says, "I am not ashamed" (1:12). We tend to hear those words in a psychological sense, something like,

"Don't worry. I'm not embarrassed to be in jail." But the Pastor is talking about a very different understanding of shame here. In an honor-shame society, public moral regard fell into two categories: that which was pure, good, true, and wise was worthy of honor, that which was vile, deceitful, and evil was worthy of shame. "Paul" is not speaking primarily of emotional embarrassment; he's talking about a final verdict on his life and work. The statement, "I am not ashamed" means "When all is said and done, I will not be put to shame." He is saying, "Here in the shadows of this age, the world has judged me to be worthy of shame, but when the light of dawn comes, I will be seen for who I truly am, Christ's faithful advocate."

And when is this dawn in which all will be revealed? Already the first bright streaks of light are on the horizon in the resurrection of Jesus. "It has now been revealed through the appearing of our Savior Christ Jesus, who abolished death and brought life and immortality through the gospel" (1:10) No one ever appeared more shameful than did Jesus on the cross, but on Easter we saw him as he truly is. Just so, when the promise of Easter floods creation at the end of all things, Paul's ministry will be seen not as a matter of shame but as a sign of the power of God in the world (1:8).

When "Paul" says, "I am not ashamed, for I know the one in whom I have put my trust, and I am sure that he is able to guard until that day what I have entrusted to him" (1:12), he is saying in essence, "I know and trust the risen Christ, so I am placing my wager on him and his gospel. For the moment, it will cause me to suffer and to be imprisoned, just as our Lord suffered and was imprisoned. But on 'that day,' the Great Last Day, my trust, my wager on the gospel, will be validated." As the African American spiritual says, "O, nobody knows who I am until the judgment morning!"

"Paul," thus, beckons to "Timothy," and to all the good leaders in Ephesus, to "join with me in suffering for the gospel" (1:8), because, when all is said and done, this is the ministry that will count, this is the life that will endure, and even now, if one knows how to squint, it can be seen as the life-giving path. The invitation to join in suffering is not an expression of masochism but instead an acknowledgment that service to the gospel puts one inevitably in the crosshairs of the powers that be. The Pastor is not suggesting that the leadership at

Ephesus seek out suffering just for the sake of suffering but, rather, should recognize that suffering goes with the territory when one puts one's life in the service of the gospel. As the second-century bishop Polycarp, squinting himself, said in a letter he wrote to the Christians at Philippi, "I rejoice that you have shown love even to those among the faithful who have been placed in chains. These shackles are, after all, the jewelry of the saints and the crowns of those who belong to God."[13]

When Dietrich Bonhoeffer was himself a prisoner in a Nazi jail, he wrote to his friend Eberhard Bethge about the upcoming baptism of Bethge's son, who was also Bonhoeffer's godson. Bonhoeffer was struck with the daring gesture of participating in a baptism in a world full of war and air raids, a world in which evil seemed to have the upper hand, a world in which he himself was in chains. He wrote to Bethge:

> If in the middle of an air raid God sends out the gospel call to his kingdom in baptism, it will be quite clear what that kingdom is and what it means. It is a kingdom stronger than war and danger, a kingdom of power and authority, signifying eternal terror and judgment to some, and eternal joy and righteousness to others, not a kingdom of the heart, but one as wide as the earth, not transitory but eternal, a kingdom that makes a way for itself and summons men to itself to prepare its way, a kingdom for which it is worthwhile risking our lives.[14]

1:15–18 Reason 4: Friends in Ministry

This passage puts the spotlight on a man named Onesiphorus, who "refreshed" Paul, visited him in prison, and was not offended by Paul's imprisonment. The verb translated "refreshed" may mean that Onesiphorus showed care and hospitality or that he provided financial support—perhaps both.[15] The affection showed by Onesiphorus to Paul is in sharp contrast to Phygelus, Hermogenes, and all the others in Asia who have turned away from Paul. Onesiphorus not

13. A paraphrase of Polycarp, "Letter to the Philippians," 1:1.
14. Dietrich Bonhoeffer, *Letters and Papers from Prison* (New York: Touchstone, 1997), 304.
15. See Johnson, *The First and Second Letters to Timothy*, 361.

only bucked the trend by backing Paul, he is also described as well-known for his good ministry in Ephesus.

Interestingly, Onesiphorus, Hermogenes, and Demas (whom we will meet later in 2 Tim. 4:9) all show up in the fictionalized second-century document *The Acts of Paul and Thecla*, which presents a very different portrait of Paul than the Pastoral Epistles, a Paul who has much in common with the false teachers (see the discussion of this document in the comments on 1 Tim. 2:8–15). There Paul and two companions, Demas and Hermogenes, are on a missionary tour and come to the town of Iconium, where Onesiphorus lives. Onesiphorus warmly greets Paul as a "servant of the blessed God" but oddly ignores the other two men. Demas and Hermogenes immediately get their noses out of joint over this snub. Aggravated by Onesiphorus and envious of the greeting Paul received, they challenge Onesiphorus, demanding to know why he gave them the cold shoulder and why he didn't recognize that they, too, are servants of God. In one of the great put-downs in all of ancient literature, Onesiphorus tells Demas and Hermogenes that he didn't greet them with hospitality because he took one look at them and failed to see "any fruit of righteousness" in them. Sure enough, before the tale is ended, Demas and Hermogenes have proved Onesiphorus to be perceptive by swinging completely over to the dark side and becoming saboteurs of Paul's ministry.

How is it that we encounter some of the same cast of characters here in 2 Timothy? One obvious possibility is that the author of *The Acts of Paul and Thecla* had read 2 Timothy and simply borrowed the names of Paul's friends and foes. Another possibility is that it was the other way around, that the Pastor got the names from *Paul and Thecla* (which would also imply that we have the dating backwards, that 2 Timothy, in fact, postdates *Paul and Thecla*). The most likely scenario, however, is that neither borrowed from the other and that both documents are drawing from a common well, namely the lore about Paul that circulated in the early church. The Christians in Asia Minor surely told stories about their legendary missionary pastor, and names like Onesiphorus, Phygelus, Hermogenes, and Demas would appear in those stories as well-known supporters or opponents of Paul.

Quite apart from the historical and literary questions, this passage about Onesiphorus is designed to underscore the importance of friendship and mutual support among those who labor for the gospel. He is pictured as traveling to Rome and searching eagerly until he found his friend, the imprisoned Paul. Onesiphorus is the kind of friend every "Paul" needs, the kind of friend every "Timothy" needs, the kind of friend to others every "Timothy" is called to be. Like "Paul," who encountered fierce opposition, the good leaders at Ephesus face formidable opponents. And like "Paul," these leaders will need companions like Onesiphorus who encourage and support them in their work.

Theologians Karl Barth and Eduard Thurneysen were lifelong friends and mutual supporters. When the two of them became part of a circle of theologians who took on the theological establishment and challenged the reigning European theology of their day, they were bolstered by their friendship. The same was true when, in the name of the gospel, they spoke out against the rise of Nazism. Even at the end of life, their friendship kept them strong in the faith. According to Barth's biographer, Eberhard Busch, the day that Barth died, peacefully in his sleep, he had been working on a lecture he hoped to give to an ecumenical gathering in Zurich. As he worked into the evening, Barth was interrupted by two telephone calls. The first was from his nephew Ulrich Barth, and Barth closed that call by quoting a stanza from a hymn about Christian hope. Then later, his old friend Thurneysen called. As Busch tells the story,

> The other person who wanted to speak to him so late at night was his friend Eduard Thurneysen, who had remained faithful to him over sixty years. They talked about the gloomy world situation. Then Barth said, "But keep your chin up! Never mind! 'He will reign!'" When the telephone rang, he had been writing a few sentences of the draft for his lecture in which he was saying that in the church it is always important to pay attention to the Fathers who have gone before in the faith. For "God is not a God of the dead but of the living."[16]

16. Eberhard Busch, *Karl Barth: His Life from Letters and Autobiographical Texts* (Philadelphia: Fortress Press, 1977), 498.

Barth, Thurneysen, Onesiphorus, Paul, Timothy, and the old teachers of the church gathered around each other in a communion of friendship and sainthood, reminding each other amid the gloom of this world and the tribulations of those who try to stay faithful, that Christ will indeed reign. Indeed, "Paul" wishes for his friend that he would "find mercy from the Lord" on the day of judgment, that he would, in fact, be one whose acts of friendship would prove to be the kind of godliness that counts "for both the present life and the life to come" (4:8).

2 Timothy 2:1–3:9

2:1–7
Keep Your Eye on the Ball

1:1–2 Strong in Grace

Having rehearsed in the previous chapter several sources for endurance in ministry, the Pastor now softens his voice and speaks again in an intimate and fatherly tone. He urges "Timothy," his "child," to "be strong in the grace that is in Christ Jesus" (2:1). How is it that one is "strong in . . . grace?" In order to understand this, one is tempted to latch onto the word "grace," to run to Romans and Galatians to retrieve a Pauline theology of grace as opposed to "law" and to apply it here. But actually the Pastor is working here with a somewhat different definition of grace than we find in Romans or Galatians. He is saying something equally profound but in some ways simpler.

The word translated "grace" here can also be rendered "gift," which is probably the sense meant in this passage. Timothy has the gift for leadership and ministry, a gift that is not an intrinsic part of his character but instead a gift that is given over and again by Christ. Sometimes we say things like, "Marilyn has such marvelous gifts for ministry. She should think about seminary" or "We ought to nominate Jim to serve on the vestry. He has all the gifts for it" or "Everyone has a spiritual gift. You should seek to discover what your gift is." While these statements may be true in their own ways, they mean "gift" as certain qualities or characteristics that people possess—a gift for public speaking, a gift for making wise judgments, a gift for keeping the peace in tense situations, and so on. The Pastor is talking about "gift" in a more dynamic sense, not as what people already have that makes them good leaders, but instead as what they don't have in and of themselves, but need. "Gift" here is the power God gives, and continues to give, in the exercise of ministry and leadership.

Many pastors are keenly aware of this sense of "gift" in their ministries. They may have many marvelous skills and attributes. They may
be intelligent, articulate, and perceptive, but when they stand in the
pulpit to preach, they become aware of what they don't have. So they
utter the silent plea, "Speak to me that I may speak."

For the Pastor in 2 Timothy, those who lead the church are set
apart for service by the laying on of hands, and again, this ordination is not merely a ritual validating talents and gifts that those being
ordained already possess. Rather, for the Pastor ordination is a gift-
ing event, and ministry is empowered by "the gift of God that is
within you *through* the laying on of [human] hands" (1:6). In other
words, ordination is not just a ceremony recognizing gifts; it is an
experience in which the gift needed to serve Jesus Christ is *received.*

So the Pastor, as he did in chapter 1, is here tenderly encouraging
the leaders at Ephesus to remember their ordinations, to "rekindle
the gift of God" first received there, and to derive the strength to
endure in good ministry from the confidence that they are not out
there on their own abilities alone. For the Pastor, good ministry is a
tightrope act, balanced between too little confidence and too much.
The false teachers, with their self-made "gospel" and their spiritual
elitism, are over-confident. They are puffed up and "conceited" (1
Tim. 6:4). On the other hand, those good leaders at Ephesus who
hold back out of a sense of inadequacy, who cede the field to the
false teachers because of a "spirit of cowardice" (1:7), fail to trust
that God will fill the empty places in them with power and boldness.
They don't remember their ordinations and have forgotten the gift
kindled within them then, the gift, the empowerment of Jesus Christ
himself. As Karl Barth once said of his own faith and work,

> I know the rather sinister figure of the 'atheist' very well, not
> only from books, but also because it lurks somewhere inside me
> too. But I believe I know even better the real God and the real
> man who is called Jesus Christ in the unity of both. He let the
> atheist depart once and for all and long ago, completely. . . .[1]

---

1. Karl Barth, *Fragments Grave and Gay*, ed. M. Ruscheidt (London and Glasgow: Collins
Fortress Library, 1971), 45–46.

2:3–7 *Soldiers, Athletes, and Farmers*

The Pastor knows that the leaders at Epehesus, the "Timothys" who are charged with guiding the community in faith, will need all the strength they can muster. Good leadership in the church is never easy. Their job is the painstaking one of receiving the gospel, which has at great cost been passed down to them, and building a company of faithful teachers who will pass the gospel along to the next generation (2:2). There will inevitably be opposition—jealousy, obstructionism, people who believe they have a better "gospel" than the real one, rejection—and because there is opposition, there will be suffering (2:3).

The only way to remain true to one's calling as a leader is to trust and cherish the gift given by Christ and to stay focused like a laser on the mission itself. The Pastor illustrates this focus with three images—the soldier, the athlete, and the farmer. Good ministry is like serving as a soldier—as a "soldier of the cross," so sings the spiritual "Jacob's Ladder." Good soldiers don't get distracted from the mission but stay on task and do everything in their power to please their superior officer. Good ministry is also like being a disciplined athlete who knows the rules of the game and the discipline necessary to play well. And finally, good ministry is like being a farmer who wipes the sweat of hard work off his brow every day and whose labor finally finds its reward in the harvest.

In other words, good leaders in the church keep their "eyes on the prize" and, when their ministries encounter opposition, they resist doubt and despair, as well as the temptation to substitute something that seems in the moment to be more attractive or persuasive than the gospel. The British theologian R. E. C. Browne once observed that there comes a point for every minister when the gospel seems too little to go on. Even so, said Browne, "they must not go beyond their authority in a mistaken attempt to make their authority strong and clear. That going beyond is always the outcome of an atheistic anxiety. . . ."[2]

---

2. R. E. C. Browne, *The Ministry of the Word* (Philadelphia: Fortress Press, 1976), 40.

2:8–13

The Paradox of the Gospel, and of the Ministry

2:8–10 Mountaintops and Valleys

In the Book of Acts, Paul stood before King Agrippa and announced that he was on trial because of his hope (Acts 26:6). And now the "Paul" of 2 Timothy announces that the apostle who was tried for his hope in the gospel has now been convicted, sentenced, and imprisoned.

This passage begins oddly: "Remember Jesus Christ, raised from the dead, a descendant of David." What makes this odd is that it seems backward. We would expect the statement to be in chronological order: "descended from David, raised from the dead." A similar formula in Romans 1:3, in fact, has it in the expected order, first David, then the resurrection. But maybe this reversal of order is part of the point. It at least serves to reinforce the literary structure of the passage and, perhaps, as Luke Johnson has suggested, to undergird its theology as well.[3]

The passage moves up and down, from mountaintop to valley and back again. It begins on the mountain crest with a trumpet blast and a proclamation of the resurrection, the manifestation of divine power in the risen Christ. But then it moves quickly to the valley, to the humanity of Jesus and his Davidic ancestry. Then it lingers in the valley long enough to see Paul doing hard time in a Roman prison, suffering and "chained like a criminal," only to climb the mountain once more with a proclamation of the freedom of God's word: "But the word of God is not chained!" Then we plunge back down to the valley of Paul's suffering, which he endures "for the sake of the elect," who will—now we go back up the mountain for the denouement of this text—"obtain the salvation that is in Christ Jesus, with eternal glory."

Viewed this way, this up and down movement is a piece of theological choreography, moving back and forth between the mountaintop

---

3. Luke Timothy Johnson, *The First and Second Letters to Timothy,* The Anchor Bible, vol. 35a (New York: Doubleday, 2001), 380–81.

where the Easter victory is full and complete and the valley, where
this hope must be lived out in human history with all its labor pains
and suffering. As such, it stands as a counter to the false teachers, who
proclaim a gospel that is only up, up, and away—and never down.
We learn later that these false teachers claim that the "resurrection
(of all humanity) has already taken place" (2:18), meaning that the
way is open for the truly spiritual to depart the encumbrances of this
fleshly life and to enter now into the perfect realm of constant bliss.
Not so fast, says the Pastor. We have our hopes set on Easter, to be
sure, but we live out those hopes in a Good Friday world, a world
in which even revered figures like David have feet of clay, a world in
which even apostles go on trial for hope and get thrown behind bars
for the sake of the gospel. The light of Easter has dawned, and we see
it beckoning us toward eternal glory. But don't forget, as the false
teachers tempt you to forget, that the Christian life is not putting on
sweet angels wings and flying away into the ether. It's lacing up your
shoes and putting one foot in front of the other, faithfully living out
the gospel hope in the messy relationships and conflicted circumstances of this world. After all, that's the way Jesus himself did it. He
was no angel; he was "a descendant of David," who kept his eye on
hope even as he suffered in the flesh. As the creed used by the Masai
tribe in Africa expresses it:

> We believe that God made good his promise by sending his
> son, Jesus Christ, a man in the flesh, a Jew by tribe, born poor
> in a little village, who left his home and was always on safari

---

**What Jesus offers [in] Holy Week is not an escape from loss but a better way
of losing. In each Passion account, and especially in the Gospel of John, Jesus
suffers humiliation and defeat but does not relinquish his identity as the Son
of God. His final cry is addressed to his Father. His divinity is confirmed not by
coming down from the cross but by his gestures of love while impaled upon
it. From the cross he provides for his mother and forgives his tormentors.
From the cross he draws a world of lost souls to himself. As it turns out, what
remains in each of us is not the bravado of mastery but the vulnerability of
love.**

Richard Lischer, "Stripped Bare: Holy Week and the Art of Losing," *The Christian Century*, 127/9
(March 12, 2012): 11–12

doing good, curing people by the power of God, teaching about God and man, showing that the meaning of religion is love. He was rejected by his people, tortured and nailed hands and feet to a cross, and died. He was buried in the grave, but the hyenas did not touch him, and on the third day, he rose from that grave. He ascended to the skies. He is the Lord.[4]

2:11–13 A Baptismal Poem

The Pastor winds up this section of the letter with what many scholars believe is an adaptation of an early Christian hymn (2:11–13). These three verses have what appear to be four rhythmic stanzas, and they are, therefore, set in psalm-like, poetic typography in the NRSV. The introductory phrase "the saying is sure" (2:11) gives some weight to the idea that the Pastor is quoting something traditional here, a hymn or a well-known poem. Luke Johnson, however, has argued that there is no external reason to think of this material as a previously existing hymn or poem.[5] It could just as well be a lovely, rhythmical piece composed by the author of 2 Timothy. Even so, the rhythm of this passage almost requires that we read it in a different frame, as poetry and not as business-as-usual prose. As literary critic Barbara Herrnstein Smith says,

> It is simply the fact that as soon as we perceive that a verbal sequence has a sustained rhythm, that it is formally structured according to a continuously operating principle of organization, we know that we are in the presence of poetry and we respond to it accordingly . . . expecting certain effects from it and not others, granting certain conventions to it and not others.[6]

The four stanzas of this piece of poetry in 2 Timothy are "if-then" statements—i.e., if this is true, then something else is also true. These

4. The text of the Masai Creed is found in Larry Dinkins, "Towards Contextualized Creeds: A Perspective from Buddhist Thailand," *International Journal of Frontier Missiology*, 27/1 (January–March 2010): 8.
5. Johnson, *The First and Second Letters to Timothy*, 378–79.
6. Barbara Herrnstein Smith, *Poetic Closure: A Study of How Poems End* (Chicago: University of Chicago Press, 1968), 23.

four statements are coupled into two pairs: the first two statements are a pair of positive statements, and the second two are a pair of negative statements. One important key to understanding this poem is the recognition that these paired statements are instances of a distinct feature of biblical poetry, namely parallelism. A good example of parallelism can be found in the opening verse of Psalm 103:

> A Bless the Lord, O my soul,
> B and all that is within me bless his holy name.

Notice how line B says almost the same thing as line A, but in different words. Since they express approximately the same idea twice, the two lines obviously reinforce each other. But biblical scholars have pointed out that providing reinforcement is just the beginning of the work accomplished by line B. It echoes the thought of line A, to be sure, but it does not merely repeat it in new words. It extends it and expands on it. One biblical scholar says that the two lines, A and B, "strengthen, heighten, and empower each other."[7] Another says that, in parallelism, line B often "intensifies" line A.[8]

The same repetition and intensification pattern is at work in the poem in 2 Timothy. Here is the first couplet:

> A If we have died with him, we will also live with him;
> B if we endure, we will also reign with him (vv. 11–12)

Since lines A and B are placed next to each other in parallel structure, we have two interpretive questions before us: What does line A mean, and how does line B intensify that meaning? As for line A, it speaks of dying then living, and even though the words "with him" are not technically in the original Greek, they are implied and almost surely refer to dying and living with Christ. So how does a Christian die and live with Christ? One possibility is that this poem is speaking literally of dying a martyr's death—Paul's death, Timothy's death, anyone's death who risks taking up the gospel cause in a dangerous

---

7. J. G. Herder, *Vom Geist der Ebräischen Poesie* (Dessau: publisher unknown, 1782), 23.

8. Robert Alter, *The Art of Biblical Poetry, Revised and Updated* (New York: Basic Books, 2011), 15 et passim.

world—and then living with Christ in the resurrection after death. Much more likely, though, is the possibility that the poem speaks metaphorically and liturgically and that line A is an allusion (or even a quotation) from the liturgy of baptism, a reverberation of what the historical Paul said of baptism, "But if we have died with Christ, we believe that we will also live with him" (Rom. 6:8).

If line A is a baptismal reference, and the "death" it speaks about is dying with Christ in baptism—death to the old self and death to sin—then living with Christ is both a future promise and a present reality. It comes to fullness, of course, in the world to come—"For if we have been united with him in a death like his, we will certainly be united with him in a resurrection like his" (Rom. 6:5)—but it is also a present-tense assurance that the Christian life, even in times of suffering, is a life joined with Christ here and now and is already a participation in that eschatological promise.[9] The first line of the poem, then, continues the down and up, valley to mountaintop movement of the previous passage. One who has the "valley experience" of being buried in the waters of baptism and who walks the "valley path" of taking up the cross and serving in Christ's name receives the "mountaintop" promise of living with Christ, both now and in the Day of Resurrection.

Now, how does line B of this poem intensify the claim of line A? If line A spoke of "dying" with Christ, line B speaks of "enduring" with him. So what was a moment in line A, baptism, is now stretched into a season in line B, the whole Christian life. Participating in Jesus' suffering and death in baptism now is elongated into a life's journey, marked by faithful endurance. This is what Paul was talking about when he described the afflictions and sufferings of his own ministry as "carrying in the body the death of Jesus." He wrote to the Corinthians,

> But we have this treasure in clay jars, so that it may be made clear that this extraordinary power belongs to God and does not come from us. We are afflicted in every way, but not crushed; perplexed, but not driven to despair; persecuted, but not forsaken; struck down, but not destroyed; always carrying

9. See Philip H. Towner, *The Letters to Timothy and Titus* (Grand Rapids: Eerdmans, 2006), 509–10.

in the body the death of Jesus, so that the life of Jesus may also be made visible in our bodies. For while we live, we are always being given up to death for Jesus' sake, so that the life of Jesus may be made visible in our mortal flesh. So death is at work in us, but life in you (2 Cor. 4:7–12).

Line A said "we will . . . live with him," and line B intensifies this as "we will . . . reign with him." This means that when all is said and done, and the bright light of the resurrection shines on all creation, those who endured in this world, living a life with Christ, will find that life validated. As John Howard Yoder put it, "[P]eople who bear crosses are working with the grain of the universe."[10]

What is true about the Christian life generally gets applied, here in 2 Timothy, particularly to "Timothy" himself, that is, to the leaders at Ephesus. Because the work of ministry and service takes those leaders down the path of suffering, and because that path was Jesus' path, too, the Pastor is saying that these servants of the gospel can feel Christ's comforting presence as they travel, and they can trust the promise that this path may lead to Calvary and all hell may break loose around them, but it leads to Easter victory as well.

This means that ministers and leaders like those at Ephesus have bread for the long journey of trying to guide congregations, in joy and in pain, come what may. In other words, they can endure through thick and thin, and, as the second line of the poem says, "If we endure, we will also reign with him." So what does good ministry look like? It looks like loving God's people so much that one stands with them in all of the broken places of life, not dishing out the false promises of spiritual escape but standing there, in season and out of season, at bedside and graveside, standing there with the gospel that has been guarded for us as a treasure and passed to us in trust, standing there not in our own power but in the power of the Spirit, a gift given over and again. It means "suffering like a good soldier of Christ Jesus" (2:3), even if that means experiencing the dank of a prison in Rome or Flossenbürg or Birmingham or Robben Island, even if it means trying to keep a congregation faithful that is riddled with conflict, deception, and accusation. It means knowing that such a

10. John Howard Yoder, "Armaments and Eschatology," *Studies in Christian Ethics*, 1/1 (January 1988), 58.

ministry, although perhaps shamed for the moment, will finally not be put to shame. It is a ministry that counts, really counts, because it is a ministry that is finally gathered up into the eternal mercy and reign of God.

"Heartaches are not cured by ministry," writes theologian Richard Lischer, "they are caused by ministry." He goes on to say,

> Having this ministry is like having children. Yes, in some respects they are an answer to prayer, but they also stimulate a lot of desperate prayers. And all the joy they bring into your life is sharpened by the possibilities of new pain.
>
> One Sunday in our congregation, we baptized a baby the day after its mother's funeral. It fell to our minister to "make sense" of these two events in words. I can still see him pacing up and down the center aisle with the baby in the crook of his arm. Through his tears he spoke of the promises of God, as if to say, "This is the ministry we have. It's a hard gift. Let's not lose heart."
>
> This ministry is like love: it never ends. It never comes to the end of its rope. It never wrings its hands and says, "There's nothing more to be done." By its very nature it can never run out of material, because the very conditions of its defeat only create the possibilities for its rebirth.[11]

Turning back to the poem, the first couplet is followed by a second one. If the first was positive, about endurance and life with Christ, the second is decidedly negative.

A if we deny him, he will also deny us;
B if we are faithless, he remains faithful—
   for he cannot deny himself. (vv. 12–13)

Line A may or may not be quoting Matthew 10:33 ("whoever denies me before others, I also will deny before my Father in heaven"), but the two verses certainly share the same view. If remaining faithful to Christ through endurance and suffering means

---

11. Richard Lischer, "Odd Job: The Secret Gift of Ministry," *The Christian Century*, 121/7 (April 6, 2004): 25.

sharing in Christ's life, both now and in the life to come, then denying Christ means a commensurate loss of relationship to him.

Line B, as we would expect, expands and intensifies line A, but it
also smuggles a surprise into the equation. Just based on the rhythm
and flow of the passage, we would expect this fourth line to read, "If
we are faithless to him, then he will break faith with us." But no ... no
amount of denial or faithlessness on the part of humanity can break
the promise of God in Jesus Christ. "He remains faithful," because
faithfulness and keeping promises is his very character, and he cannot deny his own character.

The Pastor has placed this poem in the letter, both as an encouragement to the good leaders at Ephesus and as a warning to the false
teachers, indeed as notes for a "come to Jesus" sermon he hopes the
good leaders will preach to the false teachers. "Remind them of this,
and warn them before God," says the Pastor in the next verse (2:14).
The warning, of course, is that the false teaching being promulgated
at Ephesus is tantamount to a rejection of baptismal identity and a
denial of Christ. To deny Christ runs the risk of being denied by him

But what does that mean in this context? It is possible, of course,
to turn this snippet of poetry from the Pastor into an end-of-time
nightmare scene, with the false teachers and all their flighty followers standing in astonished horror before the judgment seat of Christ
and hearing his stern voice say, "You denied me in life, so I deny
you in the afterlife. Depart from me, you evildoers. I never knew
you." Indeed, this is a tough word, and one does not want to take
too much of the iron out of this text. The Pastor does mean it as a
stern warning, and he does take with eternal seriousness the choices
that people make in the life of faith. But it is also possible to read it
as something other than the wrath-filled horror show depicted by
medieval painters of the last judgment like Jan Van Eyck and Hiero-
nymus Bosch.

The poem essentially reminds all readers that the goal of humanity is life—life full and abundant, lived out in communion with
others and with God. It's just that when we come to the fork in the
road, the sign pointing to abundant life in Christ looks hard, narrow, rocky, salted with suffering, and strewn with crosses. The other
way, by contrast, seems broad, pleasant, well-lit, and bubbling with

happiness. There are the false teachers, halfway down the cheerful looking path beckoning, "Come on. *This* is the path to true spirituality." The poem warns us; don't be fooled by the bright lights and the paved road. It is, as it has always been, the way of the cross that leads home.

But the broad path is indeed inviting, and at Ephesus (and every Ephesus the church has ever known) many choose unwisely. If the Pastor's poem were truly harsh and rigid, then it would portray a God who watches them skipping merrily down a fool's route and who says, "They have chosen the path of destruction; to hell with them"—like the angry St. Peter in a *New Yorker* cartoon, who glowers at a man standing at the gates of heaven and snarls, "You picked the wrong religion, period. I'm not going to argue about it."[12]

But this is a God who will not counter deceit with deceit, faithlessness with faithlessness. Indeed, this is a God who cannot do so, because it is not in God's character to do so. This God dashes after those who have gone astray, seeking them like a good shepherd, calling them home. And this God sends out his ministers to seek them as well, to be patient and to display all gentleness (2:24–25). And God pursues those who have wandered from the faith not mainly because they have wrong ideas that need correction, or the wrong religion that needs replacing, but because they are missing the gift God wishes to give—life full and abundant, lived out in communion with others and with God—in other words, the gift of the very self of God. Even the Pastor, trapped as he is in the middle of a brutal church conflict, holds out the hope that the whole company of humanity, even his opponents, will be gathered into the great mercy of God (2:25). For all of the acrimony of this conflict at Ephesus, the "Paul" of these letters even holds out hope that those famous "shipwrecks" of the faith—Hymenaeus and Alexander—will finally be restored to the fold (1 Tim. 1:20). So this poem does in fact serve as a warning to the false leaders—not as a warning that they will be abandoned and crushed by a vengeful God but that they will miss the fullness of life possible in communion with a merciful, promise-keeping God.

12. Charles Barsotti, "You Picked the Wrong Religion, Period. I'm Not Going to Argue about It," *The New Yorker* cartoon (June 12, 1995).

2:14–21

Good Advice, Bad Conflict

In this section of the letter, the Pastor returns to the task of giving wise pieces of advice about good ministry, but not very far beneath the surface one can see, yet again, the jagged edges of the conflict with the false teachers.

2:14 Tussling Over Words

The leaders are wisely told to "avoid wrangling over words," which is, of course, good advice. But the fact that it had to be said at all implies that a great deal of wrangling over words was taking place, probably flare-ups started by the false teachers over obscure word puzzles in Scripture. Good study of Scripture does, of course, pay attention to words. It is like diving for pearls. The student descends deep into the text, attending to details—the words that are used, the etymologies of the words, the arrangement of the words into sentences, the connections between what is said in one verse to other verses in the passage, and so on. But then, when the student has found a pearl of insight, she swims with it back to the surface and places it in the box of all of the pearls that have been discovered. Each pearl is important, but it is the collection of pearls that has the greatest value.

Sometimes, though, Bible students get stuck under water and don't resurface. They get fascinated by a single verse or a single word and try to construct a whole theology perched precariously on the tiny surface of that lone insight, forgetting the larger context. For example, many years ago some advocates of the Christian temperance movement wrangled over the possible meanings of the Greek word *oinos* (wine), insisting that the story of Jesus turning water into wine at the wedding at Cana (John 2:1–11) was actually the story of Jesus turning the water into unfermented grape juice! Or again, several years ago a popular devotional writer latched onto a few sentences in 1 Chronicles 4 in which an obscure character named Jabez prayed, "Oh, that You would bless me indeed, and enlarge my territory, that Your hand would be with me, and that You would keep *me* from evil, that I may not cause pain!" (1 Chr. 4:10 NKJV). The writer jacked up this one verse and placed a whole theology of prayer on it. Forget the Lord's Prayer, forget Gethsemane, forget the Psalms, this single text in which Jabez petitions God for more territory became the complete key to prayer. "How would your day unfold," the writer breathlessly asked in his runaway best-seller *The Prayer of Jabez*, "if you believed that God wants your borders expanded at all times with every person and if you were confident that God's powerful hand is directing you even as you minister?"[13]

How would your day unfold? Some critics of *The Prayer of Jabez* were quick to go on attack, carping that if one took a daily dose of this thinking that God always wants one to have more and more, then the day would likely unfold right into a gimme, gimme prosperity gospel. It didn't help that the author of the book had a tendency to crow cheesy sentiments such as, "If Jabez had worked on Wall Street, he might have prayed, 'Lord, increase the value of my investment portfolios. . . .'"[14] The *New York Times* review of the book was titled: "Lord, Won't You Buy Me a Mercedes-Benz?"[15]

The whole Jabez uproar was, of course, an example of what the Pastor meant by wrangling over words. It could have been avoided had the devotional writer looked at the full witness of Scripture about prayer and constructed a prayer theology out of the breadth of Scripture instead of fabricating a prayer palace out of a single text, like an upside down pyramid with the point resting on the tip of a biblical pin. Interestingly, the Jabez theology, like the false teaching at Ephesus, tended to disfigure the gospel by turning it into a self-serving, over spiritualized abstraction, out of touch with the realities and the sufferings of everyday Christian disciples. As one reviewer in an evangelical journal said,

> Throughout [*The Prayer of Jabez*], there is no example of enduring faithfulness at humble and thankless tasks—like counseling a troubled couple for years, or caring for an elderly parent in one's home, or daily visiting a dying aids patient for weeks, or toughing it out for three decades in Saudi Arabia,

13. Bruce Wilkinson, *The Prayer of Jabez: Breaking Through to the Blessed Life* (Colorado Springs, CO: Multnomah Press, 2000), 78.
14. Ibid., 31.
15. Judith Shulevitz, "Lord, Won't You Buy Me a Mercedes-Benz," *New York Times,* May 20, 2001, BR47.

where a lifetime of conversions can be counted on two hands.
. . . [The book] is long on the individual's existential meaning and on exploiting the chance, short-term encounter for
God, but short on the meaning of perseverance and ordinary
suffering.[16]

2:15–18 Profane Chatter

If the leaders are encouraged to avoid splitting hairs over words,
they are also to steer clear of "profane chatter" (2:16), repeating a
warning given in 1 Timothy 6:20. By "profane chatter," the Pastor
is probably not talking about cursing but spiritual Gummy Bears,
inspiring-sounding but finally superficial nonsense that passes
for the gospel—fool's gold instead of the real thing. Again, the
advice to avoid this kind of talk implies that the air is full of it at
Ephesus.

The only specific example the Pastor gives is the claim made by
two of the false teachers, Hymenaeus and Philetus, "that the resurrection has already taken place" (2:18). We have run into Hymenaeus
before (1 Tim. 1:20) as one of the "shipwrecks" in the faith that
had to be disciplined because of blasphemy (Philetus appears only
in this passage). These two, charges the Pastor, have "swerved from
the faith," (2:18), gotten off course, and are leading others astray.
They are theological Typhoid Marys, infecting the community with
the disease of their teaching, which spreads "like gangrene" (2:17)
destroying healthy tissue in the body of Christ.

So the "resurrection," these false teachers claim, has already
occurred. They are not talking about Jesus' resurrection, which
indeed would have already taken place, but the promised resurrection of the faithful in the *eschaton*. Why is this a problem? We can
identify at least two reasons why the Pastor labeled this view as "profane chatter" and as a threatening and gangrenous infection:

First, it changes the character of the gospel. The Pastor would have
seen himself in the tradition of Paul regarding the theology of the
resurrection. For Paul, Jesus' resurrection was a foretaste of the

16. Mark Galli, "Significance in a Small Package: The Prayer of Jabez: Breaking Through to the
Blessed Life," *Christianity Today*, 45/8, (June 11, 2001): 98.

resurrection in store for all creation at the end of all things. This future resurrection is the kingdom of heaven, the reign of God, the fullness of "the victory through our Lord Jesus Christ" (1 Cor. 15:37), in which "the creation itself will be set free from its bondage to decay and will obtain the freedom of the glory of the children of God" (Rom. 8:23).

Of course, almost all well-meaning human beings long for the world to be made a better place, for freedom, and for wrongs to be set right. These are dreams expressed in poetry and song, but for Paul, the gospel is distinctly different from these human aspirations. The kingdom of God is not "when you wish upon a star," not our desires cantilevered forward into the future, not the dreams of our hearts brought to fruition in God. It is, rather, the other way around, the life and glory of God brought to fruition in us and in all of the creation. Therefore, since this life of God is larger than our capacity to imagine, we hope for something we have been promised but have not yet seen (Rom. 8:24–25), and we do not have the language to describe God's coming glory. What we do have is a glimpse of it in the risen Christ, who is the "first fruits" of our resurrection (1 Cor. 15:23). All of the New Testament's descriptions of the future of the creation and the future for the faithful are elaborations and projections based on what has been witnessed in the resurrection of Christ.

Despite what is sometimes said about Easter in popular Christianity, the risen Christ was not a resuscitated corpse—a Jesus who was dead on Friday and back alive just as he was, good as new, on Sunday. Rather, the risen Christ was an appearance of God's eternal glory in the world of time, place, and history, a glimpse in advance of what we now wait for in patience: "the redemption of our bodies" (8:23). What we see in the risen Christ is a coming together of our world of earth and flesh and God's future. On the one hand, the risen Christ still had a body, "flesh and bones" like ours, and even the marks of his embodied life, the wounds from the cross, are still present (Luke 24:39). This is to say, the resurrection gathers up and validates Jesus' history as an embodied human being. On the other hand, the body of the risen Christ is not exactly the same body he had three days before. He is recognizable, but also not. This is the Gospel writers' way of describing what cannot be described in ordinary words, that the risen Christ has a body, but a glorified body. He is the same, but altogether new. He is the Jesus we knew in Galilee and Judea, and he is also the Christ beyond all human imagining. And here, too, the transfiguration of Jesus' body is a foretaste of what lies ahead for the bodies of those who belong to him:

> Listen, I will tell you a mystery! We will not all die, but we will all be changed, in a moment, in the twinkling of an eye, at the last trumpet. For the trumpet will sound, and the dead will be raised imperishable, and we will be changed. For this perishable body must put on imperishability, and this mortal body must put on immortality. When this perishable body puts on imperishability, and this mortal body puts on immortality, then the saying that is written will be fulfilled: "Death has been swallowed up in victory." (1 Cor. 15:51–54)

The different view, attributed to Hymenaeus and Philetus, namely that the resurrection had already taken place, was almost surely the first sprigs of what comes to full flower in later gnostic Christianity. For the gnostics, the accounts of Jesus' resurrection were not to be taken literally as an embodied event but spiritually. "Some gnostics," writes Elaine Pagels, "called the literal view of the resurrection the 'faith of fools.' The resurrection, they insisted, was not a unique event of the past: instead, it symbolized how Christ's presence could be experienced in the present. What mattered was not literal seeing, but spiritual vision."[17]

So the claim that the resurrection had already happened involved more than simply changing the timing of the resurrection; it was also altering the nature of it. In the hands of these false teachers, the resurrection was no longer a future event in which God would glorify all creation in the same manner as Jesus was glorified; the resurrection became an inner spiritual experience, an awakening, available to the mystical elite here and now. In Paul's understanding of the gospel, the resurrection had some size; it was the renewal of all things, the gathering up of all time, space, history, and matter into the eternal victory of Christ. For the false teachers, the resurrection

---

17. Elaine Pagels, *The Gnostic Gospels* (New York: Vintage Books, 1989), 11.

was something one could experience in a moment of mystical reverie or on a weekend retreat.

Second, it changes the character of the Christian life. The claim of the false teachers about the resurrection not only threatened to change the content of the gospel, it also implied drastic changes in the way the Christian life would be lived. The gnostic *Gospel of Philip*, dating from the late second- or early third-century, probably gives us a glimpse of some of the trajectories of the thought of the false teachers at Ephesus. Like Hymenaeus and Philetus, the *Gospel of Philip* also teaches that the resurrection is already fully present: "Those who say they will die first and then rise are in error. If they do not first receive the resurrection while they live, when they die they will receive nothing."[18] In *Philip*, this resurrection is an experience of enlightenment, one that Jesus experienced in his life as well: "Those who say that the master first died and then arose are wrong, for he first arose and then died."[19]

So the first implication of this alternative view of the resurrection is that the Christian faith is not a matter of hoping for the renewal of creation and the redemption of our embodied lives but instead a yearning to be spiritually enlightened. The Christian faith moves from being a hope for the salvation of all things to a quest for a spiritual high. This view naturally divides the community. Instead of the church as the unified body of Christ, weak and strong laboring together on behalf of the redemption of the world, the fellowship is instead divided into the enlightened and unenlightened, those who are truly spiritual and those who aren't.

Second, if the resurrection happens only in the tiny compartment of our little souls, then it follows that we lose interest in the wider material world and the larger embodied life. The Pastor has already accused the false teachers of rejecting the goodness of God's creation (1 Tim. 4:3–5), and by the time we get to the *Gospel of Philip*, the false teachers have developed a good reason for doing so: God

18. Madeleine Scopello and Marvin Meyer, "The Gospel of Philip," in Marvin Meyer, ed., *The Nag Hammadi Scriptures: The Revised and Updated Translation of Sacred Gnostic Texts Complete in One Volume* (New York: HarperCollins, 2008), 177.
19. Ibid., 165.

didn't create the world, not the God of Jesus Christ anyway. This world is the work of an inferior god, and the pure and immortal soul bridles against its constraints. "The world came about through a mistake," states *Philip*. "For he who created it wanted to create it imperishable and immortal. He fell short of attaining his desire. For the world never was imperishable, nor, for that matter, was he who made the world."[20]

Naturally, then, those who believe that the resurrection has already happened as a bright spiritual light inside the soul would pursue an ascetic lifestyle, with picky diets and a distaste for fleshly entanglements, such as ordinary marriage, family, and childbearing (see 1 Tim. 4:3). *Philip* speaks of ordinary marriage as "defiled" as opposed to "undefiled" spiritual marriage, which is "not fleshly but pure. It belongs not to desire but will. It belongs not to darkness or night but to the day and the light."[21] These spiritual marriages—and we may be seeing the first hints of them in the Pastoral Epistles— were either sexless or, more likely, marked by sex that the parties had convinced themselves was "spiritual," the product of their enlightened wills and not of lust or base desire.

So the Pastor believes that the hope for the resurrection calls on Christians to live in paradoxical relationship to this world. This world is both the good creation of God, whose gifts are to be received with thanksgiving, and the arena of sin and death in need of salvation. This world is both the fallen creation, full of sorrow and pain, and the treasure of God, the environment where the love and mercy of God in Christ are experienced. For the false teachers, however, the call is not to live paradoxically but dualistically. The world of flesh is defiled and impure. The goal is to become pure and to acquire the spiritual knowledge Jesus wishes to impart (to experience the "resurrection" in our souls here and now), which allows us to break free from the shackles of the world around us. For the Pastor, the Christian life is a wager that the spiritual and the material have become intertwined, just as they were in the word become flesh in Jesus, and that the suffering experienced by those who walk the paths of this world as God's children is not gratuitous but is instead our

20. Ibid., 179.
21. Ibid., 183–84.

> What seems so central in Jesus' teaching as it lies there in the Gospels is that he is speaking of a future coming of the kingdom of God, a consummation of Israel's history in the apparently near future that would bring about a radical change in human life. This change would not be brought about so much by human effort but by a definitive action of God at the end of time, at least time as we know it. "Thy kingdom come" is a very central petition of the Lord's Prayer itself.
>
> Some scholars contend that that was all later Church apocalyptic fantasy; that wasn't Jesus himself at all. To them Jesus was simply this wise sage and Cynic philosopher telling everybody just to realize the presence of the invisible presence of the kingdom right in their own everyday lives. . . . We may have found this Jesus figure useful to wake us up but basically then—in true American fashion—we are self-saved because we realize how wonderful we are.
>
> John P. Meier in John Booker Feister, "Finding the Historical Jesus: An Interview with John P. Meier," *St. Anthony Messenger*, December 1997, http://www.americancatholic.org/Messenger/Dec1997/feature3.asp.

participation here and now in Christ and in the labor pains of a creation groaning in hope for redemption.

2:19–21 Building the House, Putting the Dishes on the Table

Now, in contrast to the wind-blown chaff of the false teachers and their word games and silly chatter, the Pastor introduces two sturdy images, one about God and the other about the good leaders. In the first, God is pictured as having laid the foundation of the church (see similar images in 1 Cor. 3:10–14 and Eph. 2:20) and as having written two inscriptions on the stones: "The Lord knows who are his" and "Let everyone who calls on the name of the Lord turn from wickedness." These inscriptions sound vaguely biblical, and they do reflect biblical themes (see, e.g., Num. 16:5 and Isa. 52:11), but they are not direct biblical quotations. The import for the Pastor is clear, however. While the church at Ephesus may be in the middle of a cat fight over what the gospel is and what it isn't, down at bedrock God is neither confused nor amused. Those who stay true to the gospel as delivered by sound teachers are those whom God recognizes as God's own, and any who want to be in the worshipful presence of this God need to turn away from false alternatives.

The second image is also about a house, but this time we are not inspecting the foundation but opening the cupboard. In a well-provisioned Roman home one is likely to find two kinds of dining utensils. There is the everyday stuff, made of clay and wood, and then there are the special implements, made of gold and silver and saved for extraordinary occasions. Those leaders who "cleanse themselves" by heeding the Pastor's counsel on the urgent concerns before the church will "become special utensils, dedicated and useful to the owner of the house, ready for every good work" (2:21). This is quite a nice image, since it blends beautifully the Pastor's concerns about holy ministry and everyday Christian service. Taken as a whole, the image implies that good leaders are like instruments of gold and silver, and it also implies that they are put to good use day in and day out. In God's house when there is faithful leadership, the table is set with the finest every day.

The idea of the Christian life as the extraordinary lived out in the ordinary is one of the themes of Flannery O'Connor's short story "The Temple of the Holy Ghost."[22] In the story, the mother of a twelve-year-old girl is taking care of two relatives for the weekend, both teenaged girls. With great mirth, the older girls tell the mother and her daughter about Sister Perpetua at their convent school. They tell them that Perpetua, the oldest nun at the school, gave them a lecture once about what they should do if some boy should start acting "ungentlemanly" in the back seat of an automobile. Sister Perpetua told them to say, "Stop sir! I am a Temple of the Holy Ghost!" The report of this lecture set the girls to giggling again, and it also explained why they teasingly referred to themselves as "Temple One" and "Temple Two."

The mother, however, did not laugh but instead said, "I think you girls are pretty silly. After all, that's what you are—Temples of the Holy Ghost." The teenagers can hardly believe their ears. This mother was just like Sister Perpetua. But the daughter heard her mother's words powerfully. "I am a Temple of the Holy Ghost, she said to herself, and was pleased with the phrase. It made her feel as if somebody had given her a present."[23]

22. Flannery O'Connor, "The Temple of the Holy Ghost," in *The Complete Stories* (New York: Farrar, Straus and Giroux, 1971), 236–48.
23. Ibid., 238.

2:22–3:9

One More Time: Good Leadership and Bad

Coming out of the previous passage, the Pastor has portrayed good leaders in the church as the finest implements of gold and silver adorning the table in the household of God, which is built on a firm foundation. He now circles back around to spell out exactly what "gold and silver" excellence means in terms of practical leadership style. Good leaders do not immaturely pursue their own passions and interests but seek out the interests of the gospel—righteousness, faith, love, and peace—and they do so in the company of others who are single-minded in their devotion to the gospel (2:22). They should avoid the tactics of the false teachers who "breed quarrels" and stir up a hornet's nest of "stupid and senseless controversies" (2:23).

This is all familiar territory. The pastor has honed in on this since the first verses of 1 Timothy. But suddenly a new ingredient is added. Up until this point, the false teachers have been viewed as the enemy, as the ones to be avoided. But now the ministry of the good leaders expands to include not only the loyal faithful but the false teachers, too. The good leaders are not to engage in theological duels with the false teachers but instead to be "kindly to everyone" (2:24). They are to correct the opponents, but with gentleness (2:25). The hope is, now that the table in the house of God is reset with the fine dishes and the exquisite tableware of sound leadership, even those who have swerved from the truth will change direction, repent, and come back home.

3:1–9

Culture Wars, Church Wars

The Pastor rounds out this broad section of the letter by placing the little controversies in the church in Ephesus in the context of larger shifts in the culture. Today we would say things like, "In the postmodern climate, there has been a collapse of trust in all metanarratives."

The Pastor in his context says, "In the last days, distressing times will come." It may be that the Pastor thinks that he is literally living "in the last days," on the brink of the end of the world, a conviction that we, now nearly twenty centuries later, know not to be the case. Or it may be that the Pastor is referring, more metaphorically, to a world that is always passing away in the light of the world that is promised in the great resurrection victory of God in Christ.

It almost doesn't matter. The Pastor is right, something about this world is in its "last days." Paradoxically, the world is the creation of a loving God, who proclaimed it to be "very good," and it is, at the same time, the fallen world in decay. It has shining oceans, stunning wildlife, and humanity bristling with the kind of creativity to produce works of genius in music, art, theater, and literature. And beneath that brilliance burns the bonfire of the vanities, consuming the greed, shame, and violence that lurk in all things. The Colombian philosopher and aphorist Nicolás Gómez Dávila was not unmindful of the world's beauty and richness when he nevertheless looked at our contemporary culture and said, "The Gospels and the Communist Manifesto are on the wane; the world's future lies in the power of Coca-Cola and pornography."[24] In other words, look closely at the world around us, and we will see that something out there is in the "last days."

There are always people who sense that the world as we know it is passing away, and with the old verities no longer secure, they grasp desperately for the next new thing. For the Pastor, the results of this are disastrous. People hoist anchor to escape a dying age but they have no charts to reach the next safe harbor. So people imagine that they are sailing on a perpetual party boat, turn in toward themselves, and become "lovers of themselves, lovers of money, boasters, arrogant, abusive, disobedient to their parents, ungrateful, unholy, inhuman, implacable, slanderers, profligates, brutes, haters of good, treacherous, reckless, swollen with conceit, lovers of pleasure rather than lovers of God" (3:2–4). That's a pretty dispiriting

24. Nicolás Gómez Dávila, *Escolios a un Texto Implícito: Selección* (Bogatá: Villegas Editores, 2001), 477. Uncredited English translation accessed at http://don-colacho.blogspot .com/2011/03/2983.html.

list, and things don't look up when it comes to religion. There, says the Pastor, people put on a pious show, wearing a holy face, but they don't take the faith seriously, telling the Gallup pollster that they are devoted to the church but living in ways that are tantamount to "denying its power" (3:5).

This is pretty strong negative language, and one has to raise an eyebrow here at the Pastor's sour analysis of culture. He sounds a bit like an old man living alone in a bleak house with all the shades drawn, a man who comes out onto the porch just long enough to blink in the sunlight and to bellow nasty insults at the neighborhood kids who have ventured into his yard to retrieve a soccer ball. "Get off my yard you arrogant, abusive, disobedient, ungrateful little slanderers!" Moreover, when has there been a time when there weren't lovers of money, conceited people, and pleasure seekers in the world? When was the "golden age" when people showed up for church with a completely unblemished conscience and really, really serious about Christian discipleship? The Pastor seems to think of these social breakdowns as signs of the end when they actually seem for all the world to be situation normal.

But even though we may think that the Pastor's language is overly dramatic and harsh, the voice he is using here is not grumpiness; it is the voice of apocalyptic. In apocalyptic language, the book of Revelation being a notable example, the world is described in highly symbolic, very dramatic, black and white terms. Worldly powers, such as the Roman Empire, are not merely earthly political forces; they are "the many-headed Beast with blasphemous names written on its heads" (see Rev. 13:1). In ordinary theological speech, we might say, "God will overcome all evil," but in apocalyptic language this gets ratcheted up a few notches to become, "Death and Hades will be thrown into the Lake of Fire" (see Rev. 20:14).

Often, educated Christians step around apocalyptic language, finding it "unreal" and leaving it to the fundamentalists and the fire-breathing preachers on the far end of the AM radio dial. But "apocalypse" actually means "unveiling," and far from being unreal, apocalyptic language is intended to disclose the hidden truth about reality so often disguised by banality and to show it at its most real. Apocalyptic language works like those moments in movies when there is a character we like and trust, but then the camera catches this character at a certain angle and we see a strange glint in his eye or hear a revealing hesitation in his voice, and suddenly we realize with a shock, "Oh my heavens, he's the villain!" Everything we had thought before must now be rethought. Apocalyptic language takes the beige landscape of ordinary life and turns up the color contrast, disclosing the battle between good and evil raging beneath the seemingly placid surface.

In Luther's time, Europe was changing economically. An economist would say that it was moving from a feudal economy to an early form of capitalism and that it was marked by unregulated markets. What Luther saw, however, was a sudden surge of the sin of avarice. Old relationships were breaking down and being replaced by selfishness and the profit motive, and money itself was being bought and sold by usurers at extortive rates of interest. So Luther described it as he saw it, and he employed apocalyptic language to do so:

> Accursed avarice and usury have utterly destroyed Germany.... Leipzig is sunk in avarice: in short *mundus est diabolic, Genitivi causus, Nominativi causus* ["The world is the Devil's, and the people in it have become pure devils."].... Come Lord Jesus, come, hearken to the sighing of Thy church, hasten Thy coming; wickedness is reaching its utmost limit; soon it must come to an end. Amen.... God must intervene and make an end, as He did with Sodom....[25]

When the historian R. H. Tawney read Luther's words about capitalism, he scoffed that Luther didn't understand economic complexities and that he was like a "savage introduced to a ... steam-engine. ... Attempts to explain the mechanism only enrage him; he can only repeat there's a devil in it."[26] Philosopher Norman O. Brown, however, recognized the unveiling power of Luther's apocalyptic language. "Tawney never sees," said Brown, "that the proposition 'there's a devil in it' is Luther's most profound attempt to explain."[27]

So when others would simply see everyday life rolling along as

---

25. Luther as quoted in Norman O. Brown, *Life against Death: The Psychoanalytical Meaning of History* (Middletown, CT: Wesleyan University Press, 1985), 219.
26. R. H. Tawney, *Religion and the Rise of Capitalism* (London: J. Murray, 1926), 89.
27. Brown, *Life against Death*, 219.

normal, the Pastor looks through apocalyptic lenses and sees "the last days" and the world unraveling before his eyes. He sees people scurrying through life, loving themselves, loving money, loving pleasure, and he sees not business as usual but what happens when people believe they are running out of time and kidding themselves that they are not. As a character in Walker Percy's novel *The Moviegoer* said, "Losing hope is not so bad. There's something worse: losing hope and hiding it from yourself."[28]

There was a television game show a few years back in which the contestants were given ninety seconds to race around the aisles of a supermarket with a cart, filling it with whatever they could grab. Pounds of filet mignon from the butcher's case, gallons of fudge ripple ice cream, boxes of doughnuts—whatever one desired. It was quite a parable of everyday life, normal, respectable people grabbing for themselves desperately, suddenly thrown into a frenzy all because they believed they were running out of time.

The main purpose of the Pastors' apocalyptic speech, and he considers this a matter of great significance ("You must understand this. . . ." [3:1]), is to set the troubles at Ephesus in context, to let the good elders know that the distress caused by the false teachers is a local outbreak of a larger cultural loss of faith and not simply an easily remedied local flap, and to heighten their resolve to stay firm in the gospel. The false teachers, like many others in these "last days," have lost their love for God and have become, in their own ways, house burglars, insinuating their way into the homes and the house churches at Ephesus (3:6–7). There they have taken advantage of (at least intellectually, perhaps sexually as well[29]) the vulnerable, especially some of the young, immature, impressionable, and unattached younger women.

In the NRSV translation, the Pastor calls the victims of the false teachers' deception "silly women" (3:6), but the Greek is literally the diminutive form of the word "women," that is "little women."[30] This may take a bit of sting out of the label, but even so, it is hardly flattering, and if the Pastor had known his short letter would end up

---

28. Walker Percy, *The Moviegoer* (New York: Knopf, 1961), 193.
29. Johnson, *The First and Second Letters to Timothy*, 414.
30. Jouette M. Bassler, *1 Timothy, 2 Timothy, Titus* (Nashville: Abingdon Press, 1996), 160.

in the Bible and could read his own words from the perspective of later generations, chances are good that this is yet another passage where he would have thought a second time about this irritable jab. There are two ways to attack false teachers, to condemn their ideas and to disparage their followers, and the Pastor employs both. Earlier he took on directly their ideas about the resurrection, and now he makes light of their admirers.

There is no way to avoid the patriarchal implication of this passage, and in fact, the Pastor is not inventing this swipe at "little women" who are always ready for instruction but who never gain true knowledge. Instead, he is drawing on a cultural reservoir of prejudice about women and philosophical learning. Epictetus, for example, snickered at certain women in Rome who carried around copies of Plato's *Republic* but completely misunderstood it, "for they attend only to the words of Plato, not to his meaning."[31] Beneath the stereotype, however, there was a two-sided reality, and we should look at both sides.

On the one hand, young, unattached women, some of them widowed at an early age, were a social concern for this Christian community (see comments on 1 Timothy 5:11–15). These women, either by virtue of their own wealth or because they had been placed on the widows charitable roll were people of means but not of occupation. They were unmarried, childless, and, because of the customs of the ancient world, formally uneducated. They were too old to be supervised by parents and too young and undeveloped to be seen as wise "mothers of the church," so they essentially lacked a well-defined social role. Along come the false teachers, with their mumbo-jumbo exegesis of Scripture, telling these young women how their talents had been hidden, how spiritually extraordinary they were or could be. This was a flattering message, one these women were eager to hear, and they had the financial means to make life good for the teachers who espoused it, so it was an arrangement that worked well for both parties. The women were mobile, moving freely among the various houses of the church and whispering that they had learned some truths that were far more interesting and meaningful than the

---

31. Epictetus, *Fragments*, 53, in *The Discourses of Epictetus with the Encheiridion and Fragments*, trans George Long (London: George Bell and Sons, 1877), 417.

dreary old message of the cross and the resurrection being taught by the traditional elders. Before long, the whole community erupts into a dispute over the "old faith" and the "new spirituality," and that is why we have the Pastoral Epistles in the first place.

So, from this point of view, we can understand the Pastor's exasperation over these "little women." The false teachers have preyed on their vulnerabilities and infected them with spiritual gibberish. Then the women spread the contagion from house to house, and the whole thing has blown up in the faces of the responsible elders. But there is another side to this, of course. The false teachers were deceptive, to be sure, but they did something the good elders neglected to do: they paid attention to the intellectual life of women in the community. We don't think for a moment that their motives were pure—there was money, and perhaps sex, involved. But the young women responded to them not because they were silly gossips or salacious but because they wanted to be alert, informed, and significant members of the church. The Pastor is putting out a roaring brush fire and, consequently, can see only one side of the equation. Fortunately, subsequent generations of Christians have realized the urgency of the other side too.

> What she didn't understand, she being spiritual and seeing religion as spirit, was that it took religion to save me from the spirit world, from orbiting the earth like Lucifer and the angels, that it took nothing less . . . eating Christ himself to make me mortal man again and let me inhabit my own flesh and love her in the morning.
>
> Walker Percy, *Love in the Ruins* (New York: Picador, 1999), 254.

As a way of encouraging the good elders to carry on faithfully, the Pastor trots out a piece of folklore: the story of Jannes and Jambres (3:8–9). According to legend, these two were magicians in Pharaoh's court who used their magic tricks to oppose Moses and Aaron and to seduce the Hebrews away from the worship of Yahweh.[32] In other words, the Pastor is saying, don't think that the false teachers at Ephesus are all that innovative. People have been trying to lure the

---

32. Benjamin Fiore, *The Pastoral Epistles*, Sacra Pagina Series, ed. Daniel J. Harrington (Collegeville, MN: Liturgical Press, 2009), 12:168.

faithful away with hocus-pocus deceptions since the very beginning. Jannes and Jambres were foiled, and so will be the false teachers, because when all is said and done, "their folly will become plain to everyone" (3:9).

2 Timothy 3:10–4:22

This letter, which has been personal from the beginning, becomes even more intimate now as it draws to its close. The Pastor, speaking as always in the voice of the apostle Paul, introduces personal details from Paul's life as examples of the kind of enduring ministry that the entire letter has advocated. So personal is this section that, in many places, we will find ourselves referring at times to Paul (meaning the historical figure) as well as to "Paul" (the symbolic author of the letter) and to "the Pastor," the actual author, in order to underscore the deeply autobiographical character and intention of this section of the letter.

3:10–17
Staying on the Path of Faith

3:10–13 What Persecutions I Endured!

We can imagine that a candidate for President of the United States, in the middle of the long series of state primaries, might give a speech with this rhetorical flourish: "We were strong in Iowa, victorious in New Hampshire, triumphant in South Carolina! Now it's on to Florida and Michigan!" Here "Paul" also lists a series of geographical locations—Antioch, Iconium, Lystra—and it is no less powerful rhetorically, even though the theme here is not joyous triumph but faithful suffering.

Antioch, Iconium, and Lystra were towns in Asia Minor visited by Paul on his first missionary journey (see Acts 13–14), and in each town Paul's preaching generated both positive response and enraged opposition, including threatened or actual violence. The accounts of Paul's missionary exploits were surely well-known among the early Christian communities, the tales of his experiences told and retold in Ephesus and in the other churches. Just to say the names "Antioch, Iconium, and Lystra" was like saying "Birmingham, Selma, and Memphis" in the recounting of the history of the civil rights movement. The readers of 2 Timothy remembered these stories, so what they read in the letter was the drumbeat of the names—Antioch, Iconium, Lystra—but what they remembered in their minds was something like "run out of town in Antioch, received death threats in Iconium, pummeled with stones in Lystra, all for the sake of the gospel." Then it is almost as if "Paul" lifts his quill from the papyrus, looks off into space, shakes his head in wonder, and writes, "What persecutions I endured!" This is a rhetorical device, of course, a naming and thus a confirming of what the readers are already feeling: "My goodness, did Paul forever take a beating in his ministry!"

This moment of poignant reflection on the texture of Paul's work, the memory of his relentless commitment, unshakable faith, and unwavering determination in the face of severe opposition, moves in two directions. First, it looks back over the life of Paul and lifts up Paul's own ministry ("my teaching, my conduct, my aim in life, my faith, my patience, my love, my steadfastness, my persecutions, and my suffering" 3:10–11) as a powerful example of what is essential and good about Christian ministry in the middle of a hurricane of conflict. Second, it serves to encourage such steadfastness and faith in the leaders at Ephesus. The Lord rescued Paul from every snare and danger (3:11), and the good elders at Ephesus can expect the same.

In fact, the good elders at Ephesus can expect to receive the same as Paul did in both senses: the protection of God *and* the persecutions of opponents. When "Paul" says, "Indeed, all who want to live a godly life in Christ Jesus will be persecuted" (3:12), he means something far more profound and mysterious than "the other high school students will tease you because you bring your Bible to class." Whenever faithful people and congregations embody in this world the life of God, the values of "the beloved community" promised for all in the reign of God, the snakes start coming out of their holes. When Christians try to follow the "Prince of Peace" and take seriously his command to "put your sword away," the gun zealots go on an angry offensive, including some mangled congregations that sneer at the word of Jesus by raffling off automatic weapons in worship. Let a neighborhood church decide to offer the hospitality of Christ by providing hot meals and a warm overnight shelter for homeless, and the cries of "you're destroying property values" are soon to come. Let a pastor try to display the wideness of God's mercy and love by presiding at the wedding of his lesbian daughter, and someone will try to run him out of the ministry.

Why? These are not simply honest disagreements over hot-button cultural issues; this is roused hatred. When the reign of God is a spiritualized abstraction, no one minds. It poses no threat. But when someone tries to live out God's life in this time and place, it is bound to stir up a fight. And this is not merely because one opinion is set out against another or that people who are not religious snub their noses at people who are. This is because when the light of God's future shines into the present, it exposes the decay and injustice of the world as it is. Wall Street glitters, glitters that is until a St. Francis or a Mother Teresa shows up, then the seamier side of greed is thrown into sharp relief.

Not only does the lived gospel unmask the decay in the world as it is, it also exposes the impermanence of this present age. War, racism, economic injustice, and oppression aren't just evil, they are also obsolete, passé, destined to be thrown on the scrap heap by the coming of God's kingdom. When God's life is made visible in advance to those who have sunk all of their investments into this world, it signals clearly that they have made a foolish investment. As philosopher Nicolás Gómez Dávila once quipped, "The fool is disturbed not when they tell him that his ideas are false, but when they suggest that they have gone out of style."[1]

In the book of Revelation, there is an apocalyptic scene in which a war breaks out in heaven between the forces of God, represented

---

1. Nicolás Gómez Dávila, *Escolios a un Texto Implícito: Selección* (Bogatá: Villegas Editores, 2001), 62. Uncredited English translation accessed at http://don-colacho.blogspot .com/2010/01/intelligence-wisdom-stupidity.html.

by Michael and the angels, and the forces of evil, in the form of a dragon and his angels. The dragon is mortally wounded and cast out of heaven down to the earth, where the old serpent writhes around in fearsome power and rage. It is a metaphor for evil in this world—powerful, angry, dangerous, and seemingly unstoppable—but then the heavenly chorus sings a word both of warning and reassurance. The bad news? "Beware of the dragon; he is vicious and angry." The good news, "The reason he's so angry is that his time is short; his time for destruction is passing away" (see Rev. 12:7–12).

Paul agrees with Revelation. The old snake is stirred up by the presence of the holy, and it's only going to get worse before it gets better (3:13). The false teachers are not only deceivers but also deceived themselves. They are blind pilots flying an off-course airliner full of hoodwinked passengers.

> The New Testament is a brutal destroyer of human illusions. If you follow Jesus and don't end up dead, it appears you have some explaining to do. The stark signifier of the human condition is one who spoke up for love and justice and was done to death for his pains. The traumatic truth of human history is a mutilated body.
>
> Terry Eagleton, *Reason, Faith, and Revolution* (New Haven: Yale University Press, 2010), 27.

3:14–17 But as for You

"Paul" returns to a familiar theme, the need for "Timothy" to continue on the path of the traditional faith that he was taught and which he has believed (3:14). "Paul" reminds him of the two main reliable resources that have served to carve out this reservoir of faith in him: the people who have taught him and Scripture.

As for the people who taught him the faith, "Paul" encourages "Timothy" to remember "from whom you learned it" (3:14). The word "whom" in Greek is singular in some manuscripts that we have of this letter, but it is plural in the most reliable manuscripts. "Timothy" learned the gospel from Paul, but not just from Paul. His teachers were also his grandmother Lois, his mother, Eunice, and probably others (1:5). The text implies a constellation of faithful people gathered around "Timothy" from his childhood on, forming and preserving in him the Christian faith. Probably some later scribes who were copying this passage, either desiring to underscore Paul's importance or believing that the text itself referred to Paul alone as Timothy's teacher, changed the plural "whom" to a singular form.

The point of this advice for "Timothy" to remember his teachers is not just that Timothy should recall what they taught but also that he should remember who they were: people who held steady to the gospel when others wandered away, people who were sustained by God in times of trouble and persecution. The doctrinal content they imparted to "Timothy" is important, but so is the texture of their faithful lives.

The second resource for "Timothy" is Scripture, the "sacred writings," which Timothy has known since his childhood (4:15). Ironically, what the Pastor says here about Scripture has, over the generations, been the occasion for that "wrangling over words" (2:14) that the Pastor wants good leaders to avoid. The church, especially the Protestant wing, has been eager to get to the point of precision about the nature and authority of Scripture as an inspired text, and this is one of the few passages in the canon in which the Bible seems to be talking about itself.

What the Pastor says is that "all Scripture is inspired by God." The word "inspired" in Greek is *theopneustos,* which literally means "God-breathed." Some have latched onto that phrase in order to argue that every word of the Bible—nay, every syllable, every consonant and vowel—was dictated by the breath of God, that is, by the Spirit of God. Since God is perfect, the argument goes, then whatever comes from God's breath must be perfect and without error. Others counter, "But wait, there *are* errors in the Bible, errors of scientific and historical fact, errors of grammar." And then the response, "Well, if those are truly errors, then they were introduced by later scribes. They weren't there in the original writings, which were free of any flaws." And on the wrangling goes.

It is important to note that this text, on which so many theories of biblical inspiration have been erected, is actually not all that clear. In the first place, in Greek, this verse can be rendered in at least three possible—and equally valid—constructions. Is the Pastor saying "*all* Scripture is inspired and is useful" (which would mean that every part of Scripture is "inspired"), or is he saying "taken as a whole, Scripture is inspired" (thus placing the emphasis on the core truth of Scripture rather than specific texts, sentences, and words), or is he saying "every Scripture *that is* inspired is useful" (meaning some writings are inspired but not all of them)? The latter reading would fit into the dispute at Ephesus since the false teachers surely had writings they looked to as authoritative, so "Paul" would be saying, "They have their writings and we have ours. Don't trust every writing, only those that are truly inspired and able to instruct us." The Greek, however, can be rendered in any of these various ways.

The NRSV, as is the case with most English translations, chooses to go with the former: "all Scripture is inspired. . . ." But even here, it is not fully evident what the Pastor would consider to be "Scripture." Almost surely the Old Testament, which was the first Bible of the early Christians. But anything else? It's too early for a New Testament canon, but biblical scholar John P. Meier, among others, has found an allusion, perhaps a quotation, from the Gospel of Luke named as "Scripture" in 1 Timothy 5:18. So maybe, Meier suggests, the Gospel of Luke is "on the fast track to canonization" in the Pauline churches and is included by the Pastor in inspired Scripture.[2] How about the other Gospels? Or letters of Paul? What about 2 Timothy itself? Surely the Pastor doesn't mean to include his own letter in "all Scripture," but of course, later Christians have made it a part of the scriptural canon. What exactly constitutes "Scripture" for the writer of this letter? We don't know for sure.

However we decide these questions, though, the main point is that 2 Timothy 3:16 is not a systematic theology of Scripture and was not intended to be. The Pastor is not arguing that the Scripture is inspired; he's assuming it and moving on to his real point, which is not what Scripture *is* but instead how Scripture should be *used*—"for teaching, for reproof, for correction, and for training in righteousness" (3:16). Taken as a whole, the sentence conveys the sense, "Since we all know that the holy writings are the gift of God's Spirit, don't neglect to use them to inform, shape, and correct your own faith and the faith of the church."

2. John P. Meier, "The Inspiration of Scripture: But What Counts as Scripture? (2 Tim 1:1–14; 3:14–17; cf 1 Tim 5:18)," *Midstream* 38/1–2 (January–April 1999): 77–78.

> We must not try the Scriptures by our apprehensions, but our apprehensions by the Scriptures.
>
> Richard Baxter, *The Practical Works of the Rev. Richard Baxter* (London: James Duncan, 1830), 5.559.

The dispute at Ephesus is never far from the mind of the Pastor. Consequently this passage about the usefulness of Scripture probably has in mind the misuse of Scripture at the hands of the false teachers. *They* use Scripture to run right past the traditional interpretations and to play word games with the holy writings, finding there all kinds of strange spiritualized myths and genealogical codes with secret meanings (1 Tim. 1:4), but that's not the real purpose of Scripture, which is to "instruct you for salvation through faith in Jesus Christ" (3:15). "Salvation" here refers to a whole way of life, living the life of those who are redeemed by Jesus Christ, not to a momentary decision of belief. Scripture trains the faithful, "everyone who belongs to God" (3:17), in the life of salvation so that the church can body forth in the world proficient in the gospel and "equipped for every good work" (3:17).

FURTHER REFLECTIONS
How Seriously Should We Take the Pastor's Alarm?

This swath of 2 Timothy, which places the dispute at Ephesus into an apocalyptic context, shows with increased intensity just how seriously "Paul" takes the threat posed by the false teachers at Ephesus. They are house burglars and deceivers whose very appearance is much more than a simple irritant in the life of an early congregation. The dust-up at Ephesus is, in the Pastor's view, an ominous sign of the "last days" and the treacherous, unholy, godless blasphemies that age will usher in.

The question for readers today is, How grievously should we take this problem in our own time? Conversations about the kind of spirituality advocated by the false teachers, a spiritual escapism that sets one free from the strictures of the body, including the institutional church, are commonplace today in a "spiritual but not religious" culture. And alternative views of the resurrection, which the pastor fears "will spread like gangrene," are the routine curriculum in many adult education classes in churches these days. People who look very much like the "false teachers" of Ephesus are still very much with us, indeed are key players and leaders in many Christian communities.

In some ways, the Pastor's warnings should come to us like Charles Dickens's tale *A Christmas Carol*. Old Ebenezer Scrooge is visited deep in the night by three spirits, the Ghost of Christmas Past, the Ghost of Christmas Present, and the Ghost of Christmas Future. He learns who he was, the terrible truth of who he has become, and what might lie ahead in the future. Terrified by what he sees and hears, Scrooge wakes up a new man, ready to be what he has not been before: loving and generous. In the same way, Christian leaders today can see the words of the Pastor, especially these apocalyptic sections, as the visits of the ghosts of Christmas. They are exaggerated, they are frightening, they haunt us, but we do wake up from them, alert and ready to exorcise the past and to exercise sound and generous ministry in the church.

What we see in the Ghost of Christmas Past is the powerful heritage we have from the gospel of Jesus Christ. Taught to us by parents and patient teachers, modeled by fearless leaders like Paul and Luther and Sojourner Truth and Dorothy Day and Martin Luther King Jr., this gospel faith has given new meaning and life. What we learn from the Ghost of Christmas Present is that the leadership of the church has, in a spirit of cowardice, allowed weeds to grow in the garden of the church. "Better" gospels and more "sophisticated" spiritualities have crowded into church and culture to rival and replace the gospel. What the Ghost of Christmas Future warns is that, left unchecked, these new renditions of the gospel will leave people ethically adrift, without anchor, wind, or harbor.

The upshot is that the gospel always needs strong teachers and advocates. In a very practical sense, people may momentarily be flattered by a spirituality that emphasizes airy freedom, creativity, and escape, but eventually all of us will come face-to-face with our embodiment and our place as creatures in time and place. Our own bodies will age. We will, most of us, deal with marriages needing vigilant care, with vexed parenting relationships, with demanding friendships, with parents in bodily and perhaps mental decline. If we do not have an embodied theology that makes sense of the suffering entanglements of real human relationships, we will be given over to despair. But, as the Pastor would counsel, look at Jesus. . . . look at Paul . . . there you see the true gospel, grace made perfect in weakness and suffering. Therein lies life.

What this finally calls us to do is not to go on the hunt for heresy and heretics—which of us could stand a full theological checkup anyway? Even the Pastor, in the heat of the battle, has at his best more charity than that. What it calls on us to do is to "proclaim the message" (4:2), to be good, patient, diligent, caring pastors and leaders, to preach the gospel "whether the time is favorable or unfavorable," to hang in there with people "with the utmost patience in teaching" (4:2).

Perhaps no Reformation figure was more insistent on right doctrine and piety than the pastor and theologian John Calvin. He faced his own false teachers, and he, like the Pastor, did not indulge in niceties. In fact, in his commentary on 2 Timothy, he said that the false teachers' claim about the resurrection, namely, that it had already happened, "means that they invented some kind of allegorical resurrection, as has been attempted in our day. Through this trick Satan overthrows the fundamental article of our faith concerning the resurrection of the body." Calvin urged his contemporaries that "such an example should arouse us to diligent watchfulness so that we are quick to ward off such plagues from ourselves and others."[3]

This sounds, of course, like a shrill call to arms to purge the church of wrong thinking, but Calvin was a pastor as well as a theologian, and what this translated into in the life of the church at Geneva was not witch hunting but pastoral care. The minutes of the meetings of the Consistory (the pastor and the elders) of the church in Geneva in Calvin's day show that members of the community were routinely asked to meet with the elders and to "explain the creed," that is, to talk about their understanding of the gospel. Some could, some stammered, some drew a blank. These church members were also expected to speak to the elders about their personal lives, and the

---

3. John Calvin, *1, 2 Timothy and Titus* in *The Crossway Classic Commentaries*, ed. Alister McGrath and J. I. Packer (Wheaton: Crossway, 1998), 139.

elders encountered the usual manifestations of human weakness, from lax church attendance to drunkenness to divorce to fornication and more. The counsel of the elders was mostly some combination of sincere repentance, going to "the sermon" (worship), and saying daily the creed and the Lord's Prayer.

In short, like the author of the Pastoral Epistles, the leaders in Geneva took with profound seriousness the great gospel tradition and jealously guarded it. But for those members of the community who had fallen prey to bad teaching, or who had no teaching, or who couldn't manage to drag themselves out of bed or tavern to attend worship, or for whom life had become morally frayed, the Geneva leaders, also like the author of the Pastorals, met their ethical and doctrinal faltering not with a club but with a parental hand, desiring that "everyone who belongs to God may be proficient, equipped for every good work" (3:17).

4:1–5

To Sum It Up: Carry Out Your Ministry Fully

The Pastor is now circling the airport, getting ready to land. Here he sums up the essence of everything he has been saying to "Timothy," and therefore to the leaders at Ephesus. The Pastor signals the importance of these concluding instructions by uttering a solemn oath. If he were in a court of law he would have placed his hand on the Bible, raised his right hand, and said, "I do solemnly swear. . . ." But the Pastor is in no ordinary courthouse. He is standing instead in the great court of God at the end of time, the court where Jesus Christ is the judge of the living and the dead. "In the presence of God and of Christ Jesus, who is to judge the living and the dead, and in view of his appearing and his kingdom, I solemnly urge you . . . ," intones the Pastor.

Why the solemn oath language? The Pastor is not trying to frighten the leaders at Ephesus, saying in effect, "You'd better do what I say because you're going to be judged by Christ if you don't." He is rather casting the light of God's ultimate kingdom on the everyday practice of ministry. When all is said and done, what will really count is what matters in the light of Jesus Christ. This is important to say because, in this world, other standards of evaluation compete for our attention. Pastors today are notorious for comparing (sometimes secretly) their success in ministry by the size of membership or budget or building, and the Pastor is saying, "None of that matters. What matters is only that ministry that can stand unashamed on that day when Jesus Christ is revealed as all in all."

Thornton Wilder's play *Our Town* is set in the small town of Grover's Corners. In one pivotal scene, a young woman, Emily, has died in childbirth, and the townsfolk have gathered in the cemetery for her funeral. But when the funeral is ended, the deceased Emily is not ready to depart to the next world, not ready to go to her rest. She convinces the Stage Manager, who is a somewhat Godlike figure, to take her back for one last earthly experience, back to one happy day in her life, her twelfth birthday. So she goes, but it turns out to be a painful experience because she now sees life from the point of view of her death, and she cannot understand how her mother and the others in her family can take life for granted. So she returns to her grave, but as she goes, she makes a speech to her mother, a speech the theater audience can hear but her mother cannot:

> Oh, Mama, look at me one minute as though you really saw me. Mama, fourteen years have gone by. I'm dead. You're a grandmother, Mama! Wally's dead, too. His appendix burst on a camping trip to North Conway. We felt just terrible about it—don't you remember? But, just for a moment now we're all together. Mama, just for a moment we're happy. Let's really look at one another! . . . We don't have time to look at one another. I didn't realize. So all that was going on and we never noticed. . . . One more look. Good-bye, Good-bye world. Good-bye, Grover's Corners. . . . Mama and Papa. Good-bye to clocks ticking—and my butternut tree! . . . and Mama's sunflowers. And food and coffee. And new ironed dresses and hot baths . . . and sleeping and waking up. Oh, earth, you're too wonderful for anybody to realize you! Do any human beings ever realize life while they live it—every, every minute?

The Stage Manager, who can hear Emily's words, answers "No."

Then he pauses and adds, "The saints and poets, maybe they do some."[4]

Wilder was making something of the same point for the audience that the Pastor is making for his. When we look at life from the end of things, what counts changes. The people of Grover's Corners, caught in the swirl of everyday life, could not appreciate what really counts. Only Emily, now in the afterlife, could appreciate what truly matters. In Jesus' parable of the Rich Man and Lazarus (Luke 16:19–31), a rich man feasts lavishly every day while remaining oblivious to a beggar, a man named Lazarus, at his very gate. But then comes the dramatic end: Both men die. Lazarus is carried by the angels to be with Abraham while the rich man is tormented in Hades. Seeing things now from the perspective of the afterlife, the rich man realizes he has missed everything that was important about life, and he asks Abraham to send Lazarus to warn his five brothers so that they will not make the same mistake. Abraham replies, "They have Moses and the prophets; they should listen to them." In other words, it's all in the Scriptures; they should read them and obey. The rich man protests that if Lazarus would go to them from the dead, it would make more of an impression than the Bible, because the Bible is around all the time. Abraham rejects the rich man's request, saying, "If they don't listen to Moses and the prophets, neither will they be convinced, even if someone rises from the dead." The irony of this ending of the parable is apparent. Jesus Christ did rise from the dead, and his resurrection validated what had been said and done by Moses and the prophets. But people continue to live in oblivion, even though someone has come to them from the dead.

The Pastor is pulling back the curtains on the end of all things, when Jesus Christ will judge the living and the dead, and saying, "I am now going to tell you what will really count about ministry when the kingdom breaks through and all is seen for what it really is. I will be Moses and the prophets for you and instruct you, here in the midst of time and circumstance, about the kind of ministry that will be seen as worthy on that day."

What counts in ministry, according to the Pastor, are two things:

---

4. Thornton Wilder, *Our Town*, act 3.

faithful preaching and sound teaching. First, "Timothy" is urged to preach the word, which means more than simply "preach the Bible." It means to preach the whole gospel message—gathered up in Jesus Christ, witnessed to in Scripture, fleshed out in the lives of faithful people like Paul and Eunice and Lois, and embodied in the church that lives out the "love that comes from a pure heart, a good conscience, and sincere faith" (1 Tim. 1:5). In other words, "Timothy" is to proclaim the entirety of the Christian life, and he is to be persistent in doing regardless of the conditions for hearing that preaching. If the season is favorable or not, if the weather is fair or foul, if the soil is rich or poor, if people open their ears or close their hearts— no matter; "Timothy" is to preach the word.

> That is what we are to do, tell the good news of what God has done for us in Jesus Christ, the good news of the coming reign of God, the good news of the power of the gospel to change and transform lives even in this 21st century. It is to be proclaimed to all, even if only received by some. . . . Tell them of Jesus Christ, tell them that he was born in Bethlehem, brought up in Nazareth, baptized in the Jordan, tempted in the wilderness, preached in Galilee, was arrested in Gethsemane, tried in Caesar's court, died on Calvary's cross, and rose from Joseph's tomb. Tell it! Tell it when you are up and tell it when you are down. Tell it when all is well and tell it when all is hell. Tell it when you are well received, and tell it when you are absolutely not believed. Tell it until sinners are justified. Tell it until hell is terrified. Tell it until Jesus is magnified. And tell it until God is satisfied.
>
> Cleophus LaRue, "Why Bother?" (sermon, *Day 1 Radio*, October 12, 2008), http://day1.org/1114 -why_bother.

Second, "Timothy" is to perform the work of a sound teacher, not merely conveying content but guiding the learners so that they can "take hold of the life that is really life" (1 Tim. 6:19). The sound teacher aims to "convince, rebuke, and encourage" (4:2). To convince is to persuasively explain the faith so that it becomes clear why it is the path that leads to life. To rebuke is to warn people away from false paths that may look promising but lead only to washed-out bridges, dismal swamps, and sudden and steep cliffs of fall. To encourage is to stand along the pilgrim path of the Christian life, offering cups of water to the weary travelers, exhorting them to finish the journey and to stay on the path. Good teachers do all of these things "with utmost patience" (4:2), aware that disciples sometimes take a step or two back before moving forward, wander off the path in heavy fog, or fall in exhaustion in the middle of the journey and need tender care.

"Paul" warns "Timothy" that staying steady as a preacher and teacher will not be easy because bad times are coming. Of course, these future bad times predicted by "Paul" are the actual bad times being endured by the present church at Ephesus. "For the time is coming," cautions "Paul," and what follows is a perfect description of the current crisis at Ephesus. The people will have had their fill of sound teaching and will browse around for something new and more satisfying. They have "itching ears" or want "to have their ears tickled," or as we would put it, "they want to hear things that entertain them, make them feel good, and flatter them into thinking well of themselves." So they get what they want. They find teachers who will say what they want to hear, who will titillate them with baloney disguised as "the really spiritual truths" and cardboard myths painted up to look like the real thing.

This is, of course, a chronic problem in the church. "The time is coming when people will not put up with sound doctrine" (4:3) and that time is always coming and has always been and always will be. What goes around comes around, and a century or so after 2 Timothy, Clement of Alexandria faced his own band of false teachers—the Sophist philosophers in his case—who were willing to pump out gaseous chatter designed to tickle peoples' ears. He wrote,

> Inflated with this art of theirs, the wretched Sophists, babbling away in their own jargon; toiling their whole life about the division of names and the nature of the composition and conjunction of sentences, show themselves greater chatterers than turtle-doves; scratching and tickling . . . the ears of those who wish to be tickled.[5]

---

5. Clement of Alexandria, *The Stromata*, book 1, chap. 3, from *Ante-Nicene Fathers, vol. 2*, ed. Alexander Roberts, James Donaldson, and A. Cleveland Coxe, trans. William Wilson (Buffalo, NY: Christian Literature Publishing Co., 1885), 304.

So the Pastor says that people will forever be seeking out their gurus, their spiritual guides, their mystical personal trainers, their new age prophets, but good teachers are to stay the course. "As for you," he writes to "Timothy" (4:5), "always be sober," that is, be temperate, even-keeled, sturdy. Be ready to "endure suffering" (just as "Paul" did [see 3:10–11]), because it will surely come. And, of all the titles one could covet, the only one worth having is "evangelist," that is, one who patiently plants and nourishes the good news in peoples' lives. Finally, don't merely dabble in ministry, wishing all the while that you were somebody else, doing something else—a tailor, a goatherd, a Greek philosopher, a rock star, a therapist, or a celebrated novelist—but instead "carry out your ministry fully," with an abundance of energy, confidence, commitment, and joy.

4:6–22

Farewell

4:6–8 "Paul" as Libation, "Paul" as Athlete

"Paul" now bids adieu, both in the smaller sense of ending this letter and in the larger sense of anticipating his own departure in death. As he describes his approaching death, "Paul" employs two metaphors to summarize his life. In the first, which the Pastor probably borrowed from Paul's Letter to the Philippians (see Phil. 2:17), he says that he is "being poured out as a libation." The image, a common one in antiquity, is of a cup of wine or blood being poured out at an altar as a sign of sacrifice and devotion to a god. When Philo of Alexandria was explaining Jewish ceremonies and feasts to his Hellenistic audience, he described the blood poured around the altar in the burnt offerings as "the libation of life" and the pouring of this libation as a sign of a desire to please God:

> And the blood is poured out in a circle all around the altar, because a circle is the most complete of all figures, and also in order that no part whatever may be left empty and unoccupied

by the libation of life; for, to speak properly, the blood is the libation of the life. Therefore the law here symbolically teaches us
that the mind, which is always performing its dances in a circle,
is by every description of words, and intentions, and actions
which it adopts, always showing its desire to please God.[6]

Thus, "Paul' portrays his own life as an offering to God, a pouring
out of himself in devotion. The cup is nearly empty now, and "the
time of my departure has come" (4:6).

Then "Paul" quickly changes metaphorical direction and enters
into the world of athletics. First he presents himself as a wrestler who
has "fought the good fight," then as a runner who has "finished the
race," but the point is that he has "kept the faith" (4:7) throughout
the long course of his ministry with the same intensity as the well-
trained, single-minded, persevering athlete that he earlier encouraged "Timothy" to be (see 2:5). Olympic athletes today compete for
the gold, silver, and bronze medals, but in the ancient world the tro-
phy in an athletic contest was a garland wreath placed as a crown on
the head of the winner.[7] Just so, "Paul" anticipates that his endurance in ministry will be rewarded with "the crown of righteousness,"
which Christ, the Lord of all, will place on his head on that Great
Judgment Day. But "Paul" does not think of himself as the lonely,
long-distance runner. The winner's crown is not for him alone, but
for all the children of the kingdom who have kept their eyes on the
prize, fought the good fight, and run the race, clinging to the hope
promised in the kingdom (4:8).

4:9–22 God in the Details

As is the case in Greco-Roman letters generally and in Pauline letters in particular, the last section is reserved for closing minutiae and
details. Letters and emails today often conclude in the same fashion—"say hello to George," "enjoy the trip to France," "call us if you

6. Philo, *The Special Laws,* book 1, chap. 38, *The Works of Philo Judaeus,* trans. by Charles
Duke Yonge, adapted by Peter Kirby (London: H. G. Bohn, 1854), http://www
.earlychristianwritings.com/yonge/book27.html.
7. Luke Timothy Johnson, *The First and Second Letters to Timothy,* The Anchor Bible, vol. 35a
(New York: Doubleday, 2001), 366.

plan to be in Chicago," "hope Lisa gets good news from her doctor," "sorry I left my cell phone in your car, please send it if it's not too much trouble," that sort of thing.

These sorts of details are included here. "Paul" wants and needs "Timothy" to visit soon (4:9) and encourages him to make the trip before winter makes travel even more hazardous (4:21). He asks "Timothy" to bring his cloak and some books and parchments when he comes (4:13). Scholars have puzzled about why "Paul" would want any of these things, especially since he is ostensibly writing from prison and has just announced that he is near death. Some have suggested that, since the original readers of this letter knew that this is not from the actual Paul to the actual Timothy, these details are symbolic. The "parchments," for example, may refer to the Scriptures, the importance of which has just been discussed (3:15–17). This may be the case, but if so, the allusions are pretty subtle, and there is nothing else in the text itself to push us toward seeing cloaks, books, and parchments as anything other than what they appear to be on the surface.

We are on firmer ground when we recognize that the Pastor has shifted ground thematically and theologically in this final section of the letter. "Paul" is no longer the dying apostle leaving the legacy of his ministry to "Timothy." He is now the "Paul" who stood firm in his ministry of preaching to the Gentiles (4:17) and whose controversial ministry divided the house. Some stayed loyal to him, and some others abandoned him. Some sixteen names are mentioned in the closing fourteen verses of the letter; some of the names we recognize from elsewhere in the New Testament and others appear only here. These people are probably well known to the readers as persons who played some role in the ministry of Paul.

The theme that runs through this recitation of names seems to be the distinction between those who stayed in the Pauline camp and those who betrayed and abandoned him. Demas, for example, appears to be a coworker with Paul and in good standing when he is mentioned in Colossians 4:14. But something went wrong; he fell "in love with this present world" and has now deserted "Paul" and gone to Thessalonica (4:9). Alexander the Coppersmith opposed "Paul's" message and acted destructively toward "Paul," doing him great harm (4:14). And these two are representative of a larger group who deserted "Paul" at a critical time, when he was making his defense before the Roman authorities (see Acts 22).

On the other hand, Luke has remained with Paul (4:11), Mark is "useful" in "Paul's" ministry, Tychicus and Titus (who is the recipient of the third letter in the Pastoral Epistles) are still at work in the shared mission (4:10,12), the couple Prisca and Aquila, who once "risked their necks" for Paul (Rom. 16:3), remain in the fold, as is Onesiphorus, whom we met in 1:16 as a man not ashamed of "Paul's" chains (4:19). Eubulus, Pudens, Linus, and Claudia are among the company of brothers and sisters supporting "Paul" (4:21).

For some of the other names we have to guess on which side of the ledger they fall. Crescens, for example, is a name mentioned only in this letter. He is said to have "gone to Galatia," but why? Has he gone, like Demas, as an act of desertion or, like Tychicus, as a loyal Pauline missionary? Probably the latter, but the original readers would almost surely have known the lore about Crescens that we don't know and, thus, would have been able to fill in the missing details.

Even with the missing pieces, though, the main picture is clear: a drama of loyalty and abandonment played out in the life of Paul is now being replayed in the church at Ephesus. For Paul, some opposed his message; others supported him. Some people were "useful" to him in his ministry, and others were destructive. Some people risked their necks for Paul and the gospel, while others lost their zeal and fell in love with money and the things of this world. "Tell me the old, old story," and it is happening all over again in Ephesus.

If the contention, betrayal, and villainy that marked Paul's ministry are being reprised in the church at Ephesus, the Pastor wants to assure them that the outcome for Paul will also be reprised. What was true for Paul will be true for his legacy and for those who exercise good leadership and loyalty to the gospel: "The Lord will rescue me from every evil attack and save me for his heavenly kingdom. To him be the glory forever and ever. Amen" (4:18).

"Paul's" final words to "Timothy" may echo the liturgy of the earliest church,[8] but wherever they come from they are the blessing every minister needs: "The Lord be with your spirit. Grace be with you."

---

8. Benjamin Fiore, *The Pastoral Epistles: First Timothy, Second Timothy, Titus*, Sacra Pagina Series, ed. Daniel J. Harrington (Collegeville, MN: Liturgical Press, 2009), 12:188.

TITUS

Titus 1–3

1:1–4

For the Sake of Faith and Truth

The first two Pastoral Epistles, 1 and 2 Timothy, presented themselves as letters from the apostle Paul to a beloved coworker and disciple, Timothy. As we argued, these letters were probably actually written by an author we have called "the Pastor" near the end of the first century, late enough that Paul and probably Timothy are almost surely dead (see discussion of "Paul" in the comments on 1 Timothy 1:12). The death of Paul would have been news well-known among early Christians, so the original recipients of 1 and 2 Timothy were aware that they were receiving a letter from a symbolic "Paul." "Paul's" words of warning, encouragement, and counsel constituted the voice of the Pauline legacy projected into the life of a conflicted church a generation later. Likewise, the "Timothy" of the first two letters is a symbolic representation of an ideal minister and church leader following in the Pauline tradition.

Now, in the Letter to Titus, we find the third and shortest epistle from the hand of the Pastor. Much about this third letter is reminiscent of the first two. Again, wise pastoral leadership and faithful guidance of a Christian community are the issues on the table. And once again "Paul" is writing to a beloved companion and disciple, this time to "Titus," whom we know from other New Testament references as Paul's "partner and coworker" (2 Cor. 8:23), a Greek (Gal. 2:3) who evidently had a warm and consoling personality (2 Cor. 7:6,13) and who shared Paul's zeal for faithful evangelization (2 Cor. 12:18). In the first two Pastorals, "Timothy" is described as "my loyal child" (1 Tim. 1:2) and "my beloved child" (2 Tim. 1:2), and now "Titus" is addressed in equally affectionate terms, as "my loyal child in the faith we share" (1:4), as one who has a father-son relationship to "Paul." "Titus" is pictured as having been left behind by Paul on the island of Crete (1:5), although there is no other evidence that the historical Paul was ever on that island.

Oddly, for one with such a close relationship to Paul, Titus is never mentioned in the Book of Acts, whereas Timothy appears prominently. Some scholars have wondered if Titus is simply a nickname for Timothy and that, in the historical ministry of Paul, Titus and Timothy were actually the same person.[1] But this is a matter of speculation, and it hardly matters in our understanding of the Pastoral Epistles. Here Timothy and Titus are remembered as separate people, as two young protégés of Paul. Timothy has been left in Ephesus to take care of the church there, and Titus has been left in Crete to do the same (1:5).

As similar as these three letters are, there are differences. In 1 and 2 Timothy, "Timothy" was portrayed as dealing, at Ephesus, with a raging forest fire of false teaching threatening to leap over the fire breaks and destroy the whole church. Some of the opponents are called out by name, and at least two of them have been excommunicated by "Paul" (1 Tim. 1:20). But while "Titus" is given some pointed warnings about avoiding "stupid controversies" (3:9) and a few hints that some of the teachers in the congregation are "upsetting families" (1:11), there is no hint that a five-alarm fire has engulfed the church in Crete, no urgent crisis language indicating that an active war is underway at Crete over the soul of the church. One possible understanding of the differences in the level of rhetoric is that the Pastor wrote essentially two manuals for effective ministry in the Pauline tradition. One of them, Titus, is a guidebook on preventative medicine, while the other, 1 and 2 Timothy, is a set of protocols for the intensive care unit. Ephesus is a church in crisis mode, and a major intervention is required. Crete is a tough mission setting, to be sure, and strong and vigilant leadership is required, but the false teachers so dangerous at Ephesus do not seem to have yet gotten a firm foothold at Crete. The goal of 1 and 2 Timothy is to pull the church at Ephesus back from the brink. The goal of Titus is to encourage

---

1. See, e.g., Richard G. Fellows, "Was Titus Timothy?" *Journal for the Study of the New Testament* 81 (March 2001), 33–58.

the kind of ministry that will keep Crete from ever swerving out of control and arriving at the brink, that is, to keep Crete from turning into an Ephesus.

The Letter to Titus has all the usual opening elements of an epistle.

1:1–3 The Sender

The writer presents himself as "Paul," which is here a symbol for the legacy of the actual Paul, an expression of the authentic Christian faith as conveyed to the Gentile world through Paul, Timothy, Titus, and the others who preached throughout Asia Minor. But letter writers in the Greco-Roman world often signed their letters with their credentials, and these credentials can be indications of what is to come in the letter that follows. Here "Paul" seems eager to be quite specific about his identity; indeed, apart from the salutation in the Letter to the Romans, Titus has the longest salutation in the New Testament.[2] Some see this lengthy introduction as evidence that the Letter of Titus was originally the first of the Pastoral Epistles sequentially and that this extensive personal introduction was intended to establish "Paul's" identity for the full set of letters. "Paul" names five impressive credentials:

1. *He is first of all a "slave of God" (1:1).* In Roman society, a slave might have many tasks but really only one duty—to be submissive to the will of his master. "Paul" claims for himself the role of one who is a slave belonging to God, as one whose own desires and will have been yielded in favor of God's desires and will. This not a matter of forced labor, but in the spirit of the old hymn: "Make me a captive, Lord, and then I shall be free."

The "Paul" of this letter describes himself as the "slave of God" not merely as a self-introduction but also as a model for the kind of ministry he desires for "Titus." To think of ministers and church leaders as slaves underscores and intensifies what is true for all Christians. In the Letter to the Romans, Paul indicated that human beings are either slaves to sin or slaves to righteousness. As Bob Dylan sings,

2. Raymond F. Collins, *I & II Timothy and Titus* (Louisville, KY: Westminster John Knox Press, 2002), 301.

"You're gonna have to serve somebody. . . . Well, it may be the devil or it may be the Lord. But you're gonna have to serve somebody." Paul tells the Roman Christians that "thanks to God" they have "been set free from sin [and] have become slaves of righteousness" (Rom. 6:18). Sin pays poor wages, namely death, but God lavishes on the slaves of righteousness "the free gift of God . . . eternal life in Jesus Christ" (Rom. 6:23).

Seeing ministry and leadership in the church in terms of slavery to God strikes a balance between, on the one hand, understanding vocation in contemporary terms as purely personal fulfillment (as Apple founder Steve Jobs said about work in a commencement speech, "You've got to find what you love. And that is as true for your work as it is for your lovers. . . . So keep looking until you find it. Don't settle."[3]) and, on the other hand, viewing one's life work as an unwelcome burden imposed on us from above. "Paul" is presenting himself here as neither a vocational dreamer seeking self-expression nor a begrudging, duty-bound servant. Instead, to be in obedience to God is to find oneself summoned to a place of service one might never have chosen on one's own, but to find there deep satisfaction and a sense that every potential one has is being brought to fulfillment.

When "Paul" describes himself as a "slave," he is also striking a blow against strongly hierarchical constructions of ministry. When the acknowledged and revered "apostle of Jesus Christ" presents himself as a "slave" rather than as clothed in power, it levels the field for all church leadership and points toward the shared goal of all disciples, a life of obedience not to the power dynamics in the church but instead to Jesus Christ (Rom. 6:22).

2. He is also "an apostle of Jesus Christ." One possible way to view "Paul's" claim of apostleship would put this title in some tension with his previously claimed description as a "slave." "Slave" is a humble title, but "apostle," by contrast, is a title of significance. Thus, "Paul" could be saying, "Yes, I am a 'slave,' but don't let that diminish my authority in your eyes. I am every bit as much an apostle and

3. Steve Jobs, "Commencement Address," delivered at Stanford University, June 12, 2005, *Stanford Report* (June 14, 2005).

The idea of submitting one's life fully to God is expressed in the prayer often used by the followers of John Wesley in their annual covenant renewal services. Here is a contemporary version of the prayer from the Methodist Church in Britain:

I am no longer my own but yours.
Put me to what you will, rank me with whom you will;
put me to doing, put me to suffering;
let me be employed for you, or laid aside for you,
exalted for you, or brought low for you;
let me be full, let me be empty,
let me have all things, let me have nothing:
I freely and wholeheartedly yield all things to your pleasure and disposal.
And now, glorious and blessed God, Father, Son and Holy Spirit,
you are mine and I am yours. So be it.
And the covenant now made on earth, let it be ratified in heaven.

The Methodist Covenant Prayer, as adapted by the Methodist Church in Britain, accessed at http://www.methodist.org.uk/who-we-are/what-is-distinctive-about-methodism/a-covenant-with-god.

possess the same status as Peter, John, James, or any of the rest of the so-called eyewitness disciples of Jesus."

But finally to pit the titles "slave" and "apostle" against each other would miss the Pastor's point. Here the claim to be an apostle is less about rank and status and far more about trustworthiness. "Paul" is reminding his readers that he isn't merely spouting his opinions here or trying to mold the church into his own biased vision of the kingdom. He comes not in the role of debater or polemicist but instead as a slave who has been sent with an urgent message from his master. He comes as an "apostle," as one who is authorized by Christ, sent by Christ, concerned about the life given by Christ, a Christ to whom he is bound by an oath of obedience as surely as a slave is to a master. In sum, then, "slave" and "apostle" are companion titles, and the salutation of this letter conveys that the Pastor, Christ's slave, has also been commissioned by Christ as an apostle. Therefore, what follows in the letter and that what is said comes straight from the source, from one who has been in the presence of Jesus Christ (see commentary on 1 Tim. 1:1, pp. 17–29).

3. When "Paul" describes his ministry, he gives a sneak preview of what is to follow. He expands his self-identification when he says that his ministry is "for the sake of the faith of God's elect and the knowledge of the truth that is in accordance with godliness," and, by doing so, he lists the two key elements he believes are essential for vital church life: strong faith and sound doctrine that leads to ethical expression. Strong faith is the wind that fills the sails and powers the vessel from the safe harbor into the excitement and adventure of the open sea. Sound doctrine is not a checklist of correct things to believe but the sextant and the compass, the navigational instruments that keep the ship on course as it cuts through the waves and battles storms. In other words, the Pastor writes to encourage "Titus" to have the kind of ministry at Crete that will build up among the people a confident trust and hope in God and will teach the truth of the gospel in such a way that it guides people in living peaceable lives full of faith and good works.

4. *"Paul" raises a banner over his life when he says that all that he is and does is "in the hope of eternal life that God, who never lies, promised before the ages began."* As we saw in 2 Timothy (see commentary on 2 Tim. 1:8–14, pp. 193–95, and 2:11–13, pp. 204–10), the Pastor sees the Christian faith and the work of ministry as a wager on God's future kingdom. In the Pastor's context, to commit oneself to peacefulness, the unity of the church, and to works of loving kindness, and, in our time, to devote one's efforts to peacemaking, racial harmony, and economic justice, can easily be ridiculed as naïve, given the harsh and unrelenting conditions of hatred and brokenness in the world. Establishing kindness, justice, and peace are, frankly, not in the political cards. But the Pastor is not playing the political cards; he is relying instead on the promise of God, and in that promise he is betting all

The only philosophy that can be practiced responsibly in the face of despair is the attempt to contemplate all things as they would present themselves from the standpoint of redemption. Knowledge has no light but that shed on the world by redemption: all else is reconstruction, mere technique. Perspectives must be fashioned that displace and estrange the world, that reveal its fissures and crevices, as indigent and distorted as it will one day appear in the Messianic light.

Theodore W. Adorno, *Minima Moralia: Reflections from a Damaged Life* (New York: Verso, 1978), 247.

that he is and all that he does, confident that when all is said and done his confidence will not be in vain.

I once took a guided tour of one of the newer major league baseball stadiums. It was designed in the retro fashion in vogue now, and almost every feature of the ballpark was intended to evoke the memory of the classic old parks of yesteryear, from the bleacher benches to the irregularly shaped outfield. But there was one aspect of this stadium that had no reference in the past. In fact, when I took my tour, this feature had no reference in the present, either. Beneath the stadium, down near the home and visiting team clubhouses, were dressing rooms for the umpires—two dressing rooms, one for men and the other for women. At that point, of course, there were no women umpires, only men. So the architects had clearly designed the stadium for a future that had not yet appeared. Since square footage is never inexpensive, one could even say that the builders of this stadium had wagered on that future.

Just so, the Pastor considers good ministry is that which places all its chips on the promise of God's coming reign. What that means in practical terms is that ministry often teaches as being true claims that are validated only in the kingdom and not in the way the world is at present and encourages an ethical life that may seem foolish in the harsh light of this age.

Some years ago, Peter Gomes, then the minister at Harvard's Memorial Church, preached the commencement sermon at a private girl's school in Manhattan. The graduates were daughters of New York's best and brightest and were heading themselves to exclusive colleges and to lives of accomplishment. He preached that day on Jesus' word in the Sermon on the Mount urging his hearers not to worry or to be anxious about life, but instead to strive first for the kingdom of God (Matt. 6:25–34). The sermon seemed well-received by the girls, Gomes thought, but at the reception afterward he was approached by a father of one of the graduates, a man, said Gomes, with "fire in his eyes and ice in his voice." He told Gomes that his sermon was pure nonsense. Gomes pointed out that the message actually came from Jesus. "It's still nonsense," replied the father. "It was anxiety that got my daughter into this school, it was anxiety that kept her here, it was anxiety that got her into Yale, it will be anxiety that will keep her there, and it will be anxiety that will get her a good job. You are selling nonsense."[4]

What Gomes was "selling," of course was the ethics of a different kingdom, the reign of God. If one lives only in this world, then the advice not to have any anxiety appears foolish and counterproductive. Only if one is wagering on the promise of God's future is such counsel received as holy wisdom.

Whether people serve themselves or serve others is not in their power to choose. This is decided wholly in terms of the kind of world in which they think they live, in terms of the kind of power they see ruling the roost. The issue lies at the level of the god they worship and not in the kind of person that they may want to be. In New Testament terms, they live or die according to the king that holds them and the kingdom to which they belong.

Arthur C. McGill, *Suffering: A Test of Theological Method* (Philadelphia: Geneva Press, 1982), 92.

---

5. Finally, "Paul" presents himself as one entrusted with the proclamation of the gospel (1:3). The syntax is significant here. Notice what God sent "in due time," that is, at just the right moment, was not a preacher, but the proclamation, the preaching itself. The identity of "Paul" as preacher is completely derivative of God's activity as proclaimer, God's action in making the gospel known. "Paul" is not a clergyman with a reserved parking space and "REVPAUL" vanity plate on his car. He is a slave of God whose life's labors are gathered up into what God is doing in the world, and what God is doing is revealing the good news. Paul is not president of the Ministerial Association, he is a trustee of God's work of proclamation. He is the lantern, not the light; the waiter at the banquet, not the guest of honor at the feast.

To be entrusted with the proclamation of the gospel is to be placed in a paradoxical situation. On the one side, it is frail human beings who have been entrusted with God's word. As Karl Barth rightly asked, "What are you doing, you [human], with the word of *God* upon *your* lips? Upon what grounds do you assume the role of

---

4. Peter J. Gomes, *The Good Book: Reading the Bible with Mind and Heart* (New York: William Morrow and Company, 1996), 178–79.

mediator between heaven and earth?"[5] On the other side, it is God who has chosen to entrust the gospel to human lips. The paradox is that the preacher is nothing, the preacher is everything. As Luther said, "Tis a right excellent thing, that every honest pastor's and preacher's mouth is Christ's mouth, and his word and forgiveness is Christ's word and forgiveness. . . . For the office is not the pastor's or preacher's but God's; and the Word which he preacheth is likewise not the pastor's and preacher's but God's."[6]

In this preface to the letter, the Pastor speaks both of "God our savior" (1:3) and "Christ Jesus our savior" (1:4). These are not competitive or contradictory terms but, as Jouette Bassler has observed, an affirmation that it is "God's unwavering promise of salvation that lies behind the proclamation," but "it is only through Christ that the promised salvation can be realized."[7]

1:4 The Recipient and the Greeting

The letter is addressed to "Titus," who, as we have said, is presented in the letter as a protégé of Paul, a kind of missionary worker who is charged with the pastoral care of the Christian community on the island of Crete. In this "addressee" section of the letter, "Titus" is described as "my loyal child in the faith we share." The use of "child" is an indication of the age difference—an older "servant of God" is writing to a younger pastor, in the manner of a father to his son—but it is also a fascinating description of the relationship between these two. "Titus" is said to be "my . . . child in the faith," which is probably an indication that "Paul" played a significant part in bringing "Titus" to the Christian faith, and, as a result, "Titus" is "loyal" to "Paul," his father not only by age but also by parenting him in the faith. But the fact that this faith is now "the faith we share" has made equals of them. In one sense, then, they are father and son, and in another sense they are brothers in Christ.

---

5. Karl Barth, *The Word of God and the Word of Man* (New York: Harper & Row, 1957), 125, emphasis in the original.
6. From Martin Luther's 1534 sermon on John 20:19–31, as quoted in Karl Barth, *Church Dogmatics 1:1: The Word of God, Study Edition* (London: T&T Clark, 2010), 93.
7. Jouette M. Bassler, *1 Timothy, 2 Timothy, Titus* (Nashville: Abingdon Press, 1996), 183.

"Paul" greets Titus with "grace and peace," an abbreviated version of the greeting found in both letters to "Timothy" (see commentary on 1 Tim. 1:2, pp. 17–29, and 2 Tim. 1:2, pp. 185–87).

1:5–9

Business Letter

Usually one would expect in an ancient letter like this, right after the salutation and formal greeting, a section of warm affirmation and thanksgivings (see, e.g., 2 Tim. 1:3: "I am grateful to God...."). But it is missing here, and the Pastor wastes no time getting down to business. This omission is odd, especially in what purports to be a tender father-to-son letter, and the fact that it is lacking may be yet another clue that we are dealing in the Letter to Titus with a set of instructions for church leaders cloaked in the garb of a personal letter.

The business at hand is putting the church in order, and the first task is to gather a community of leaders, to appoint some coworkers to help in teaching and guiding the house churches in Crete. The Pastor uses the terms "elder" and "bishop," and while these may be two distinct roles, it is more likely at this point that the Pastor is simply employing two terms for the same office. Eventually "bishop" and "elder" will become different offices. "Elder" will be the leader of a local church (something like our use of "pastor" or "priest" today), and "Bishop" will evolve into a supervisory position over a number of elders. But this evolution has probably not yet occurred. The qualifications for the role of elder/bishop are essentially that these persons be of sterling character, blameless both in behavior and temperament, ethical stipulations quite similar to those given for bishops in 1 Timothy (see commentary on 1 Tim. 3:1–7, pp. 88–92).

Every pastor entering a new charge has to decide where to start: What of all the possible pastoral interventions and approaches is the most urgent? Is it to renew the worship, to strengthen stewardship, to engage in Bible study, to love unconditionally the people who may have been bruised by destructive leadership in the past, to challenge old attitudes or destructive behaviors, or something else? The answer depends on the circumstances, of course, and here "Paul" sets out as the number one priority the appointment of local leaders for the house churches of Crete. Why leaders? Putting good leadership into place on Crete is crucial, not merely because the church needs to be put "in order" and demands, therefore, some solid organization, but rather because the people of Crete desperately need the church to be a place of trust. They need to trust the church, which means that the leadership should be "blameless" (1:6) and the word they speak and teach must be "trustworthy" (1:9).

Trustworthiness here is a countercultural value. In North America today, we almost expect our politicians to speak in self-serving duplicities, our schools to "teach to the test" rather than to convey wisdom, our professional athletes to game the system by taking illegal hormones, and television commercials to hype the truth (the late comedian Bill Hicks once described the United States as "the United States of Advertising"). The culture of Crete in the ancient world also (see 1:12) had the reputation for inflated rhetoric and easy talk. When the words spoken in everyday life have become cheap and unreliable, the first priority of the church is to be a place where the leadership is carved in oak, in which the words they embody, proclaim, and teach can be relied on without fail.

Therefore, the Pastor underscores one piece of the elder/bishop's equipment: a firm grasp of the gospel tradition. The elder/bishop needs to be grounded in the word as it has been trustworthily transmitted so that he can be a sound preacher and teacher and can also be a defender of the faith when it is challenged (1:9). This is an underscoring of the idea that an elder/bishop is "God's steward" (1:7). The steward in a Roman house was someone, often a slave, who managed and protected the property of the head of the household,[8] and an elder/bishop is to exercise the same accountability with the treasure of God.

In our own time, the spotlight often shines on books and television shows that fancy themselves as daring and inflammatory, boldly challenging this or that aspect of Christian faith. What often goes unnoticed is the harder more painstaking task of good teaching, of making the Christian faith vibrant and clear to a new generation. At

---

8. Jerome D. Quinn, *The Letter to Titus* (New York: Doubleday, 1990), 88.

least one well-publicized bishop in our day has taken on a role, not as a steward of "the word that is trustworthy" but instead as a provocateur, not as a patient teacher of the apostolic faith but as a cultured despiser of it. Biblical scholar Luke Johnson quipped, "Having a bishop with opinions like these is a little like hiring a plumber who wants to rethink pipes."[9]

1:10–16

The Church's Troublemakers

1:10 The Troublemakers Described

The Pastor closed his discussion of the qualification of elder/bishop with the suggestion that these leaders might well be put in the position of debating folks who contradict the gospel. Now he proceeds to specify just exactly who these contradicters might be, and not surprisingly, they are people who embody qualities diametrically opposed to the good leaders. If a good leader is to be a steward, obedient to the gospel, these folks are "rebellious." If a leader is to have a firm grasp on the word and to preach the solid gospel, these babblers are "idle talkers." If a leader is to be a blameless teacher of the truth, these troublemakers are "deceivers" (1:10). In short, "Paul" presents the tension at Crete as not between one set of ideas and another but rather as between a trustworthy word and a deceptive, self-serving one.

One of the phrases the Pastor uses to describe the troublemakers—"especially those of the circumcision" (1:10)—is odd and ambiguous. "Those of the circumcision" can simply mean Jews generally, but here the phrase probably functions to evoke the memory of a particular occasion in Paul's ministry, one that involved Titus and about which the readers of this letter might well be aware. This is the incident, described in Galatians 2, in which Paul returns to Jerusalem to meet with the leaders of the church and to account for his ministry among the Gentiles.

---

9. Luke Timothy Johnson, *The Real Jesus: The Misguided Quest for the Historical Jesus and the Truth of the Traditional Gospels* (New York: HarperOne, 1997), 33.

At that point, Paul's missionary appeal to Gentiles was still hotly controversial, and some of Paul's critics would have preferred that evangelism be confined to Jewish circles altogether. At the very least, they would have insisted that any Gentiles converting to the faith must adopt the practices of Jewish Christians, such as circumcision. But Paul reports that the potentially volatile meeting initially went well, and "even Titus . . . was not compelled to be circumcised, though he was a Greek" (Gal. 2:3). But, after this promising start to the meeting, matters must have swiftly deteriorated when, according to Paul, some "false believers" were secreted into the meeting, and they tried to question "the freedom we have in Christ Jesus" (Gal. 2:4), probably meaning that they broke the peace of the assembly by rallying once again the anti-Paul, pro-circumcision troops.

Taken as a whole, then, the force of this section seems to be not a warning about hazards in Jewish-Christian relations but a more general caution about controversy in ministry. Having set forth the desired credentials and qualities of church leaders, "Paul" goes on to alert "Titus" to the hard truth that good leaders with excellent credentials will always encounter their opposites in the life of the church. "You can count on it," "Paul" seems to be saying. "You remember it happened to me in my ministry when I defended my work to those in Jerusalem—you were there—and it will happen in your ministry too. That's the way things go, so be prepared."

1:11 The Strategy for Remediation

The Pastor goes straight in with the scalpel. If the work of trustworthy and good ministry is disrupted by deceitful and lying people trying to take over the life of the church, and be assured that this will inevitably happen, then silence them. What they teach is wrong, they do it only for money, and they have the potential to upset "whole families" (that is, entire house churches) with their nonsense.

We have here a glimpse into the life and organization of a missionary church at this point in Christian history. As we saw in 1 Timothy, what we call "the church at Corinth" or "the church at Ephesus" or, in this case, "the church in Crete" is actually not a single church at all but a cluster of house churches. Each house church is led by an elder, who is a combination of pastor, preacher, teacher, and guide. The health of each house church, therefore, is very much dependent on the soundness of the elder in charge. If the elder loses his compass bearings and begins to teach something less than the gospel—and in the religious stewpot of the ancient world, there were plenty of rivals to the gospel—then that house church inevitably suffers. Because there were many informal lines of communication among the house churches, an infection in one house church could easily spread to others.

As we saw in 1 and 2 Timothy, the house churches of Ephesus had indeed become corrupted with "false teaching," and some of the elders were not only passing along a defective, highly spiritualized version of the faith, they were also being rewarded financially for doing so. Elders received a stipend for their leadership, and some of the wealthy members of the church, who fancied these new spiritualized teachings, were sweetening the pot for these wayward elders.

It may be that such wrong teaching is already rooted in the church in Crete, as it was in Ephesus, and the Pastor here is urging, as he did in 1 and 2 Timothy, to root it out. It is more likely, however, that this is a warning in advance to nip it in the bud. There are a lot of rebellious, idle-talking, and deceitful people in this world, the Pastor is warning. We have seen them undermining the church at Ephesus, and we had to deal with them sternly there. They have the capacity to upset "whole families" (that is, whole house churches), and they do it for money (1:11). So if and when you find this happening in Crete, these "idle talkers . . . must be silenced" (1:10–11).

At first glance, the Pastor's counsel, "they must be silenced," may seem both unrealistic and unnecessarily harsh. Silencing one's opponents, after all, is easier said than done, and it hardly seems a good and graceful pastoral care strategy to tell certain people in the church simply to "shut up." But if this is an advance and general warning to the young pastor "Timothy," and not specific instructions about some actual problem at Crete, it begins to make more sense. The Pastor is saying, in effect, "Look, young minister, in forming a newborn church, nothing is more essential than trustworthy leaders with a trustworthy grasp of the gospel, and nothing is more threatening to the life of the community than untrustworthy leaders with a false word to preach and teach. So don't go to sleep at the switch. At the first hint of deception among the leaders, declare this as a pastoral 'situation red' and move swiftly." Later in the letter, the Pastor will hint at a more moderate and gradual pastoral care process to deal with false teachers, one involving several admonitions to the troublemakers (3:10–11). But here the general caution is clear and decisive: nothing is more urgent than to keep the church clean from false teaching, otherwise the community of Christ is at risk.

1:12–16 But Seriously, Titus

The Pastor has not won many accolades from contemporary readers for this section of the letter, which appears to be a somewhat mean-spirited and culturally insensitive rant at people from Crete, who are described as "always liars, vicious brutes, and lazy gluttons." But people who get worked up over this passage can perhaps loosen up a bit when two factors are taken into account. First, the Pastor is quoting well-known epithets about Crete, and second he is attempting to make a joke.

The statement "Cretans are always liars, vicious brutes, and lazy gluttons" is probably the result of gluing together two proverbial sayings. An analog would be, "As they say in Europe, 'All Americans are rich and obese.'" Two independent stereotypes pasted together, neither of them technically accurate, but each with a grain of evocative truth. Whether the Pastor did the gluing in this case or it was done before, the final product is a negative stereotype of people from Crete.

Now the joke. The Pastor is using a classic example in philosophical logic, one that goes back at least to Eubulides in the fourth century BCE and that has become known as the "Liar's Paradox." Versions of it appear in college logic books today, and the simplest construction is this:

Statement: *I am lying.*

Question: *Is that statement true?*

Well, let's think. If the statement is true, then the one who made it is indeed lying, which must mean that it isn't true. But if isn't true that he's lying, then he's telling the truth, but the truth he's telling is that he's lying, and so . . . Think about this long enough, and it will spin your head.

The Pastor's version is, "A certain prophet of Crete said, 'All Cretans are liars . . . ,'" and while we are doing a double take trying to figure out whether the prophet of Crete is one of the Cretan liars and what is true and false, the Pastor throws in the punch line: "This is true!" What is true? Who knows? That's the joke, and while we may or may not think this funny, the Pastor did.[10]

Imagine a pastor from Korea who is being sent to the United States, in fact to north Georgia, to establish a new multicultural church. In his farewell dinner in Seoul, his pastor friends might toss in a couple of jokes. One might say, "We pray that your work in America will be fruitful, but don't forget what Gandhi said when asked what he thought of Western civilization. He said, 'I think it would be a good idea.'" Another pastor friend might say, "As you try to plant that new church in Georgia, keep in mind that it won't be easy. I heard a man, a Georgian himself, say, "If you've ever made change out of a collection plate, you *miiiight* be a redneck!"

These would be jokes, of course (jokes that people nineteen centuries into the future would probably not get), but they would also be serious. They would remind our Korean evangelist that he was going into a very different culture and subculture and that he should be prepared to work doubly hard to establish a mission. Likewise, once the Pastor's joke has been cracked, he becomes more serious. Behind the stereotypes and jokes about Cretan culture, he says, there are some social realities, and anyone attempting to form a church in Crete would do well to take them into account. In the culture of Crete, the pastor warns, truth is often a slippery concept, and therefore, you must always be vigilant to live, preach, and teach only that which is trustworthy and true.

Many years ago, the church I attended was contemplating setting up an overnight shelter for homeless people, a place where street folk could find a warm bed, a safe place to stay the night, and a nutritious meal. The church did eventually establish the shelter, and it has

---

10. See a clear discussion of the "Cretan Liar Paradox" in N. T. Wright, *Paul for Everyone: The Pastoral Letters: 1 and 2 Timothy and Titus* (Louisville, KY: Westminster John Knox Press, 2004), 147.

expanded its services greatly over the years. But I will never forget when the church was in the initial planning stages, and we invited a local minister with long experience in homeless ministry to come and give us advice. "Well," he said, "if you're dealing with homeless people, I hope your fire insurance is good, that you're prepared for frequent thefts, and that you have an item in your budget to clean the church grounds every day." We were shocked. What he said seemed callous and also to dehumanize the very people we were hoping to serve. But, of course, he wasn't callous; he was realistic. No one had a more devoted and compassionate ministry with homeless people than he, and no one knew more about the demanding realities of such a work than he.

Some of this commentary was written while on summer vacation along the beautiful Eastern Shore of the Chesapeake Bay in rural Maryland. Looking out at the blue water and the crab boats plying the lovely coves, one can hardly imagine that this territory was once occupied by pirates and a local population of hard-drinking, hard-living people who gave their settlements names like "Devil's Island" and "Rogues Point."

In the late eighteenth and early nineteenth centuries, young "Tituses" in the form of Methodist itinerant preachers sailed in small boats from island to island and from village to village, holding camp meetings and revivals, establishing congregations, building churches, and evangelizing the land. There are many reports of local ruffians disrupting the meetings and of fistfights breaking out at the revivals, sometimes leaving the preachers beaten and bloody. One can imagine some "Paul" in 1815 writing to some "Titus" about the perils awaiting him as he went out to bring the gospel to the "treacherous people" of the Eastern Shore.

So the Pastor is speaking to "Titus," who is beginning a tough ministry in Crete, a culture legendary for being sometimes brutal and hard-edged. "This is not badminton," says the Pastor. "This is ministry, rough and tumble ministry. And this is not a rose garden; this is Crete. This is no place for fainthearted pastors. So buckle up your cleats, brother, and get ready to do God's work in a tough environment."

The Pastor puts the finishing touch on this discussion of lies versus truth by warning "Titus" of the form this conflict is likely to take in Crete. He may have been joking earlier, but now he is very serious. The very gospel is at stake. He is keen that the same doctrinal distortions that he battled so furiously in the two letters to "Timothy" not get planted in the church garden at Crete. He refers to "Jewish myths," which is almost surely the same sort of speculative and over-spiritualized exegesis of the Old Testament that was in play in Ephesus (see "The False Teaching" in the commentary on 1 Tim. 1:3–11, pp. 34–36).

Significantly, the Pastor insists that conflict over false teaching in a newly developing church is not some mere freshman dormitory theological debate. It is not an abstracted discussion in which "you have your opinions about religion and I have mine; isn't that interesting!" No, for the Pastor, sound teaching about the gospel comes from a conscience transformed by Christ. Teaching the truth of the gospel is not a matter of getting it exactly right on the fine points of the doctrine of the Trinity. It is, rather, a way of seeing the world in the light of Jesus Christ. It is what the Pastor described in the very first verse of this letter: "the knowledge of the truth that is in accordance with godliness" (1:1). So the surface question to ask about teachers in the church is whether they are true or false, right or wrong, but the deeper question has to do with their faith and godliness. Have they been transformed by the gospel or not? "To the pure, all things are pure," says the Pastor, "but to the corrupt and unbelieving, nothing is pure" (1:15). So don't entrust the teaching of the gospel to those who have not been claimed by the gospel. They may claim to know God, but they don't. Down deep, such people are "detestable, disobedient, unfit for any good work" (1:16).

That's a severe judgment. It would be difficult, if not impossible, to take the Pastor's counsel here strictly and literally. On the ground and in the reality of living together as a Christian community, people cannot be so easily sorted into "pure" and "un-pure." Most of us, even when we are at our best, are a conflicted and perplexing mixture of purity and impurity, godliness and brokenness. No wise pastor today would divide her congregation into the "worthy and admirable" on the one hand, and the "detestable, disobedient, and utterly unfit" on the other.

The Pastor is no fool, of course; he knows the untidiness of the human condition, even among the faithful. What the pastor is doing, however, is reminding "Titus" that, in the midst of the tangled snarl of trying to organize and lead a Christian community, composed of real people with messy lives, it is crucial to keep one's eye on the ball. No one is a perfect leader or teacher, but there is leadership and teaching that flow from a heart and conscience transformed by the gospel, and there is leadership and teaching that flow from other less worthy sources. It is important to keep this distinction in view when guiding the church and choosing its leadership. "Don't be fooled," the Pastor warns. "If the dipper of water drawn from the well is poison, there's a good chance that the well itself is poisonous. If people claim to love God but what flows out of them is teaching that confuses, divides, misleads, and destroys the faithful community, there's a good chance that this is more than clumsy pedagogy. The well itself may be poisoned."

<h1 style="text-align:center">2:1–15</h1>

Order in the House

2:1–10 All in the Family

In one of the most startling incidents in the Gospels, Jesus is speaking to the crowds, and his mother and brothers show up and ask to speak to him. Someone interrupts Jesus' teaching to tell him that his family is waiting outside to see him. That prompts a stunning response from Jesus. "Who is my mother, and who are my brothers?" And then, sweeping his hand out toward his disciples, he adds, "Here are my mother and my brothers! For whoever does the will of my Father in heaven is my brother and sister and mother" (Matt. 12:48–50). With this one remark, Jesus relativizes all human and social family structures. His family is defined by the kingdom of God; his true relatives are not determined by bloodline but rather by doing the will of God, the heavenly parent.

But how does Jesus' radical word about God's true family bear on the actual households in which we find ourselves? Sometimes,

Christians simply assume that the way the culture defines stable families must be God's will, which ends up baptizing the prevailing social pattern of families as "the Christian family." But the fact is that the prevailing social pattern for families varies from society to society and keeps changing over time.

For example, many people in North America today would probably describe a satisfying marriage in terms of mutual love and personal fulfillment. Indeed, a popular Christian online dating site uses the slogan "Find God's match for you" and implies that God endorses love and personal fulfillment as proper goals of marriage by prominently placing on their Web site such biblical verses as "Delight yourself in the LORD and he will give you the desires of your heart" (Ps. 37:4 NIV) and "Let love and faithfulness never leave you" (Prov. 3:3 NIV). In some other cultures, though, young men and women would never dream that they were in charge of finding "God's match" for themselves or that the main criteria for choosing a mate should be love and personal fulfillment. Marriages in those societies are customarily arranged by the parents and for reasons having little to do with the desires of their children's hearts. Or again, the seventeenth-century Westminster Confession of Faith, a creedal document still honored by many Presbyterian and Reformed churches, has an entire chapter on marriage, and the word "love" is not mentioned a single time. In seventeenth-century England, husbands and wives may well have loved each other, but the main purposes of marriage were viewed not as love and personal fulfillment but as mutual help, childbearing, and the building of a steadfast society. It only takes a little probing across cultures, or across time, to reveal that what some defend as "traditional family values" aren't actually all that traditional but are instead simply the values of a particular cultural moment.

By contrast, occasionally in church history a few Christian groups have taken a more radical approach. They seize on Jesus' redefinition of the family as the impetus to reject altogether society's norms for marriage and family and to attempt to establish purer "kingdom families." However, these experiments—such as the celibacy practiced by the Shakers and the Harmony Society or group marriage as observed in the Oneida Community in New York—almost inevitably turn out to be fragile, internally flawed, and short-lived.

Most of the time, Christians take a middle road between simply endorsing cultural values about the family and rejecting those values outright. In this middle way, Christians inherit family structures from the society around them and then attempt to redeem them from within. That is, they take the given cultural patterns of the family and inhabit them as best they can with Christian vision. By doing so, Christians contribute to the reform of families as social institutions, reforms that start from within but that sometimes end up reshaping family structures, legally and ethically.

This middle way of reform from within is precisely what the Pastor is attempting in Titus 2 (and in other places throughout the Pastoral Epistles). His inherited model for the family is the Greco-Roman household, a model he applies both to the domestic household and to the church as the household of God (when we say today that an effective pastor-parish relationship is like a "good marriage," we are doing the same kind of blending of domestic and ecclesial images).

The Greco-Roman household was patriarchal and hierarchical, characteristics that Christians today call into question, just as future Christians will readily be able to point out the ethical blind spots in our own domestic patterns. But as we argued earlier in this commentary, envisioning a completely different set of social structures was unimaginable for the Pastor, just as thinking of legalized same-sex marriage would have stretched the imaginations of most Christians in 1950. Jesus envisioned a radically different alternative to the family, but for the Pastor, as for all pastors since who work on the ground, Jesus' vision translated into the question, "How do you live out the kingdom to the best of your ability within the limits of what is possible and imaginable?"

The Pastor's goal is for the Christian household to be a model of calm stability. Others outside the church ought to be able to look at the house churches and homes of Christians and sense the peace and integrity there. Critics of the Pastor today read his counsel and wish that he had more appreciation for less domesticated and tamped-down virtues—such as freedom and equality—but the Pastor's experience with freeform Christianity as advocated by the false teachers in

Ephesus had been a disaster. No, in his view, the time had come for the Christian household to trim the sails and tighten the rigging.

The Pastor gives "Titus" guidelines for the instruction of five groups of people found within the church and also within a typical Roman household: older men, older women, younger women, younger men, and slaves. For the most part, the instructions are beautiful but unremarkable in terms of ethics (2:2–10). Older men should be serious, loving, faithful, and constant. Older women should be reverent, good role models for the younger women, and should temper the alcohol consumption (which was at least as much an issue in Greco-Roman society as it is today). Younger women should listen to the wisdom of their elders, love their husbands and children, manage their households well, and submit to the authority of their husbands. Younger men should be models of good works and should train themselves to be sound teachers. Slaves should submit to their masters and show perfect fidelity (for the vexed issue of slavery and early Christianity, see the commentary on 1 Tim. 6:1–2, pp. 162–69).

Once again, we can see the Pastor not challenging the prevailing family systems of his day but instead investing them with Christian virtues. The reasons are two: the good graces of the church's neighbors and the saving grace of God. As for the neighbors, the Pastor wants the world to look at the church and to see nothing but peace and goodness. He doesn't want unruly family life to discredit the word of God (2:5) or to give opponents any occasion to speak evil of the Christian community (2:8). As for the grace of God, a kind, generous, self-disciplined, faithful church family, full of integrity and trustworthy speech, is a publicly visible expression ("an ornament," 2:10) of an inner peace created by the saving grace of God. Those who know that God has granted them the deepest gift of all know to their core that they have no more need to fight and struggle over the small prizes and little flatteries of life.

2:11–15 Saving Grace

Here we see one of the basic convictions of the Pastor in action, namely, that theological doctrine is not some abstraction that can be taught like the multiplication tables but is rather living truth, shaping and guiding the Christian life toward joy and hope. Having described how Christians of various sorts ought to behave with one another in the family of God, he now swings the doctrine of saving grace into view, showing how this grace animates the everyday lives of the faithful.

Grace, says the Pastor, has a past, a present, and a future. In terms of the past, the grace of God "appeared, bringing salvation to all." This appearance was, of course, in the incarnation, in the life, ministry, death, and resurrection of Jesus Christ. Saving grace is not just an idea or a sweet sentiment; God did not merely arrange the clouds to spell out "I love you." Grace is an embodied event in our history. Jesus "appeared," he showed up, speaking graciously, acting graciously, healing graciously, bringing in and through his own body "salvation to all" (2:11).

In terms of the present, the saving grace that appeared in Jesus continues among us as a kind of trainer and coach. Living the Christian life, the life that responds to God's saving action, is not automatic or easy. It takes hard work and practice, and therefore, grace sticks around to put us through the drills and to teach us how to love God in return and "to live lives that are self-controlled, upright, and godly" (2:12).

In terms of the future, grace gives to the faithful the hope that the saving action of God will, when all is said and done, rescue humanity from the power of death raging in this broken and sinful world.

If any doctrines within the whole compass of Christianity may be properly termed fundamental they are doubtless these two—the doctrine of justification, and that of the new birth: the former relating to that great work which God does *for us*, in forgiving our sins; the latter, to the great work which God does *in us*, in renewing our fallen nature. In order of time neither of these is before the other. In the moment we are justified by the grace of God through the redemption that is in Jesus, we are also "born of the Spirit"; but in order of thinking, as it is termed, justification precedes the new birth. We first conceive his wrath to be turned away, and then his Spirit to work in our hearts.

John Wesley, "Sermon XLV, The New Birth" in Alice Russie, ed., *The Essential Works of John Wesley* (Ulhruchsville, OH: Barbour Publishing, Inc., 2011), 199.

In the fullness of God's beloved community no one will be on death row, no one will put makeup on her cheek to cover the bruises of domestic violence, no one will go to sleep hungry and frightened, no one will be banished from his home because of his sexual orientation, no one will be abused by her father, no one will be beholden to some addictive substance. We don't experience the fullness of this now, but we see it on God's horizon, and so "we wait for the blessed hope and the manifestation of the glory of our great God and Savior, Jesus Christ" (2:13). While we wait, we focus our energies to live as those who already belong to this beloved community, and we do everything in our power not to behave as those who have nothing to wait for, nothing to hope for.

> Why do I preach? Why do I sit up here? What do I live for? For this one thing alone: that together we may live with Christ! This is my passion, this is my honor, this is my fame, this is my joy, this is my one possession! . . . But I do not want to be saved without you!
>
> Augustine, *Sermon* 17.2, in William Harmless, SJ, *Augustine and the Catechumenate* (Collegeville, MN: The Liturgical Press, 1995), 188.

3:1–8a

Heading out the Door, Singing a Hymn, Remembering Baptism

In chapter 2, the Pastor gave counsel for how Christians should live in households. Now in this chapter, he takes that advice on the road and counsels Christians about how to live out in the world. The same model of quiet, humble integrity prevails here, too. Christians are to be law-abiding, gentle, and ready to perform good works, avoiding quarreling and showing courtesy to everyone (3:1–2). This may seem tepid until we imagine someone actually putting this into practice at work, at Walmart, driving in rush hour traffic, in a parent-teacher conference, at a top-level sales meeting at corporate headquarters, or at the "Black Friday" door-buster sale at Best Buy.

What is intriguing theologically is that the Pastor backs up this counsel to gentle, peaceable behavior by immediately breaking into a poem-like recitation, probably a hymn borrowed from the baptismal liturgy. Although most of what we know about the baptismal liturgy of the early church comes from later than this letter, we can see in this hymn the outline of an emerging practice:

> (a) *Repentance.* Baptism was viewed as repentance and conversion, a turning away from the old world and the old self and a turning toward Christ and the new understanding of oneself as a child of God. Repentance here is larger than simply feeling sorry for one's sins; it's a change of citizenship, a renunciation of the customs and laws of the evil age and a taking on of the customs and laws of the kingdom of God. Eventually in the development of the liturgy, baptismal candidates would turn toward the west, would renounce Satan and all his empty promises, and would repent of the life they once lived under Satan's power. In a beautiful baptismal sermon from the fifth century, the old bishop Theodore of Mopsuestia told those who were about to be baptized what was going to happen to them. He said, "You will kneel on the floor, and you will face the West, the region of evil and darkness, and you will point your finger at the accuser, and you will say, 'Satan, I renounce you and all your vanities, and all your angels and all your ministries.'"[11] We catch the flavor of that in the opening stanza of the hymn quoted by the Pastor:

> > For we ourselves were once foolish,
> > disobedient,
> > led astray,
> > slaves to various passions and pleasures,
> > passing our days in malice and envy,
> > despicable,
> > hating one another (3:3).

> (b) *Turning toward Christ.* Then those being baptized would do an about face, would turn away from Satan and sin and death and turn toward the east, that is, they would "orient" themselves and would turn toward a new life in Jesus Christ. Bishop Theodore even described how in his day the bishop

---

11. The description of the baptismal ceremony is abbreviated from Theodore of Mopsuestia, "Baptism Homily II," trans. Edward Yarnold and found in Yarnold, *The Awe-Inspiring Rites of Initiation: Baptismal Homilies of the Fourth Century* (Slough: St. Paul Publications, 1972), 176–88.

presiding at the baptism would change into bright vestments
so that when the candidates turned away from darkness and
toward Christ, they would be dazzled by the light. "Then you
will face the East," Theodore preached, "and you will find
that the Bishop is in new clothes which are resplendent and
dazzling and light, a symbol of a new world which you are
entering. They dazzle because you will shine in that world.
They are graceful and delightful for you will be graceful and
delightful."[12]

The hymn in Titus also describes how those who turn away
from the old life and toward Christ are dazzled by what they
see:

> But when the goodness and loving kindness of God our
>   Savior appeared,
> he saved us (3:4–5).

Jouette Bassler has underscored what we observed earlier (see
commentary on 2:11) that the idea of Jesus "appearing" as
savior is a distinctive feature of the Pastor's Christology.[13] For
him, part of what God was and is doing in the saving work of
Jesus is making an appearance, showing forth to all who will
look the saving intention of God. In Jesus, God pulls back the
veil so that we can comprehend what God is truly like, seeing clearly the "goodness and loving kindness of God" that
appeared in Christ (3:4). This is only one of many ways to
describe the work and meaning of Christ, of course, but it fits
well the baptismal liturgical emphasis and is also particularly
apt in churches where the main threat is a form of enlightenment spirituality. Over against a kind of gnostic whispering of
secret insights meant only for the elite, God *appeared* in Jesus
Christ—God in the flesh—a comprehensive, visible, accessible, world-embracing reality.

(c) *Going through the waters of baptism to the "promised land."*
Then the candidates for baptism, stripped of the clothing of
the old world, go down into the baptismal pool. When they
emerge, they are given a baptismal robe, the new clothes of
righteousness, an anointing with oil as a sign that they had

12. Ibid.
13. Bassler, *1 Timothy, 2 Timothy, Titus*, 183.

received the Holy Spirit, and they rejoiced that they had been given a new identity, a new family of the faithful, and a new hope of eternal life. The Pastor sings of this, when he says that this salvation comes,

> . . . not because of any works of righteousness that we had
>   done, but according to his mercy,
> through the water of rebirth and renewal by the Holy
>   Spirit.
> This Spirit he poured out on us richly through Jesus Christ
>   our Savior,
> so that, having been justified by his grace,
> we might become heirs according to the hope of eternal
>   life.

The theological claim that salvation comes by God's mercy and not by any human works of righteousness is a major Pauline concept (see, e.g., Rom. 1:16–17; 3:27–28), and it was a rallying cry for Luther and the other reformers. Luther was reading Romans 1, and he found there claimed, "For in [the gospel] the righteousness of God is revealed through faith for faith; as it is written, 'The one who is righteous will live by faith.'" Luther's theological world tilted on its axis. He wrote,

> I saw the connection between the justice of God and the state-
> ment that "the just shall live by his faith." Then I grasped that
> the justice of God is that righteousness by which through grace
> and sheer mercy God justifies us through faith. Thereupon I
> felt myself to be reborn and to have gone through open doors
> into paradise. The whole of Scripture took on a new meaning,
> and whereas before the "justice of God" had filled me with
> hate, now it became to me inexpressibly sweet in greater love.
> This passage of Paul became to me a gate to heaven.[14]

At its best, the conviction that human beings are "justified by grace" does not undercut works of righteousness but, in fact, stimulates good works as a sign of gratitude for the saving initiative of a merciful God.

The Pastor concludes the recitation of the baptismal hymn with a

14. Martin Luther, *Luther Works* (Philadelphia: Fortress Press, 1960), 34:336. Contemporary English translation by Roland Bainton, *Here I Stand: A Life of Martin Luther* (Peabody, MS: Hendrickson, 1977), 48.

It is precisely where we are under pressure to justify ourselves and we feel the threats of the law in our everyday life that God's justifying love encounters us. It shines through wherever we step back from ourselves—in fact, we feel it most when we can laugh at ourselves. It also comes out in self-forgetful work where we are fully absorbed in what we are doing. Again, it is evident in conversation when we give ourselves completely to the other. God's justifying love is especially powerful when it comes to us in the middle of unfinished work that screams out at us—when we can drop off to sleep, despite all the things we have to leave undone, "without any merit or worthiness on our part." "It is in vain that you rise up early and go late to rest"—sitting at the desk, for example—"eating the bread of anxious toil, for he gives sleep to his beloved" (Ps 127:2).

Oswald Bayer, "Justification," *Lutheran Quarterly* 24/3 (Autumn 2010): 338–39.

phrase that the NRSV translates as "[8]The saying is sure" (3:8). With this note of confidence, the Pastor is in effect saying, "This is the gospel. Amen."

3:8b–15

The Closing

The Pastor has given "Titus" many words of advice and instructions for the life of the church in Crete. He has ranged over topics like church leadership, the difficulty of mission in Crete, the importance of sound teaching, the conduct of Christians in house, church, and society, and more. As the letter now draws to a close, the Pastor expresses his desire that "Titus" should not receive this letter as a set of mere suggestions but rather should "insist" that all of these instructions be put into effect in Crete.

The reason for this insistence? "So that those who have come to believe in God may be careful to devote themselves to good works" (3:8b). Some commentators note that the phrase "who have come to believe in God" doesn't quite catch the meaning of the text.[15] Perhaps "those who have come into this faith" would capture better how the Pastor here is continuing the baptismal

15. See, e.g., Collins, *I & II Timothy and Titus*, 367.

imagery. In *The Apostolic Tradition*, a patristic-era document describing worship and other church practices, there is a description of newly baptized Christians being given a cup of milk mixed with honey. This symbolizes God's promise to bring the children of Israel into a land flowing with milk and honey, and the cup says to the new convert, "Welcome to the promised land!" The Pastor is imagining "Titus" gathering the new flock at Crete. They have turned from their old ways, been taken through the waters of baptism, and now have been ushered into a new world and a new life in Christ. They have come into this faith, into the promised land. So the Pastor is stressing to "Titus" the importance of giving these new disciples the good stuff, the sound teaching, the firm guidance in how to live this faith. He wants "Titus" to give them the milk and honey.

If "Titus" does form them well, then they will do "good works," that is, they will live the kind of lives in their homes, in the church, and in society that are useful, beneficial, and "profitable to everyone" (3:8c). This idea of beneficial lives becomes the organizing theme for the rest of the letter. Theologically, God pours out the rich benefits of grace and mercy on the believers through the waters of baptism and the renewal by the Holy Spirit (3:5). Therefore, God in Christ is of great and abundant benefit to all who have entered into this promised land of faith. In the baptismal ceremony, the believers, who have turned away from worldly passions and toward Christ in repentance, now turn again toward the world, but this time in love and mission. The goodness and mercy that has flowed toward them from God now flows through them to everyone around them. The abundance of God wells up in the world through the abundant generosity and kindness of the faithful.

This gospel of grace and mercy has great size and reach. Thus, Christians who stoop to engage in stupid controversies and cat fights about Scripture, such as quarrels over genealogies and the Old Testament law (see commentary on 1 Tim. 1:3–11, pp. 29–48) miss the point about the spaciousness of the Christian life. Such distractions are to be avoided because they are not beneficial—they are "unprofitable and worthless" (3:9). And people who, after a couple of warnings, still want to plunge the church into energy sapping quarrels need to be quarantined (which is an extreme measure, but one intended to correct and restore [see 1 Tim. 1:20]).

The Pastor mentions several names of people in the Pauline orbit: Artemas, Tychicus, Zenas the Lawyer, and Apollos. Tychicus and Apollos are mentioned elsewhere in Acts and in the Pauline letters. Artemas and Zenas appear only here in the New Testament but would probably be people known in the lore of Paul. "Titus" is urged to visit Paul while he winters in Nicopolis (there were several places named Nicopolis; it hardly matters which one is meant here).

Taken as a whole, the picture this listing of names gives is of a busy and productive collection of church workers. Artemas and Tychicus are being sent by Paul to relieve Titus in Crete so that Titus can be free to visit Paul. Titus is to send Zenas and Apollos off on a trip (a missionary journey?), making sure they are fully provisioned. There is energy, activity, and fruitfulness here, which segues into the instruction to teach the Christian on Crete to be devoted to good works, so that they too can be about the business of supplying needs and "so that they may not be unproductive" (3:14). The Greek word translated "unproductive" is technically "unfruitful."

This circle of fruitfulness and usefulness in the name of Christ is expanded by the closing words, as "Paul" sends greetings from the company of believers who are with him and sends a special salute to those in Crete who return the blessing, those "who love us in the faith. Grace be with you all" (3:15). And so these three letters, called the Pastoral Epistles, end as they began (1 Tim. 1:2), surrounded by the grace of God.

Final Thoughts

One day I was hiking on the Scottish island of Iona, and I reached the island's highest point, a rocky knoll overlooking the North Atlantic Ocean. The top of the hill was scarred with weather-sculpted indentations, each filled with rainwater. At first the landscape appeared barren, almost a moonscape, but as I paused over each rock-hewn pool I was amazed to find every one of them to be teeming with life, rich with small plants and tiny aquatic creatures. I have had something of the same experience as I have worked carefully with the texts of the Pastoral Epistles. In these letters, which so many find barren and foreboding, I have found great beauty and astounding pools of meaning swarming with life and energy. Like the vitality hidden in the pools of Iona, the treasures of the Pastoral Epistles are also easily overlooked.

Part of the reason for this is that the Pastorals bear witness to truths that are not only deeply countercultural but also that run against the grain of many of us who self-assuredly tell ourselves that we are already countercultural. Take, for example, the Pastor's intense focus on what seem at first to be the most mundane details of church life. He frets about the qualifications of leaders, the way money is managed—or mismanaged—in the church, the number of women on the widows' charity roster, and how people dress in worship. All of this apparent triviality seems so bourgeois to us over against our confident and expansive view of an inclusive God who loves everyone equally and whose presence transcends the little boxes of institutions and creeds and ecclesial structures.

But it is precisely this emphasis on particularity by the Pastor who wrote these letters that is so radical, challenging, and ultimately life-giving. An abstracted and universal God is easy to avoid, but not one whose life is bound up in the everyday details of a real community of people. Sometimes in the name of ethics we find it useful to refer to so-called communities, such as "the deaf community" or the "transgendered community," but however effective these references are as political shorthand, they do not actually refer to communities—not real ones. These are instead abstractions. Real communities live together, have arguments, make compromises, have to come to difficult decisions about their common life, and often find their true character expressed not in the fact that they share this or that grand vision but in the ordinary and grounded realities like who gets to decide about the budget or who gets to sit at the head of the table at the banquet.

In focusing on the fine-textured details of the life of the church— not the abstracted church, but the real one with real people in it— the Pastor is not bourgeois at all, but deeply theological and allegiant to the Scriptures. For him, the church is not an arbitrary and finally disposable institution but the place and the people among which God has chosen to dwell, not to create a sect but on behalf of the whole creation. This is the irony of biblical faith, that the God who transcends all and who is utterly unknowable nevertheless attaches God's own life to the sweat, blood, and turmoil of a particular people. Theologian Michael Wyschogrod observed, "The divine presence in the created order had to become embodied in a people of flesh and blood." Israel, claims Wyschogrod, was God's "habitation."[1] So for the Pastor, the church—again not the imaginary church or the idealized church but the real one with vexatious people in it—is God's habitation.

For the Pastor, the universal truth of the gospel and the cosmic plan of salvation are revealed not in some ethereal music that floats through the universe but in the flesh and blood of Jesus Christ and in the flesh and blood of the community gathered in his name. The universal, in other words, is always attached to the bodily particularity. As Lesslie Newbigin has said,

---

1. Michael Wyschogrod, *The Body of Faith: God in the People Israel* (Northvale, NJ: Jason Aronson, 1996), 10.

> From the beginning of the Bible to its end we are presented with
> the story of a universal purpose carried out through a continu-
> ous series of particular choices. God, according to the biblical
> picture, although he is the creator, ruler, sustainer and judge
> of all peoples, does not accomplish his purpose of blessing for
> all peoples by means of a revealer simultaneously and equally
> available to all. He chooses one to be the bearer of his blessing
> for the many. Abraham is chosen to be the pioneer of faith and
> so to receive the blessing through which all the nations will be
> blessed. Moses is chosen to be the agent of Israel's redemption;
> Israel is chosen to be a kingdom of priests for the whole earth.
> The disciples are chosen that they may be "fishers of men" (Mark
> 1:17) or, in another metaphor, that they may "go and bear fruit"
> (John 15:16). The church is a body chosen to "declare the won-
> derful deeds" of God (1 Peter 2:9).[2]

In a recent radio interview, well-known rock musician Tom Petty
was describing how it is that his spiritual quest has broken free from
the constraints of the institutional religion. "I was raised with the
Bible," he said, "but I've read the New Testament for myself now.
Jesus had some beautiful thoughts, but he never said anything about
going to a meeting once a week." Perhaps Petty should read the New
Testament again. He'd find there a Jesus "who went to the synagogue
on the sabbath day, as was his custom" (Luke 4:16), who assembled
a community of disciples, and who established the church. But even
deeper, he would find there a Jesus who was thoroughly Jewish, who
was formed by the community of God's people living out—and
failing to live out—the commandments of God in the rhythms of
everyday life.

That is why the Pastor is so zealous to confront the gaseous, disembodied form of spirituality that is the central problem of these
letters. The Pastor is not some theological scold, slapping people on
the wrist when they depart from orthodoxy. He is instead a pastor,
a shepherd, who is alarmed when the sheep wander into places of
danger. Airy spirituality, he knows, appears to be a lovely meadow,

---

2. Lesslie Newbigin, *The Open Secret: An Introduction to the Theology of Mission*, rev. ed. (Grand
Rapids: Eerdmans, 1995,), 68.

but it leads to a steep and perilous cliff. His voice sometimes sounds like a rebuke, but it is actually the alarm of love.

One surprising benefit of spending so many months preparing this commentary, which is based on letters presented as wise words between pastors, has been to remember with gratitude those pastors who have been shepherds to me from my youth until now, pastors who have even at times sounded the alarm of love over my life. For the most part they were poorly paid, and compared to doctors and lawyers and business people, they always seemed a little awkward and out of place. But there they were, in their J. C. Penney suits, preaching the gospel week-in and week-out, hovering over hospital bedsides, standing defiantly beside cemetery grave plots saying, "O death, where is your victory?" Like the Pastor of these letters, they worried about the details of worship, the minutiae of the charity rolls, and the quality of the Sunday school curriculum. Every now and then, I am sure, in the loneliness of a dark night, they, too, had to remind themselves of their call and their ordination just to muster the courage and energy to get up the next day and to keep at the task of embodying the gospel. But keep at it they did, and because of their labors, I and many others in their flock were able to take a little firmer grasp on "the life that is really life" (1 Tim. 6:19).

Selected Bibliography

Bassler, Jouette M. *1 Timothy, 2 Timothy, Titus.* Nashville: Abingdon, 1996.

Collins, Raymond F. *I & II Timothy and Titus.* Louisville, KY: Westminster John Knox Press, 2002.

Dibelius, Martin and Hans Conzelmann. *The Pastoral Epistles.* Hermeneia. Philadelphia: Fortress Press, 1972.

Fiore, Benjamin, SJ. *The Pastoral Epistles: First Timothy, Second Timothy, Titus.* Sacra Pagina Series. Edited by Daniel J. Harrington, vol. 12. Collegeville, MN: Liturgical Press, 2009.

Johnson, Luke Timothy. *The First and Second Letters to Timothy.* The Anchor Bible, vol. 35a. New York: Doubleday, 2001.

Osiek, Carolyn A., and David L. Balch. *Families in the New Testament World: Households and House Churches.* Louisville, KY: Westminster John Knox Press, 1997.

Quinn, Jerome D., and William C. Wacker. *The First and Second Letters to Timothy.* Grand Rapids: Eerdmans, 2000.

Tamez, Elsa. *Struggles for Power in Early Christianity.* Maryknoll, NY: Orbis, 2007.

Towner, Philip H. *The Letters to Timothy and Titus.* Grand Rapids: Eerdmans, 2006.

Wall, Robert W., with Richard B. Steele. *1 & 2 Timothy and Titus.* Grand Rapids: Eerdmans, 2012.

Young, Frances. *The Theology of the Pastoral Letters.* Cambridge: Cambridge University Press, 1994.

Index of Ancient Sources

Apocrypha and Septuagint

PHILO

Apostolic Fathers

1 CLEMENT

Nag Hammadi Codices

New Testament Apocrypha and Pseudepigrapha

Classical and Ancient Christian Writings

HIPPOLYTUS

Index of Subjects

liturgy
  baptismal, 272–77
  See also sayings "sure and worthy of
    full acceptance"
logic, 263–64
Lois, 189–90, 192, 231, 240
Lord's Prayer, 218
Lord's Supper. *See* Eucharist
love
  Christian, 42, 44, 48, 93, 131, 136,
    240
  God's, 62–63, 96, 118, 162, 230
  good theology and, 41–42
  ministry and, 208
  of money, 88, 172, 177, 222, 224, 245
  parental, 41
  rebuke and, 282
  showing, in difficult community, 82,
    131
  strong, loving, and wise leadership,
    187–98
  "that comes from a pure heart, a good
    conscience, and sincere faith," 42,
    44, 48, 131, 240
loyalty, 51, 245
Lucifer, 226. *See also* Satan/the devil
Luke, 245
Luke, Gospel of, 233
Luther, Martin, 223, 235, 257, 275
Lutheran Church, 96, 276
Lystra, 27, 228–29

Madoff, Bernie, 42–44
magicians, 226
Mark, 245
marriage, 124–27, 235
  bishops/deacons and, 148
  cultural views of, varying, 267–68
  false teachers on, 78, 141
  in the first century, 37
  group, 268–69
  "kingdom families," 268–69
  "married only once," 148
  pastor-parish relationship compared
    to, 269
  Plutarch's advice for newlyweds, 73

rejection of, 80
same-sex, 40, 230, 269
sexless, 217
"spiritual," 217
young widows and, 34, 38, 141,
  150–51
martyrs/martyrdom, 4–5, 205–6
Masai tribe in Africa, 203–4
McGill, Arthur C., 256
mediator, Christ as, 66, 256–57
"medical" advice, 158–59
Meier, John P., 6–7, 218, 233
Meilaender, Gilbert, 187
men
  natures, masculine and feminine,
    69–71
  older, 31, 137, 139–41, 270
  and salvation, 78, 82
  and worship, 57, 72
  younger, 139, 141, 270
  See also gender roles in the Christian
    community
*Men Are from Mars, Women Are from
  Venus* (Gray), 70–71
mercy of God, 44, 49, 62, 135, 230, 277
merit. *See* works, good
Metheun, Charlotte, 33
Methodist Church, 253, 265, 271
Methodist Covenant Prayer, 253
Michael, 231
middle way of reform, 269
ministry, 237–42
  and authority, 24, 201
  carrying out fully, 237–42
  of church leaders, 175
  controversy in, 261
  discontented, 173
  early church, key ministries of, 31,
    142–46
  effective, 199–210
  to false teachers, 173, 220
  four strategic patterns of good,
    127–30
  friends in, 195–98
  and godliness, 173
  good, 127–39, 201, 255

responsibility, 6
of Christian life, 272–77
early church and, 31, 142–46, 152,
157
moral, 65
positions of, 5, 137, 174, 192
resurrection, alternate view of/claims by
false teachers, 35, 203, 213–16,
234–35
"resurrection," experiencing in our souls,
217
resurrection of Jesus, 27, 119, 194,
202–4, 239, 271
Pauline theology of, 213–15
resurrection of the body, 236
hope for, 217
risen Christ as "first fruits" of our,
214–15
Revelation, book of, 126, 222, 230–31
rich, the, 177–80
the Pastor's counsel for, 178–79
two ways of getting rich, 171
See also money; wealth
Rich Man and Lazarus parable, 239
Ricoeur, Paul, 162
righteousness
"crown of," 167, 243
slaves to, 251–52
works of, 275
Roberts, Charles, 28
Roman Empire, 164, 222
Romero, George, 106–8

Sabbath, 119, 281
sacraments, 134
Christian faith as sacramental, 102
See also baptism; Eucharist;
ordination/ordained ministry
sacrifice, 61, 68, 126, 242
self-sacrifice, 242–43
salutations, 258
"grace and peace," 29, 258
to 1 Timothy, 17–30
to 2 Timothy, 183–92
to Titus, 251, 253, 257–58
salvation, 50–53
for all, God as desiring, 62

Christian life and, 26
the church as about, 141
community created by, 135
God's saving action, 63, 135, 187,
271
God's will and, 62, 187
gospel as about, 49–54
grace and, 270–72
by grace vs. works, 160–61, 275
hope and, 26, 62
Jesus, salvific role of, 26, 50, 65, 67
life-giving work of, 187
the Pastor's view of, 161
Pauline view of, 78
power of God for, 27, 62–63, 124
"save sinners," the phrase, 50
as way of life, 135, 234
for women (the Pastor's curious
statement about), 68–69, 78
See also under childbirth/
childbearing: and salvation
same-sex marriage, 40, 230, 269
sanctification, 42, 122–24
Sarah, 119
Satan/the devil, 25, 67–68, 113, 125,
151, 153, 223, 226, 236, 252,
273
risk of falling "into the
condemnation of," 90–91
"turned over to," 56
Savior
God taking the role of, 17–18, 20,
26–29, 110
Jesus as, 25, 59, 274
sayings "sure and worthy of full
acceptance," 49–50, 55, 84, 133,
204–10, 276
schisms, 113
Schweitzer, Albert, 132
Scripture, 231–34
good interpreters of, 9–10
good study of, 211
historical-critical approaches to, xi
as inspired by God, 232
reading Pastoral Epistles as, 8–10
as resource for "Timothy," 231–32
Scrooge, Ebenezer, 235